Democracy Without Competition in Japan
Opposition Failure in a One-Party Dominant State

Despite its democratic structure, Japan's government has been dominated by a single party, the Liberal Democratic Party (LDP), since 1955. This book ... of great dissatisfaction with the LDP, no opposition party has been able to offer itself as a credible challenger. Understanding such failure is important for many reasons, from its effect on Japanese economic policy to its implications for what facilitates democratic responsiveness more broadly. The principal explanations for opposition failure in Japan focus on the country's culture and electoral system. This book offers a new interpretation, arguing that a far more plausible explanation rests on the predominance in Japan of clientelism, combined with a centralized government structure and electoral protection for groups that benefit from clientelism. Although the central case in the book is Japan, the analysis is also comparative and applies the framework cross-nationally.

Ethan Scheiner is an assistant professor in the Department of Political Science at the University of California, Davis. He received a Ph.D. in political science from Duke University in 2001. He has been a visiting scholar at Keio University (Mita) in Tokyo, Japan; an advanced research (postdoctoral) Fellow in the Program on U.S.-Japan Relations at Harvard University (2001–2); and a postdoctoral Fellow at the Stanford Institute for International Studies (2002–4). His work examines parties and elections within both Japan-specific and explicitly comparative contexts. He has published articles on political parties, elections, and electoral systems in the *British Journal of Political Science*, *Comparative Political Studies*, *Electoral Studies*, and *Legislative Studies Quarterly*. His analyses of recent Japanese elections appears (in Japanese) in *Foresight Magazine* in Japan.

Democracy Without Competition in Japan

Opposition Failure in a One-Party Dominant State

ETHAN SCHEINER

University of California at Davis

CAMBRIDGE
UNIVERSITY PRESS

CAMBRIDGE UNIVERSITY PRESS
Cambridge, New York, Melbourne, Madrid, Cape Town, Singapore, São Paulo

Cambridge University Press
40 West 20th Street, New York, NY 10011-4211, USA

www.cambridge.org
Information on this title: www.cambridge.org/9780521846929

First published 2006

Printed in the United States of America

A catalog record for this publication is available from the British Library.

Library of Congress Cataloging in Publication Data

Scheiner, Ethan, 1968–
Democracy without competition in Japan : opposition failure in a one-party
dominant state / Ethan Scheiner.
    p. cm.
Includes bibliographical references and index.
ISBN 0-521-84692-7 (hardback) – ISBN 0-521-60969-0 (pbk.)
1. Democracy – Japan.   2. Jiyûu Minshutôo.   3. Political parties – Japan.
4. Patronage, Political – Japan.   5. Patron and client – Japan.   6. Japan – Politics
and government – 1945–   I. Title.
JQ1681.S34   2006
324.252–dc22   2004030868

ISBN-13   978-0-521-84692-9 hardback
ISBN-10   0-521-84692-7 hardback

ISBN-13   978-0-521-60969-2 paperback
ISBN-10   0-521-60969-0 paperback

To Boo Boo,
Doo Doo,
Dr. D,
and the love of my life,
Melanie

Contents

Tables and Figures

Glossary of Abbreviations

ELECTORAL SYSTEM TERMS

PR	proportional representation
SMD	single member district
SNTV/MMD	single nontransferable vote in multimember districts

JAPAN

CGP	Clean Government Party (*Kōmeitō*)
DPJ	Democratic Party of Japan (*Minshutō*)
DSP	Democratic Socialist Party (*Minshatō*)
HC	House of Councillors (also called the Upper House)
HR	House of Representatives (also called the Lower House)
JCP	Japan Communist Party (*Nihon Kyōsantō*)
JNP	Japan New Party (*Nihon Shintō*)
JSP	Japan Socialist Party (*Nihon Shakaitō*)
LDP	Liberal Democratic Party (*Jiyū-Minshutō*)
NFP	New Frontier Party (*Shinshintō*)
NLC	New Liberal Club (*Shin Jiyū Kurabu*)
SDL	Social Democratic League (*Shakai Minshu Rengō*)
SDP	Social Democratic Party (formerly the JSP) (*Shakai Minshutō*)

AUSTRIA

FPÖ	Freedom Party of Austria (*Freiheitliche Partei Österreichs*)
ÖVP	Austrian People's Party (*Österreichs Volkspartei*)
SPÖ	Social Democratic Party (*Sozialistische Partei Österreichs*)

BRAZIL

PSD	Social Democratic Party (*Partido Social Democrático*)
PT	Workers Party (*Partido dos Trabalhadores*)

GERMANY

CDU/CSU	Christian Democratic Union/Christian Social Union (*Christlich Demokratische Union/Christlich Soziale Union*)
SPD	Social Democratic Party (*Sozialdemokratische Partei Deutschlands*)

ITALY

DC	Christian Democratic Party (*Democrazia Cristiana*)
PCI	Italian Communist Party (*Partito Communista Italiano*)
PSI	Italian Socialist Party (*Partito Socialista Italiano*)

MEXICO

PAN	National Action Party (*Partido Accion Nacional*)
PRD	Party of the Democratic Revolution (*Partido de la Revolucion Democratica*)
PRI	Institutional Revolutionary Party (*Partido Revolucionario Institucional*)

SWEDEN

SAP	Social Democratic Party (*Sveriges Socialdemokratiska Arbetarparti*)

TAIWAN

DPP	Democratic People's Party (*Minchuchinputang*)
KMT	Nationalist People's Party (*Kuomintang*)

OTHER ACRONYMS

DID	densely inhabited districts (common measure of urban-ness)
FECL	Foreign Exchange and Control Law
FIL	Foreign Investment Law

FILP   Fiscal Investment and Loan Program
GDP   gross domestic product
GNP   gross national product
JEDS   Japan Elections and Democracy Study
JES   Japan Election Studies

Acknowledgments and a Note on the Use of the Online Appendix

I have many, many people to thank for helping make this book possible.

However, first, let me refer readers to a supplementary online appendix for the book. This appendix can be accessed by following the links from my Web site at *www.ethanscheiner.com*. (Yes, I succumbed to cyber-spatial egocentrism for the book.) To shorten the manuscript and keep it tightly focused, I cut many details and discussion of potential counterarguments and put them in the online appendix. Much of my work is based on multivariate quantitative analysis, but most readers of this book are unlikely to be interested in technical aspects of the statistics, even if they are intrigued by the substantive results. Therefore, I kept the substantive discussions of the quantitative work but moved the tables and technical discussions of the multivariate analyses to the appendix.

Now, on to the (very sincere) gratitude! This book began as my Duke University doctoral dissertation and my greatest intellectual debt is to my Duke advisors, Meg McKean and Herbert Kitschelt. Meg's detailed comments improved the book in numerous different ways, and her guidance has been invaluable. Herbert helped me clarify many important concepts and pushed me toward more comparative approaches and sophisticated analysis. He has done more than anyone to shape my political science brain. Great thanks too for the extremely helpful comments of my other Duke mentors, John Aldrich and Scott Morgenstern.

Five others were especially influential. Steve Reed has been a constant source of guidance and information and a tremendous sounding board for ideas. Also, I would be broke if I ever had to repay him monetarily for all the data he's shared with me. Kobayashi Yoshiaki was a magnificent host at Keio University in Tokyo, where I was a visiting scholar (May 1998 through August 1999), and an invaluable source of information and contacts. Rob "WB" Weiner has been an important colleague (and friend), always willing to discuss anything. I have learned much from Rob. My parents, Betsey and Irv Scheiner, led me to some of my most useful contacts in this project and are responsible (by association) for a huge chunk of any credibility (such as it is) I may have in the Japan field.

I was very fortunate to have people who were willing to read the *entire* manuscript. Ray Christensen, Dave Leheny, and Len Schoppa not only did so but provided detailed and insightful comments that improved the book immeasurably. Ellis Krauss and T. J. Pempel reviewed the manuscript for Cambridge University Press and offered the sort of comments every author hopes for: encouraging, but also outstanding and direct suggestions for improvement. I am also grateful to Betsey Scheiner and Melanie Hurley who copyedited the book for me. Neither ever touched a sentence without improving it.

Thanks to Kojima Aya, Ozawa Akira, Nakamichi Midori, and Tatsumi Mie, who helped me prepare for interviews and the surveys and correspondence I conducted. Indeed, it was Akira, Midori, and Mie who conducted the phone interviews/surveys on my behalf. Thanks to Yasuyuki Motoyama and Izumi Yoshioka, who helped in the United States with my Japanese materials, and to Jennifer Ramos and Shawn Southerd, for their research assistance. Thanks to Kurizaki Shuhei and Teshima Masahiro, who helped with my translations in Japan. Thanks to the Inter-University Center in Yokohama for helping bring my Japanese language ability to the point that I usually did not have to worry about accidentally saying horrible things about my own anatomy when I was intending to reference comments made by advisors. Most of my interviews would not have been possible without the very kind introductions provided by Hironaka Yoshimichi, Shinada Suguru, Yanai Satoshi, Nakajima Kaze, Iigata Kōichi, Saitō Masamitsu, Chiba Ken, Tatsu Niioka, Kobayashi Yoshiaki, and Meg McKean.

Tons of thanks to Shigeo Hirano, Andy Baker, Yusaku Horiuchi, Orit Kedar, Jun Saito, and Guillermo Rosas, who provided advice on the statistical analysis. Great thanks to Scott Seaman for numerous pieces of information he found for me. Thanks to Kataoka Masaaki, who suggested using *Bun'yabetsu Jinmeiroku*; Susan Pharr for sharing JEDS96 (1996 Japan Election and Democracy Study, conducted by Bradley M. Richardson, Mitsuru Uchida, and associates); Dennis Patterson and Misa Nishikawa for sharing their campaign platforms; Masahiko Asano for his campaign expenditures data; Kabashima Ikuo and his zemi for their urban-rural SMD measures; Yusaku Horiuchi and Masaru Kohno for their Japanese Election District-level Census Data; Kobayashi Yoshiaki for sharing the JESII (Japan Election Studies II) Version 1, panel electoral studies funded by the Ministry of Education (FY1993–FY1997); and Mike Alvarez, Dean Lacy, Liz Zechmeister, John Brehm, and Jay Patel for suggestions on multinomial probit. Thanks to Cambridge University Press's editor Lew Bateman for shepherding this book through the publication process. Thanks also to

Ernie Haim, who acted as production editor, and Sara Black, who copyedited the manuscript for Cambridge University Press.

Others offered intellectual and practical suggestions of great help: Ken Greene, Andy Baker, Christina Davis, Sid Tarrow, Kathleen O'Neill, Walter Mebane, Irv Scheiner, Peter Katzenstein, David Samuels, Bonnie Meguid, Dan Okimoto, Kenneth McElwain, Kay Shimizu, Jean Oi, Dick Samuels, Robert Pekkanen, David Laitin, Alberto Diaz-Cayeros, Beatriz Magaloni, Scott Desposato, Margarita Estevez-Abe, Orit Kedar, Susan Pharr, Christian Brunelli, Shin Fujihira, Gary Cox, Matthew Shugart, Mike Thies, John Campbell, Harlan Koff, Masaru Kohno, Aiji Tanaka, Sam Jameson, Steve Levitsky, Tomoaki Nomi, Kuba Zielinski, Karen Cox, Mavis Mayer, Paula Evans, Kären Wigen, Kris Troost, Paul Talcott, Jon Marshall, Mari Miura, Alisa Gaunder, Yamamoto Tatsuhiro, Frank Schwartz, Kosuke Imai, Thomas Berger, Bill Grimes, Yoku Yamazaki, Masami Hasegawa, David Soskice, Ronda Burginger, Brian "Skippy" Sage, Val Threlfall, Amy "B-Buster" Bantham, Heidi Glunz, Mike "Candle Man" Rothman, Andy Dodge, Allison Devore, Jeremy Weinstein, and Rachel Gibson.

I was fortunate to be able to work on this book while an advanced research Fellow at the Program on U.S.-Japan Relations at Harvard University, a postdoctoral Fellow in the Stanford (University) Institute for International Studies, and assistant professor in the department of political science at U.C. Davis. Parts of Chapters 2, 5, and 6 appeared as "Pipelines of Pork: A Model of Local Opposition Party Failure" in *Comparative Political Studies* (in press), "Democracy without Competition: Opposition Failure in One-Party Dominant Japan," which was (paper number 02-12) in the Occasional Papers Series at the Program on U.S.-Japan Relations at Harvard University, and "The Underlying Roots of Opposition Failure in Japan" in the Middlebury College Rohatyn Center for International Affairs Working Paper Series. Also, thanks to The Japan Foundation, the National Security Education Program, Sanwa Bank, the Aleanne Webb Dissertation grantees, Duke University Graduate School, Department of Education, the U.C. Davis publication assistance fund, my mom, and my wife for helping fund my research.

On a more personal – and, hence, important – note: The usual acknowledgment thanks many but then places the blame for any errors or silly analysis on the shoulders of the author; I know better than to do that. Any errors or silly analysis are entirely the fault of my friends, Vince Chhabria, Matt "Sporto" Brown, Amy Krause, and the members of the West Siyeed Fantasy Football league (and occasionally Scott Seaman and Dave Leheny). So much love and thanks to my great "steps" Margaret Chowning and Polly and Sarah Bowser, my wonderful in-laws Dick and Nila Hurley, my phenomenally supportive and smart family Betsey, Irv, and Jessica Scheiner, and, most important, my best reason for getting up in the morning, Melanie Hurley.

A NOTE ON CONVENTIONS

Throughout this book, I write Japanese personal names according to Japanese convention: family name (surname) followed by given name.

Introduction

The Puzzle of Party Competition Failure in Japan

Japanese party politics are a puzzle. In 1955, the Liberal and Democratic Parties merged to form the conservative Liberal Democratic Party. The LDP's precursors had dominated the Japanese government since the prewar period, and the LDP's formation meant that a single party was in control. Given the seemingly incompatible personalities and policy positions – as well as intraparty antagonism – of those forming the LDP, many Japanese were skeptical of the new party's ability to stay together (Calder 1988: 59–60). But power proved to be impressive glue; the party remained largely intact for decades. That power helped hold the party together is hardly shocking. However, the LDP not only stayed together but also warded off nearly every electoral challenge over the next five decades: Between 1955 and 2005 (when this book was completed), the LDP was out of power for a total of ten months and 20 days.

Two points make this puzzle all the more difficult to understand. First, Japan is a democracy. Citizens maintain all the usual civil liberties, and non-LDP parties contest elections, hoping to topple the LDP. Second, and most troubling, *the LDP is not popular*. As of the writing of this book, it had been over 40 years since the party received a majority of the vote in an election for the national House of Representatives. During the 1990s, in the face of severe economic stagnation, party corruption, and seeming paralysis on the part of the LDP when it came time to do anything about such issues, displeasure with the party grew dramatically. Nevertheless, no real challenge to the LDP was able to sustain itself.

This book attempts to make sense of this puzzle.

Note that for space reasons, I have cut from this book a number of pieces of less directly relevant analysis, responses to potential counterarguments, and, especially, technical details and results of the statistics discussed. I have placed this material in the online appendix, which can be linked from *www.ethanscheiner.com*.

THE IMPACT OF CLIENTELISM

As a Japan scholar, I recognize that this puzzle is perhaps *the* defining feature of postwar Japanese party politics and, likely, the issue that acts as the greatest obstacle to Japan in overcoming its economic problems. However, as a student of comparative politics, I am just as concerned with understanding how a competition-less party system is possible in a democracy. Democracy is founded on competition. How is democracy without competition possible?

As someone trained in comparative politics, my first efforts at making real sense of the puzzle focused on party competition and the failure of party competition in other countries, but my biggest clues came from speaking to people in Japan. In my early work on this project, I asked Japanese politicians, political party staffers, journalists, and regular citizens why they thought the opposition was unable to challenge the LDP. They tended to offer three specific explanations. First, almost without fail, opposition party politicians and staff members mentioned their party's difficulty in finding attractive candidates to run. Second, opposition members were quick to note the LDP's resource advantage. That is, the LDP was able to use the resources of the state – especially in the form of subsidies and funding of projects in areas such as construction – to encourage particular regions to support the party. This resource edge was doubly advantageous for the LDP because it also encouraged donors to contribute money to LDP candidates, who, if victorious, could continue distributing state resources. The third explanation usually came from journalists, voters, and non-opposition party politicians, who argued that many voters simply did not trust the opposition. They explained that it was not clear what the post-1993 new parties stood for, in particular noting the seeming incompatibility of the different politicians who had joined together to form the parties.

Over time I realized that the three explanations actually worked together, with an important thread running throughout. In particular, Japan's clientelist structure – whereby the LDP-led central government rewards its supporters with patronage – plays a central role in all three of the problems the opposition has faced in recent years and goes a long way toward explaining the failure of Japan's opposition.

RESEARCH DESIGN ISSUES

Case studies often note the heavy role of clientelism in Japan. But they seldom consider Japan explicitly from the larger perspective of clientelist systems more generally or examine it within the larger context of different forms of linkage (programmatic or clientelistic) between politicians and citizens. Placing Japan and its clientelist system in this larger perspective provides a greater sense of the system's importance to Japan's political outcomes such as party competition failure. And in turn, the comparative perspective allows us to use what we learn about the impact of the system in Japan to understand clientelism and programmatic politics in other countries.

I began this project seeking to understand opposition failure in Japan. However, throughout the process, I was concerned with the case study problem: How can one derive generalizable conclusions from analysis of only a single case?

To address this problem, I took three steps. First, I constantly asked how my Japan-specific findings fit (or did not fit) into the existing theoretical literature. By doing so, I was forced to consider what findings about Japan might contribute to a broader understanding of politics. Second, I made substantial use of *intra*-Japan comparisons. Intracountry (both cross-regionally and over time) comparisons are particularly useful because they can bring in variation on variables that are vital to understanding the problem under consideration, while controlling for numerous factors that are not the focus. Third, I introduced substantial analysis of other countries as well. The intensive field work of scholars in other countries allowed me to push my findings further by introducing variation in both the dependent and independent variables.

My conclusions grew out of this intersection between theory, my own field work, and secondary sources. To begin my field work, I conducted interviews aimed at looking into the plausibility of various theories of party failure. The information gleaned from the interviews pushed me to consider new theoretical frameworks, which I evaluated through additional interviews and statistical analysis. In light of the results, I added new questions to future interviews and tested new questions through statistical analyses. Then, where possible, I looked to secondary sources to consider the broader applicability of the findings.

THE ARGUMENT IN BRIEF

The leading explanations for opposition party failure in Japan focus on the country's culture and electoral system, but, as I explain in Chapter 2, there are substantial limits to both explanations. Using interviews with Japanese politicians, data on Japanese new party development, statistical analysis of public opinion surveys, and close attention to the cases of other countries, I argue that the reason for the failure lies in a combination of clientelism, fiscal centralization, and institutional protections for the principal beneficiaries of the clientelist system.

Theories of party competition usually assume competition over programmatic issues. For this reason, many observers of Japanese politics with whom I spoke referred to the LDP – with its emphasis on catch-all clientelist politics – as somehow not a "real" party. However, in reality, numerous political systems throughout the world are founded on clientelist modes, where parties elected to office reward their supporters with private goods. Clientelist parties create direct bonds with voters, usually through side payments such as pork barrel. In programmatic systems, opposition failure like Japan's is rare, but ruling party dominance and opposition failure are more common under clientelism. Clientelist systems' emphasis on administrative infrastructure and bonds created through side payments places a burden on opposition parties, which usually have little access to such benefits. In Japan, the opposition has faced a big disadvantage because of the importance of organized blocs of votes that are tightly tied into LDP clientelist networks. However, clientelism by itself is clearly not a sufficient explanation for opposition party failure as new and opposition parties do make inroads in clientelist systems, most obviously in recent years in Italy, Austria, and Mexico.

In combination with particular structures, clientelism can be debilitating for opposition parties: The combination of clientelism and governmental fiscal centralization causes especially great problems. In clientelist systems where access to funding is controlled by the central government, local governments must rely heavily on its financial graces. For this reason, in such systems, local organizations, politicians, and voters have strong incentives to affiliate with the national ruling party, and parties that are not strong at the national level have a much harder time gaining local office. In Clientelist/Financially Centralized systems, such as Italy, Austria, and Mexico, nonnational ruling parties have had great difficulty winning local elections. And, in the highly Clientelistic/Financially Centralized Japanese case, the opposition has been extraordinarily weak at the subnational level, with the primary exceptions to this rule occurring in areas that simply do not rely as much on the central government.

Local weakness has a major effect on opposition success at the national level. In Japan, where controlling organized blocs of votes is central to electoral success, it is important for national politicians that local politicians and organizations campaign on their behalf. The lack of local groups that are affiliated with the opposition greatly hinders national opposition candidates' chances of success. Also, in the highly candidate-centered electoral system used at the national level in Japan, it is critical for parties to run under their banner candidates who have substantial experience and connections. Typically, these candidates have held local office. Because they hold few local offices, Japanese opposition parties have been doubly disadvantaged: They have been both weak locally and deprived of a pool of strong candidates that would have helped them gain ground at the national level. The heart of my analysis of national level failure of Japan's opposition focuses on the post-1993 period. However, this candidate recruitment problem no doubt was even more critical to opposition failure in the pre-1993 era, as Japan maintained an even more candidate-centered electoral system at the time.

The combination of clientelism and one other factor – institutionalized protection of clients of the ruling party – has further hindered opposition party success. Strong candidacies are indeed critical to the success of parties in candidate-centered systems, but the lack of such candidates is not sufficient to explain opposition failure: The longtime dominant Christian Democratic Party was knocked out of power in Italy, another Clientelist/Fiscally Centralized system that has utilized a candidate-centered electoral system. In both Italy and Japan, opposition groups pushed for an end to their respective governments' clientelist practices and gained greater popularity as a result, but the countries' different electoral arrangements channeled these efforts into different levels of success. Compared to the Italian proportional representation electoral system in place during the time of the early decline of the DC, Japan's current electoral system, which emphasizes winner-take-all single member districts, has made it extremely difficult for the opposition to mount a challenge to the LDP in the regions most supportive of clientelism. One third of Japan's SMDs are provided to rural areas, where the heart of the pro-clientelist forces in Japan resides. In the late 1990s and early 2000s, the LDP was able to use about 50 percent of the total rural vote to win at least 75 percent of the seats in such areas. As a result, over that time, party competition largely occurred only in the remaining two thirds of the country.

Rather than having one party system, Japan has come to contain two *parallel party systems*: One is rural and LDP-dominated, whereas the other is more urban and competitive. In the early postwar period, Japan was heavily rural and dependent on government favors. The LDP was able to use government resources in clientelist exchange to dominate party politics. But, as Japan grew more urban, fewer areas required government support. In such areas – especially as Japan's economy slowed – clientelist practices and the LDP itself grew increasingly unpopular. Nevertheless, the rural areas continued to rely upon the clientelist practices, support the ruling party, and hold a sufficient number of SMDs to provide the LDP with a solid seat base. Indeed, over 1996–2003, even if the opposition had been *hugely* successful and took nearly 60 percent of nonrural seats, it would still have had only about 40 percent of all the Lower House seats.

Finally, in Japan the opposition of the post-1990 period has been made up of new parties, and the clientelist and centralized system caused them additional difficulties. The importance of close links to the central government in clientelist, financially centralized systems causes most new party formation to occur from the top-down. As a result, Japan's leading new parties have typically been made up of a number of politicians from various widely different preexisting parties, which therefore faced difficulty organizing their members and agreeing on policy positions. In the case of the formation of the LDP, which controlled government resources, this reinforced the use of clientelist practices. In the case of Japan's new opposition parties of the 1990s, parties that had no such access to resources, this top-down pattern focused party formation on national level elites and made difficult grassroots level development based on a unifying platform. This not only harmed the parties' internal dynamics but also made it less clear to the public what such a motley crew of politicians could have in common. Voters have had greater difficulty deciphering the basis of such parties and, when skeptical of their unity, became less likely to support them.

Ultimately, the first two of these problems – the difficulties opposition parties have faced as a result of their great weakness at the local level and their inability to gain representation in clientelism-supporting areas because of the dominance of particular electoral arrangements – are sufficient explanations for the failure of Japan's opposition. The third problem – lack of party organization and coherence – served to exacerbate the other obstacles the opposition faced. By taking advantage of hurdles like these, the LDP has been able to maintain its dominance despite declining popularity.

HOPE FOR OPPOSITION SUCCESS?

As I completed the final revisions on this book in the summer of 2004, the Democratic Party of Japan narrowly defeated the LDP in an election for the House of Councillors, the less important branch of Japan's government. Although the election was by no means a sign that the LDP's grip on the Japanese government was due to expire, it did act as a reminder that permanent opposition failure is by no means a given. The opposition may indeed succeed. However, it will not do so simply by finding new and more attractive issue appeals to make to Japan's voters. The foundations of Japanese politics I describe above greatly hinder the effectiveness of such appeals. Instead, as I describe in Chapter 10, future opposition success will ultimately depend on defections by LDP elites away from the ruling party or on changes in the structural foundations themselves.

The Importance of Party Competition and a Model of Party Competition Failure

> A democracy predicated on the ability to "throw the rascals out" is far less convincing when it exists only in the abstract than when it is backed up by periodic examples of rascals actually flying through the doors.
>
> T. J. Pempel (1990: 7)

This is a book about how party competition can fail.

The ability of opposition parties to challenge ruling regimes is integral to representative democracy. A viable opposition is important not just because competitive elections are a necessary condition of most definitions of democracy (e.g., Schumpeter 1942) but because opposition is in fact a critical check on a country's rulers. Writing in the Schumpeterian tradition, scholars such as Downs (1957) and Schlesinger (1991) tell us that in order to get elected, parties are drawn to reflect the public's will. In competing with each other for votes, parties are in fact vying to better represent the general public. Where one party is dominant, there is little competition, and, as a result, the dominant party need not be very responsive. Party competition forces political elites and voters alike to consider alterations to the existing political agenda; examine alternative ideological, cultural, or policy ideas; and reevaluate which societal groups should be represented by the government and how.

In some cases, the impact of competition may appear insignificant to all but the most involved observer, as it simply leads to debate over "minor" details of legislation, but in many other cases the impact is more obviously profound. Competition over ideas and office offers incentives for election-seeking politicians to avoid inefficient and stagnant policies that both harm the general interests of the country and lead the policies' proponents to get bounced from office. The quest for electoral support can also force parties to look out for the interests and desires of societal groups that might otherwise go ignored and unrepresented. Most of all, the presence of a viable opposition and party competition provides the ultimate check against unrestrained power. As long as a party fears loss of office, it will be much less likely to act arbitrarily.[1]

Outcomes such as these give observers one more reason to spout the virtues of democracy. However, if, as Schattschneider (1942) suggests, democracy needs parties in order to function, a system made up of non-responsive parties suggests problems in democracy's functioning. Under democracy, we expect a type of natural selection to occur among parties. Obviously, we expect parties to survive when they do things to make themselves electorally successful. And we expect parties that are unsuccessful over the long run to be replaced by others that are sufficiently adaptive or entrepreneurial enough to find new ways to overcome the obstacles blocking the success of their predecessors.

Ultimately, then, democratic party theory tells us that, in times of voter distress, credible alternatives will challenge the existing order. Nevertheless, democracies do exist where, even in times of distress, opposition parties have great difficulty selling themselves as credible challengers.

This book offers an understanding of which factors within a democracy can get in the way of the development of viable opposition parties and thereby lead to a failure of party competition. My argument focuses on clientelism, which I discuss in greater detail later. Clientelism is not sufficient to bring about party competition failure, but when a system is founded on clientelist exchange, opposition parties typically face some difficulty because of their lack of access to governmental benefits. More powerfully, the combination of clientelism and two other factors – centralized governmental fiscal structure and institutionalized protection of those who benefit from the clientelist distribution of resources – greatly hampers opposition party efforts to compete with the ruling party.

VARYING LEVELS OF PARTY COMPETITION

In considering party success and failure, I focus on party competition, in particular as it takes the form of turnover in office. There are numerous ways that opposition parties can be "successful" in a political system. Even small parties can enter into coalition governments and often (see, for example, the

---

[1] Individual politicians may fear electoral loss even if their party as a whole does not, but, as Kitschelt points out, "Voters do not know how their preference for a particular politician is likely to affect the ultimate outcomes of democratic decision making" (2000: 848). On top of the simple uncertainty of aggregating a large group of preferences into a single set of policies, legislators may face the problem of cycling majorities, whereby no policy outcome can ever be clear. A lack of party responsiveness is therefore a problem even when specific politicians fear electoral loss because it is parties that overcome this social choice problem by working out a collectively preferred set of policies for politicians (Aldrich 1995; Kitschelt 2000).

TABLE 1.1 *Number of Years That "Non #1 Party" Holds Power: 1950–2003 (Selected Countries)*

Country	Number of Years
United States[a]	22
United Kingdom	19
Germany[b]	18
Israel	17
Italy	10
Sweden	9
Austria	8
Mexico[c]	3
Japan	0.9

"#1 Party" refers to the party that controlled the national government for the largest number of years. Numbers here refer to the number of years that parties other than this "#1 Party" controlled the national government.

[a] Refers to the number of years the Democrats controlled the presidency. However, it should also be noted that the Republican Party only controlled the House of Representatives for 10 years and the Senate for 14 years.

[b] Includes pre-unification West Germany. Note that the figure for Germany does not include the 1966–9 period in which the Christian Democrats and Social Democrats shared power in a "grand coalition."

[c] Refers to the number of years non-PRI parties controlled the presidency. However, it should also be noted that there was a non-PRI majority in the Congress for 5 years.

Sources: McGeveran (2003), *www.worldstatesmen.org.*

Free Democratic Party in Germany) gain influence far beyond their numbers because they add enough seats to combine with a larger party to create a majority government. Also, even a semipermanent opposition party can play an important policy role if the government takes up its issues. However, in considering party *competition*, turnover in office is the gold standard. It is turnover in office – where the rascals are actually thrown out of power – that indicates that accountability genuinely exists, thereby increasing the pressure on parties to act responsively to the public. And it is responsiveness based on accountability that upholds the democratic links in representative democracy.

The extent of party turnover in office varies widely from country to country. Table 1.1 demonstrates this variation in a number of contemporary democracies.[2] Each country listed provides its citizens, at a minimum, a fair

---

[2] My case selection becomes clearer when I introduce Figure 1.1.

degree of civil liberties and allows freely contested elections. In short, each falls under Dahl's (1971) definition of polyarchy and Schumpeter's (1942) definition of democracy. For each country, I list the number of years that the "Non #1 Party" held power between 1950 and 2003. By "#1 Party," I mean the party that controlled the government for the largest number of years between 1950 and 2003. So, Table 1.1 indicates the number of years that parties other than this "#1 Party" controlled the government and therefore offers a sense of the extent to which a single party dominated the government or others were able to lead.

Substantial Competition

Within Table 1.1, the United States, the United Kingdom, and Germany have the clearest postwar tradition of party competition. In each of these countries, one party certainly controlled the government for a number of years at a time, but the longer overall trend indicates competition and turnover in control of the government.

In the United States, the Republican Party controlled the presidency for 31 years (1952–60, 1968–76, 1980–92, 2000–3), while the Democratic Party controlled it in the other 22 years. Democrats did in fact dominate Congress for a number of decades: There was a Democratic majority in the House of Representatives for every Congress except one until 1995, and Democrats controlled the Senate (except for one Congress) until 1981. Nevertheless, Republicans controlled the Senate from 1981 to 1987 and from 1995 to 2001, and the House from 1995 to 2003 (McGeveran 2003).

In Great Britain, the Conservative Party had two periods of dominance (1951–64 and 1979–97), but the Labour Party was by no means shut out. Although clearly not as impressive as the Conservatives' nearly 35 years in power, Labour controlled the government for roughly 19 years (1950–1, 1964–70, 1974–9, and 1997–2003).[3] A similar breakdown of power existed in Germany (formerly West Germany): The Christian Democrats also had two fairly long periods of rule (1950–66 and 1982–98) and were the most powerful party in government for 33 years, but the Social Democrats had their days in the sun as well. The SPD controlled the German government for roughly 18 years (1969–82 and 1998–2003) and during a three-year stretch (1966–1969) shared power in a Grand Coalition with the Christian Democrats.

To gain leverage over the general problem of party competition, it is necessary to consider cases that fall along different points on the competitive spectrum. It is therefore important to include cases of substantial competition

---

[3] Unless otherwise noted, the source for government years and coalition information for all countries is Woldendorp, Keman, and Budge (1998) and *www.worldstatesmen.org*.

like those mentioned previously. Nevertheless, my analysis focuses more on party competition failure and little turnover in office.

Longtime Dominance Turning to Competition

A number of countries faced substantial noncompetition periods, but as voter displeasure with the ruling regime grew, party competition usually increased as well.

In Israel, the Labor Party and its precursors dominated the government between 1948 and 1977. However, over time, increasing numbers of voters saw Labor policies and practices as wasteful and even unfair, and the Likud Party was able to take advantage of this displeasure. After 1977, Likud more than made up for its previous absence, leading the government for roughly 17 of the next 26 years (1977–84, 1986–92, 1996–9, 2001–3).

In Italy, the Christian Democratic Party was the largest party in every (coalition) government between 1945 and 1992 and, except for 1981–2 and 1983–7, controlled the prime ministership every year until 1993. But, pressured by judicial action and popular outrage in response to a seemingly endless string of corruption scandals, the party imploded in 1993 (Donovan 1994; Furlong 1996; Koff and Koff 2000). The remaining members of the DC reestablished themselves into new, smaller parties, each one no more than a supporting actor within a larger alliance of parties. No longer holding a dominant party, Italy alternated between a center-right and center-left alliance of parties from 1993 to 2003.

In Sweden, the Social Democratic Party controlled the (usually minority) government between 1946 and 1976. Nevertheless, economic troubles fueled a split in the party's base of support and general displeasure with the party. Beginning in particular in the 1970s, the SAP faced substantial competition and, while remaining the largest party in Sweden, found itself out of power between 1976 and 1982 and again between 1991 and 1994.

Austria provides a rather different perspective. Two large parties, the Social Democratic Party and the Austrian People's Party, each played a central role in Austrian politics throughout the postwar era, with each winning a large share of the vote and seats. At the same time, with the exception of the 1970s and the early 1980s, the two parties ran the government *jointly*, with little interference from any alternatives and, except for 1966–70, the SPÖ was always in the government. However, in the late 1980s and early 1990s the rightist Freedom Party of Austria was able to take advantage of growing unhappiness with clientelist practices of the ruling regime (as well as a tide of xenophobic sentiment) to develop greater support throughout the country. The FPÖ won enough votes and seats in the 1999 election to form a coalition government with the ÖVP, knocking the Social Democrats out of power.

It is also informative to examine cases that were undemocratic for many years.[4] These cases are noteworthy in that in all of them greater party competition emerged than had ever existed before. In part because of the undemocratic nature of Mexican politics, Mexico's ruling Partido Revolucionario Institucional was able to dominate legislative and presidential politics throughout the bulk of the postwar period. However, with increasing democracy, greater public anger over party abuse of power, and economic decline, the party lost its majority (even though it remained the largest party) in the Congress in 1997 and lost the presidency in 2000. Brazil has had two major postwar periods of democracy, during which there was party competition. Over 1945–64, there was regular turnover in the party holding the presidency. During that time, the Social Democratic Party was always the largest party in the legislature, but after 1946 it never held a majority of the seats (Skidmore 1967). After 1985, with only one exception, the party of the president changed every election. No party dominated legislative elections and the top party typically held less than 20 percent of legislative seats. In Taiwan, opposition parties were only legalized in 1989. In the 1990s, the ruling Kuomintang dominated the legislature. Nevertheless, thanks in part to a KMT split, the opposition Democratic People's Party took the 2000 presidential election and won the largest bloc of seats in the 2001 legislative election (although short of the majority taken by the KMT and its offshoot People's First Party).

Weak Competition

At the lowest end of the competitive party spectrum is the focal case of this book: Japan. Despite the country's democratic structure, a single party, the Liberal Democratic Party, dominated Japan throughout most of the postwar period. Between 1950 and 2003, non-LDP parties controlled the Japanese government for a total of ten months and 20 days.[5] In Chapter 2, I offer greater detail on the puzzle of competition failure in Japan. But, for now, suffice it to say that, while always puzzling, the failure of Japan's opposition was particularly striking after 1993. During the period that followed, the party system changed substantially, a new electoral system, which ought to have provided less benefit to the ruling party, was adopted, and the LDP

---

[4] Given the highly authoritarian/nondemocratic nature of Brazil and Taiwan for a number of years during the 1950–2003 period, I do not include them in Table 1.1 because the baseline number of years would be different from those of the other countries. An argument could be made for similarly excluding Mexico.

[5] This occurred when a coalition of small to medium-sized parties controlled the government from August 1993 through June 1994. The only other exception to LDP (or LDP precursor) dominance in the postwar period was when the Japan Socialist Party led a short-lived coalition government (with LDP precursors) from May 1947 through February 1948.

grew *very* unpopular. Nevertheless, throughout the 1990s, no opposition party appeared capable of tapping into this discontent, and, as of 2004, the LDP held a substantial advantage over its potential competitors.

THE PUZZLE

Party competition is typically the default in modern democracy,[6] so uncompetitive cases are very puzzling. Looking at the variation along the continuum, it is clear that we need to explain what permits democratic systems to fall to the noncompetition end of the spectrum. This problem is not much of a concern in cases where a ruling party remains popular: An electorate has little reason to vote out a ruling party it supports.

However, the puzzle I raise here is, how is party competition failure possible in a democratic system made up of very substantial *displeasure* with the ruling regime?

CLIENTELISM, FISCAL CENTRALIZATION, AND LIMITED ZONES OF COMPETITION: A MODEL OF OPPOSITION FAILURE

Party competition failure is more likely in certain systems than in others. Focusing on the case with the least competition, Japan, and comparing it to the other cases mentioned previously leads to an explanation of how opposition parties can remain weak, even when there is thin support for the ruling regime. Figure 1.1 provides a general framework for the resulting model, which I discuss in detail.

Ultimately, clientelism is at the center of the framework.

CLIENTELISM

Theories of party competition usually assume competition over programmatic issues, where voters cast ballots for the party that takes stands on the big "issues" of the day that most closely match their own views. However, many party systems are not founded as clearly on "issues." Indeed, numerous political systems throughout the world are founded on personalistic politics, where individual features of the candidate predominate, or clientelist modes of competition, where parties elected to office reward their supporters with private goods. Where they are led by a charismatic leader, opposition parties can find in personalistic systems a short-term opportunity to gain power at the expense of the ruling regime, but personal charisma can hold sway for

---

[6] Weiner (2003) argues that noncompetition is in fact a logical default equilibrium, but his analysis focuses on the district level.

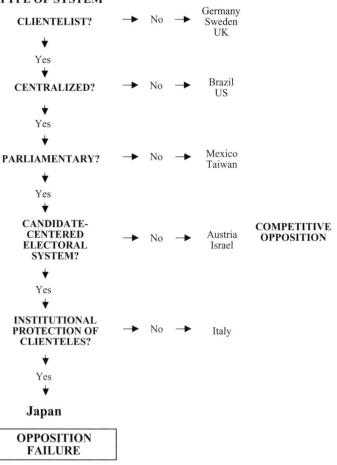

FIGURE I.I Correlates of Opposition Party Success or Failure

only a limited time, after which voters typically seek results. Clientelist systems offer a more institutionalized version of the nonprogrammatic linkage.

What precisely is clientelism? As Kitschelt (2000) explains, in contrast to programmatic systems, where parties attempt to represent sets of societal groups through packages of universally distributed, collective-goods policy programs, clientelist systems create direct and personal bonds, usually through material side payments. Resource-rich/vote-poor constituencies, particularly interest groups and economic actors who do not control votes directly, give politicians money in exchange for favors such as public works contracts. Vote-rich/resource-poor constituencies, especially economically needy electoral districts, give politicians votes in exchange for selective benefits such as public sector jobs.

The difference between clientelist and programmatic party linkage patterns is not founded on a simple distinction between collective and selective incentives. As Kitschelt emphasizes, the distinction is *procedural*. Parties are not clientelist "as long as they disburse rents as a matter of codified, universalistic public policy applying to all members of a constituency, regardless of whether a particular individual supported or opposed the party that pushed for the rent-serving policy" (Kitschelt 2000: 850). In short, clientelism, most strictly defined, refers to benefits that are awarded to people who supported the party and withheld from those who are found, on the basis of some kind of monitoring, not to have supported it. To give examples: Parties are programmatic when they create pro-union policies that help workers irrespective of the party or candidates that they support, but it is clientelistic when a party facilitates the payment of unemployment benefits to workers who are also members of the party. It is programmatic when a party enacts legislation that offers subsidies and protection to farmers – again, irrespective of a given farmer's partisan affiliation – but it is clientelistic when it offers contracts to companies that employ specific farmers because these companies and farmers support the party.

For this reason, monitoring is an important element in clientelism. Without some form of monitoring, parties cannot know if the groups that they reward with benefits are giving them the support that makes the exchange complete. However, monitoring is not necessarily easy. Under some systems, monitoring is simple, especially where, as in the pre–progressive era United States, party members escort voters to the polls and hand them a party ballot that is distinguishable (by things such as the color of the paper) from the ballot to be cast for the opposing party. Numerous ingenious methods have been used to monitor ballots even further. For example, in order to prevent ballot stuffing in nineteenth-century American elections, transparent ballot boxes were sometimes used, thereby also making it easier to monitor perfectly the ballot cast by an individual voter. In other cases, parties use immediate material benefits as a type of monitoring and enforcement mechanism: It has been reported that in elections in regions of Thailand, parties give potential supporters a single shoe (for example, the left one) but do not hand over the match (the right one) until after the ballots are counted and presumably the shoe-disbursing party has won (Ramos 2001: 10).[7] In all of these examples, because parties are able to monitor closely the behavior of their "clientele" (they can actually see that the voter is casting a vote), they can keep the provision of benefits very specific and tightly targeted.

---

[7] Other wonderful stories abound. In some cases, there are tales of voters coming to cast their ballots and then being given food or appliances by local party activists. In other cases, there are stories of campaign managers walking up to local "vote mobilizers," tearing a (roughly $100) money bill in half and explaining, "You get the other half when the votes come in."

Where campaign laws are stricter and more carefully enforced and genuinely secret ballots exist, monitoring is far more difficult. In many cases, monitoring practices of the above types are clearly impractical and illegal. Although parties can tell if particular groups or individuals do in fact provide them with contributions or mobilize groups to work on their behalf, parties are unable to monitor the precise support and voting patterns of most individuals. In such cases, it makes sense to extend Kitschelt's definition to include monitoring that occurs along more collective lines, with benefits less tightly targeted. Parties always can monitor the extent to which particular interest groups or geographic regions support the government's parties through donations, campaign volunteers, political quiescence, or, especially, a substantial number of votes. In this way, we can define as clientelist practices those in which parties give benefits to groups or regions in exchange for support of the kind I mentioned earlier or deny benefits as punishment for the lack of such support.

By defining as clientelist those systems that utilize such collective monitoring, I am perhaps stretching the bounds of the literal procedural definition. However, I am sticking to the spirit of the definition of clientelism, which emphasizes targeted, case-by-case, discretionary provision of benefits whose delivery tends to depend on support for the party or candidate.

By defining the distinction between clientelism and programmatism according to their procedures, it is very difficult to quantify clientelism or create any sort of index – for example, running from clientelistic to programmatic – by which to identify systems. As Kitschelt notes, given the multiple possible interpretations of the purpose for any given policy, it is nearly impossible to determine the proportion of a budget devoted to rent seeking or public goods items.[8] This means that the social scientist has relatively few mechanisms by which to measure whether particular practices are clientelist. Nevertheless, to examine the influence of clientelism and the attitudes toward clientelist practices, we need some sort of signal to indicate when voters and politicians are tied together through clientelist linkages. I have chosen to focus on particularistic policies, which involve the government using its discretion to dole out some sort of benefit to specific, targeted groups or regions. In some cases, these policies are disbursed to particular areas irrespective of the region's vote choices (i.e., it is not a clear votes-for-project trade). However, in many other instances, they clearly go to preferred politicians' districts. Moreover, such policies – especially when in the form of public works – are useful "tracers" of clientelism, insofar as they are usually distributed on a discretionary, case-by-case basis, and therefore tend to fall under the collective monitoring mechanism I suggested earlier.

---

[8] Carey and Shugart (1995) note similar difficulties in operationalizing a scale between party- and personalistic-oriented political behavior.

CLIENTELISM AND INCUMBENCY ADVANTAGE

A variety of factors contribute to one-party dominance in democratic systems. Certain electoral arrangements are especially advantageous for ruling parties, thereby making it more difficult to unseat them (Cox 1997). Electoral systems that promote multipartism can be advantageous as they divide the opposition. In addition, through certain types of policies, ruling parties can cultivate socioeconomic coalitions whose support is sufficient to keep the party in power for long periods (Pempel 1990). There is, as Pempel (1990) notes, an element of luck in the maintenance of such dominance. Ruling parties' bases will be less likely to collapse as long as economic conditions remain favorable for those groups whose support undergirds the government. Under such conditions, we need not expect challengers to the government to succeed.

But if opposition failure continues in the face of social or economic conditions that would appear to be unfavorable for the ruling regime, we ought to look for advantages for incumbents that exist within the political system. By definition, one-party dominance and opposition failure are a result of incumbency advantage, whether for individual incumbent politicians or for the incumbent party as a whole. And clientelism helps provide incumbents with a particularly strong advantage.

In general, incumbents have a number of advantages. Incumbent politicians are typically better known than challengers and maintain a number of perks of office that improve their ability to advertise themselves. For example, there is the American franking practice, which allows incumbents to send mail at no cost. Moreover, as Fiorina (1977) argues, incumbent politicians are especially advantaged by their casework: By facilitating voters' interactions with the government – especially the bureaucracy – incumbents generate relatively costless favor with their constituents, thereby improving their re-election chances. Because a ruling party nearly always has a larger number of incumbents than opposition parties do, name recognition, perks of office, and casework give it an advantage in running candidates for office, which carries over even when public opinion runs counter to the ruling party.

Incumbents' capacity to use governmental patronage is the most obvious advantage, especially for ruling parties, which typically control spending. Ruling parties can gain the support of numerous groups through favors such as providing public employment, offering subsidies, and creating and funding public works projects. Patronage also offers ruling parties a means to maintain the support of their primary constituents, even – perhaps especially – during times of economic slowdown, as such projects provide a type of economic safety net for many. For example, ruling parties can provide public sector jobs or increase public spending on projects that provide jobs to voters who would otherwise face economic hardship.

Incumbents can also shape universalistic, collective-goods policies in ways that may benefit them. Here I am referring to policies that benefit broad categories of people, such as the elderly or school children. The political business cycle literature focuses extensively on the ways governments manipulate the economy in an attempt both to provide outcomes that specific constituents desire and to create a strong economy shortly before the next election (see, e.g., Hibbs 1977). Moreover, these benefits can be used to lock into place different socioeconomic blocs of support for the incumbent party that otherwise might work at cross-purposes to one another.

However, socioeconomic conditions can change, and other parties can introduce new packages of policy programs that can help to divide the ruling party's base of support. Just as successful policy outcomes can be used to generate support, opponents can use negative outcomes – such as an economic downturn – against incumbent parties (Anderson 1995). As a result, such policy is at best a partial factor in generating incumbency strength and, indeed, may turn out to be more of a handicap than an advantage. Voters will tend to associate parties that rule throughout a long period of prosperity with that very prosperity, giving the parties a reputational edge even after prosperity has come to an end. Yet this edge is temporary. If prosperity does not return quickly, ruling parties' reputations – and voters' associations of the parties with prosperity – will erode.

For this reason, programmatic policies are less reliable than personalistic (i.e., based on the individual personality of the candidate) and clientelistic appeals in protecting incumbents during times of public displeasure with the ruling party. One-party dominance has been much less common outside of clientelist systems; clientelism is probably the feature that played the most potent role in preventing more credible opposition in Austria, Italy, and Japan.

Clientelist party systems emphasize administrative infrastructure, and political bonds are created through direct, material side-payments. This places a burden on opposition parties, particularly new ones with little access to such side-payments and little history of having the ability to provide them. In this way, clientelism is an obstacle to opposition party success.

CLIENTELISM AND OPPOSITION DIFFICULTIES

At the same time, new and opposition parties do make inroads in clientelist systems, as was clear in the last decade of the twentieth century in Italy, Austria, and Mexico. However, as I next explain in greater detail, when clientelism is combined with two other factors – centralized governmental fiscal structure and institutionalized protection of those in society who benefit from clientelist practices – new and opposition parties' ability to challenge the clientelist regime runs into three obstacles: weak local foundations and candidacy difficulties, limited geographic zones of competition, and poor party organization and coherence.

1. Weak Local Foundations and Candidacy Difficulties: The Impact of a Clientelistic, Fiscally Centralized System

In most systems, especially where party-generated, closed-list, proportional representation electoral arrangements do not predominate, a critical element in a party's success is its candidates for national level office.[9] In addition to its own incumbents who hold national office, a party can get potentially strong candidates from a number of different sources. It can bring in incumbent defectors from other existing parties. It can recruit nonparty political activists, such as famous celebrities (Jesse Ventura), war veterans (Dwight Eisenhower), or newscasters, who have name recognition for nonparty reasons. And it can recruit its own party members who hold office at subnational levels.[10] Naturally, attracting defectors from other parties or famous nonparty activists is hardly a reliable strategy, so parties are typically best off turning to subnational office holders from their own party. In this way, while a number of factors go into the development of a strong candidate pool for political parties, a particularly important one is the extent to which parties are strong at the subnational level.

Parties that are strong at the *sub*national level have an advantage in their capacity to recruit for national races what Jacobson (1990) calls "quality" candidates – candidates with experience in relatively high-level elected public office (e.g., state assembly).[11] Jacobson demonstrates that, in the American congressional case, the more seats a party holds in public offices at the state level, the more easily the party will be able to find quality or experienced candidates to contest national legislative races. And quality or experienced candidates are more likely to win the party a seat in the national-level race (Jacobson 1990: 58–60). Aldrich and Griffin (ND) offer a similar finding,

---

[9] Under closed- or fixed-list proportional representation, each party puts up a rank-ordered slate of candidates, and each voter casts a ballot for a party. Each party is then awarded a proportion of the total number of seats that is roughly equal to the proportion of the vote it received. (The degree to which the vote and the seat percentages are matched depends on other rules of the system.) Each party then allots its seats to its candidates according to their rank on the party list. Where a party is awarded five seats, it awards seats to the top five candidates on its list.

[10] None of this is to say that candidates without similar experiences would automatically be "weak." Nevertheless, without a proven track record in office or a large, preexisting set of supporters, parties will typically have little reason to think that such candidates would have a decent chance of winning.

[11] These candidates might be high quality for a number of reasons. Jacobson focuses on subnational office because it offers a cue that such candidates are talented and maintain important resources. Another reason that these candidates might be seen as high quality is that they have substantial preexisting bases of support.

as they demonstrate that the Republican Party was unable to do well in congressional races in the American South until it developed a base of office holders at the state level and that Republican candidates for Congress who did not have experience in subnational office were much less likely to get elected. Similarly, focusing on Germany and Great Britain, Scarrow (1996) suggests that parties – especially ones that are not yet strong at the national level – would be wise to expend energy to develop strength in local-level elections, in large measure because developing greater local electoral strength is a particularly effective candidate recruitment strategy. Moreover, developing a strong local presence helps generate greater party popularity in general and, as Curtis (1971) and Park (1998a, 1998b) demonstrate, local politicians are often the very best campaigners for a party and its national-level candidates.

However, under certain conditions, parties will be limited in their capacity to gain local strength. Where parties hold little strength at the subnational level, they will have difficulty getting their message out. They will find themselves with a dearth of strong candidates to run in national-level races and, in turn, will have much greater difficulty winning national-level seats.

The question therefore becomes, what shapes the ability of a party to be successful at the subnational level? The likely impact of party–voter linkages – that is, whether parties attract voters through programmatic or clientelist appeals – is obvious. In systems where strong links based on packages of programs or ideology bind voters and parties, local party success ought to be based on the extent to which voters approve of parties' programmatic platforms. Where party–voter linkages are founded on the clientelistic provision of goods and services, local party success ought to be based on voters' impressions of which party's candidates will be best able to provide such goods and services.

Although perhaps less obvious, local party success also ought to be shaped by the extent to which parties are dependent – in particular, financially dependent – on discretionary choices of the central government. Where subnational governmental financing depends on discretionary transfers from the central government, voters' and candidates' relationships with parties will tend to be shaped by the nature of politics at the national level.[12] This is likely to be the case even in federal systems – where subnational units are given substantial decision making autonomy of their own – if localities rely heavily upon the central government for their own financing. In contrast, where localities exhibit substantial financial autonomy, voters and candidates may be more

---

[12] Where all transfers from the central government are automatic, connections to the central government will be less important, and there is less need for local politicians and voters to be concerned with party affiliation to gain central funding. Indeed, automatic transfers even suggest a nonclientelist relationship between the center and the localities. However, my analysis is concerned with where the central government has discretionary ability to withhold (or provide) a substantial portion of subnational government funding.

inclined to affiliate with and support parties irrespective of their position in the national party context.

In the end, neither of these factors – party–voter linkages and degree of local fiscal autonomy – shapes subnational party success independently. Rather, they combine to have a substantial effect.

First, in systems like Germany's, where party–voter linkages are programmatic and subnational units do not rely heavily upon the central government for financing, voters can cast their ballots in local elections without needing to consider national-level politics (whether national policies or the strength of specific parties). In addition, the ideological or programmatic basis of politics ought to lead voters to focus primarily on local issues in making local-election decisions. Through subnational governments, voters are provided a way to get what they want at the local level. Moreover, where subnational governments maintain their own reliable financial bases, they need not worry that their local governments will suffer for being a different partisan makeup from the central government. In these cases, parties that are strong at the national level ought to have no inherent advantage in local-level elections. A party's proportion of the vote ought to be roughly the same in both national and local elections, as there is relatively little incentive to vote for the party ruling at the national level simply to ensure a stream of central governmental benefits.

Second, in systems like Britain's, where politics are similarly based on universally distributed bundles of collective goods and governmental finances are centered in the national government, voters ought to be inclined to emphasize issue-based voting in subnational elections. When localities have little power, politics tend to be nationalized. For this reason, there is little need to focus on local issues, and voters ought to be more inclined to cast ballots based on their views of the national parties at the time of voting. As a result, party success at the local level ought to be less influenced by party strength in the national parliament and more influenced by voter support for the national parties at the time of the local election.

Third, *clientelist* systems where governmental funding is highly decentralized – with subnational units exerting substantial financial autonomy – ought to lead to a very different result. Brazil and, debatably, the United States provide examples of this type. With voting based to a large degree on representatives' capacity to provide goods and services – but with this capacity not dependent upon relations with the central government – voters will be more inclined to cast votes in local-level races without consideration for politics at the national level. As a result, there ought to be very little correlation between parties' success in local and national elections, even within a single subnational unit (e.g., a state). The main exception to this pattern is when a subnational government executive maintains discretion over clientelist resources, thereby encouraging affiliation with the party of the executive.

However, in systems that are clientelist and fiscally centralized, we ought to expect a very different outcome. Italy, Austria, Mexico, and, especially, Japan are good examples. In this fourth type, voters will be most likely to cast local-election ballots for candidates of parties that are in the government at the national level. Diaz-Cayeros, Magaloni, and Weingast's (2000) discussion of voter incentives in Mexico offers a cogent micro-logic behind the behavior here: Where localities depend on the central government for funding, even voters who prefer opposition parties will be more likely to cast votes for local candidates of the national ruling party because of the danger that the ruling party will punish regions that throw their support to the opposition.

A few points ought to be added to clarify key differences between these four types of systems, as well as the incentives affecting local actors. Local dependence on the center for funding is probably not sufficient to ensure national ruling party success at the local level. Where localities are *dependent* on the central government for funding but politics are more *programmatic*, voters, by definition, ought to cast ballots according to party ties, ideology, and individual views of the parties' programs. For this reason, parties that control the national government in such systems will not necessarily own politics at the local level. Similar to voters in *clientelist* systems in which localities are especially financially *independent* of the central government, voters in *clientelist*, financially *dependent* localities will be particularly likely to cast their ballots for candidates they judge to be most capable of delivering goods and services to the locality. However, in the latter type (clientelist, financially dependent systems), local politicians rely heavily on links to the central government to gain access to these goods and services. For this reason, aspiring candidates will have great incentive to affiliate with parties that control the national-level purse strings.[13] The mechanism involves both voters and local elites.

In sum, although it is often assumed that the development of a new party is easiest to achieve at the local level, financially centralized political systems that are founded on clientelist linkages ought to hinder local new and opposition party success. Magaloni (1997) argues that the costs of entering electoral markets are lower in subnational elections. That is, in subnational elections, opposition parties can focus their scarce resources on relatively small geographical areas and voters can more comfortably take risks in trying out

---

[13] There are important commonalities here between my analysis and Greene's (2002) examination of opposition failure in Mexico. Most important, we both share an emphasis on clientelism as an explanatory variable and on what Greene calls "supply-side" analysis. That is, in both analyses, the key to party success (and failure) is the actions of elites in the party system. Many of the differences in our analysis are likely due to the presence of presidentialism in Mexico and the fact that Mexico has in many ways had an underdeveloped democracy for years.

new party alternatives (Magaloni 1997: 77). However, where politics are clientelistic and local governmental fiscal flexibility and autonomy are low, opposition parties ought to be extremely limited in their ability to win control of local governments and therefore to experiment widely in policymaking. Indeed, even if they were to win, the challengers' policy goals could very easily be held in check by the central government's ability to withhold funding. Programmatic claims and promises by local politicians would hold relatively little credibility. As a result, aspiring candidates who want to maximize their chances of holding local offices ought to avoid policy entrepreneurship that requires funds from the national government and instead prefer to affiliate with national-level politicians and parties who can help them deliver benefits to the district.

Not all politicians and voters will avoid opposition parties at the local level in such systems. Many voters and politicians with particular sets of ideologies and relationships with the opposition will continue to affiliate with and support opposition parties. And certainly, where there is party competition at the national level, local voters and politicians will not jump from party to party, in recognition of whichever party sits in power in the nation's parliament. Nevertheless, the incentives to affiliate with the national ruling party – indeed, to support the ruling party even when one prefers other parties more – are markedly greater in clientelist, financially centralized systems. Therefore, in such systems, national ruling parties ought to win a particularly large proportion of subnational-level political seats, and national opposition parties ought to win an especially small proportion.

There may be party change and development at the local level in clientelist, financially centralized systems, but this change will usually be preceded by change at the national level. That is, in such systems, party development will tend to be top-down. At the same time, there is an exception to this rule. Even in financially centralized systems, there may be variation in the level of localities' dependence on the central government. Where localities do not depend on the central government for financing, politicians and voters can affiliate with opposition parties, with less fear of ruling party retribution.

2. Limited Zones of Competition: The Limited Success of Anti-Clientelist Appeals in a System That Protects Supporters of Clientelism

According to my analysis, non-ruling parties in clientelist, financially centralized systems ought to have difficulty winning office at the local level. These parties will then face a substantial disadvantage, with weak local foundations and a fairly shallow pool of candidates to contest district races in national parliamentary elections. However, this analysis is not sufficient to explain the bigger issue of opposition failure at the national level. The opposition failed for decades in Italy, Austria, and Mexico – three cases that fall under the Clientelist/Financially Centralized heading – but especially beginning in the 1990s, new parties in these three countries found success.

It is possible that Mexico should not be placed in the same category as the other clientelist, financially centralized cases. Presidential systems such as Mexico's offer any party an opportunity for success as long as it has a single, popular candidate. Except in nondemocratic systems and wholly new democracies, presidentialism has a consolidating effect on parties and tends to lead to two-party competition (Cox 1997). One-party dominance in democratic presidential systems is unheard of. Indeed, it should not be surprising that as Mexico and Taiwan – two one-party dominant systems – grew increasingly democratic, each saw its opposition party win the presidency. Moreover, the rise of the Mexican opposition has in large measure gone hand in hand with the democratization of the country. It is difficult to find adequate comparisons in the other cases examined here to the politically motivated violence inflicted upon many who supported the opposition in Mexico, and the increased popularity of the opposition may in large part be due to a backlash against the longtime heavy-handed tactics of its ruling party, the PRI.

In addition, there is a significant difference between Austria and the other clientelist, financially centralized cases I examine here: the electoral system. Austria's electoral system makes the late 1990s' rise of its seemingly always small FPÖ and the decline of its seemingly permanent government party, the SPÖ, more understandable. Because of its large-district, party-controlled proportional representation-list system, individual candidacies are less important in Austria. As a result, even parties with relatively weak candidate bases may do well in national elections.

Nevertheless, Italy maintained neither a presidential system nor a party-centered electoral system. Neither of the explanations I suggested for Mexico and Austria can help us understand the success of new alternatives in Italy. At the same time, it appears that clientelism – or, in this case, the backlash against it – had a powerful impact there as well.

A backlash against clientelism appears to have played a critical role in shaping the success of new parties in Italy (as well as Austria). Kitschelt argues that clientelism remains viable in any country as long as it does not substantially harm the success of more "productive" (i.e., efficient and internationally competitive) sectors of the economy. Yet, in the 1980s and 1990s, "ratcheted up" costs of clientelism – a result of continued government support for inefficient sectors – and greater international competition associated with the countries' growing affluence led to a major rift between productive and unproductive segments of the economy within a number of countries that maintained large public sectors (Kitschelt 2000: 862–3). It is this rift that parties in Italy and Austria used to their advantage by appealing to those opposed to the maintenance of the clientelist system. A backlash against clientelism fueled new party growth and a solid challenge to the ruling regimes. It also appears that in Mexico the opposition PAN's free market position appealed to many voters who aimed a similar backlash at the PRI.[14] Opposition to public works and "money politics" was a serious opposition theme in Japan in the 1990s,[15] but the Japanese opposition was unable to ride it to victory.

Institutional protections for areas dependent upon clientelism and supportive of the ruling regime explain much of the reason for the different outcomes in these different cases. Even in clientelist systems, dependence upon clientelist practices vary by region. Insofar as support for the ruling regime is tied in large part to the level of dependence on clientelist practices, the result is likely to be what I call "parallel party systems": one system in heavily clientelism-dependent regions that strongly supports the ruling regime[16] and one system in other regions where party competition is much greater.

When faced with a context that includes two parallel party systems of this kind, by what mechanism will anti-clientelist appeals be successful? Parties that push anti-clientelism appeals must channel votes from people who seek the demise of the clientelist state into a substantial number of seats. This is easy to imagine in a national proportional representation system where a majority of voters are swayed by anti-clientelist appeals. But in a district-based electoral system, anti-clientelist appeals can only go so far in regions that are highly supportive of clientelism, and parties pushing such anti-clientelist appeals ought to have little chance of winning seats in those areas. Therefore, anti-clientelist parties must rely upon winning the bulk of their seats in the remaining districts. But in many less clientelism-dependent districts, interests and preferences will be mixed, leading to greater competition between clientelist parties and the rising anti-clientelist group. The likely result, therefore, is little success for anti-clientelist parties in clientelism-dependent regions and mixed success in other regions.

For this reason, in terms of the proportion of seats they win, anti-clientelist parties in clientelist systems ought to succeed only where a small proportion of seats is allotted to areas that are heavily supportive of clientelism or utilize electoral systems (such as proportional representation) that give opponents

---

[14] A similar backlash appears to have played a substantial role in ending Labor dominance in Israel in the 1970s. Moreover, although clearly not clientelist, Sweden's fusion of economic and political power had a type of functional equivalence to clientelism that generated a backlash similar to those faced in clientelist systems.

[15] Insofar as greater urbanization in Japan went along with greater public dissatisfaction with public works spending, "money politics," and the clientelist system more generally, urbanization also has a potential effect on opposition success. However, the effect is only indirect: Urbanization reduces tolerance for clientelist practices, which in turn provides the opposition with opportunities for greater success.

[16] Examples include the U.S. South of the second half of the nineteenth century and much of the twentieth century (see especially Key 1949), southern Italy, and rural Japan.

of clientelism some representation in regions where supporters of clientelism make up a plurality of the population.

None of these considerations removes the importance of quality candidates. Where fixed-list proportional representation lists do not dominate the electoral system, even anti-clientelist parties have an opportunity to win in areas supportive of clientelism if armed with a strong set of candidates. Moreover, the presence of strong candidates in other regions will be of great benefit as anti-clientelist parties seek to win a larger number of seats to make up for their deficit in unfriendly regions.

3. Party Organization and Coherence: Constraints on New Party Consolidation and Development in a Top-Down System

In determining the viability of *new* parties, the extent of party fragmentation and coherence are important. Party fragmentation refers to the extent to which parties consolidate into a larger mass or fragment into smaller pieces. Coherence refers to the extent to which new parties are able to develop into a unified whole from both an organizational and policy perspective.

Various factors can affect whether a party system consolidates into a small number of parties or fragments into a larger number of smaller ones. Where party systems are fragmented, particularly a fragmented set of new parties, the new party vote will most likely be divided, making it much more difficult for new parties to do well. Perhaps more important, where party systems are fragmented, voters are likely to be confused by the various new labels in front of them and will be fairly uncertain about what each stands for, keeping support for new parties low. Certain factors may also encourage new party consolidation, but party consolidation does not necessarily lead to greater party coherence, a critical element in the development of voter certainty about parties. That is, even when there are numerous incentives for groups to join together into a single party, getting these groups to work together can be a daunting task. In particular, the way a party forms will shape the coordination of the various groups within it and, in turn, the degree to which observers can be certain of what it stands for. Such problems ought to impede new parties' capacity to challenge ruling regimes.

Fragmentation and Consolidation of New Parties. The most obvious factor shaping party fragmentation is electoral law. There are subtle rules that encourage party fragmentation, but the most potent is probably PR, which makes it possible for parties to survive with relatively small vote percentages. In contrast, single member district systems, such as those used in elections to the U.S. House of Representatives and the British House of Commons, tend to promote greater consolidation of parties. SMD systems make the entry of new parties more difficult; however, new parties that manage to become established can grow quite strong because SMDs encourage numerous smaller parties to consolidate into a smaller number of relatively large (and therefore potentially more competitive) ones. A second factor shaping party fragmentation is constitutional structure, in particular whether the system is presidential or parliamentary. As Cox (1997) explains, under certain conditions, presidential systems tend to lead to a consolidation of parties and two-partism. In general, new parties have less of an opportunity to make headway in presidential systems, where success is dependent on widespread support. Admittedly, new parties' best chance at getting started is in pure PR parliamentary systems, but such systems also tend to set a cap on their potential because numerous parties can coexist under PR, and it is very difficult for any one of them to develop into a strong challenger.

In contrast, while new parties typically have little chance in existing presidential party systems, an attractive presidential candidate can quickly give his or her party a boost even if the party is new. Even in the strongly two-party U.S. system, it was the populist Perot candidacy that gave rise to the Reform Party, not the other way around.[17] And in party systems in flux, parties are far more likely to develop quickly when these systems include presidentialism, as the nearly successful presidential campaign of Cardenas and the PRD in Mexico demonstrates.

Another factor shaping party fragmentation is laws (if they are enforced) defining new party formation and party funding. Where such rules privilege existing parties, fragmentation will be kept at a minimum. For example, in Mexico in 1988, presidential candidates were legally bound to run under the heading of a registered party. As a result, the Cardenistas quickly joined with a preexisting party because they knew that they would have difficulty gaining legal registry of their own through the ruling PRI-led electoral commission (Bruhn 1997: 166).

New Party Coherence and Organization – Problems of Top-Down Formation. Such mergers of convenience can also create problems in the development of parties. Some new parties, such as most of the world's socialist parties, grow out of what Shefter (1994) calls "external mobilization," a process in which societal groups create parties in order to gain a voice (usually over an issue or linked set of issues) in government. (This is in contrast to "internally mobilized" parties, which are created by elites within the state seeking to create power for themselves within the government by creating linkages to a base of support in society.)[18] Externally mobilized new parties

---

[17] However, the party did little after Perot's popularity declined.

[18] Similar to Shefter's distinction is Duverger's discussion of party origins that distinguishes between parties that emerge from "extra-parliamentary" origins and those growing out of coordination within the national parliament (1954: xxiv–xxxv).

typically have a set of issues to unify them, thereby alleviating many potential problems of coordination within the organization.

However, in most established clientelist, financially centralized systems, a type of internal mobilization will lead to top-down party formation. When, as in the Mexican case discussed previously, new parties are born out of a merger orchestrated by elites who bring very different and often incompatible bases of support with them, these parties may face serious organizational difficulties. Even though they may successfully come together into one new party, they may be drawn by little other than the desire to challenge the dominant parties in the system. In essence, then, these parties are founded on the movements of elites, and therefore lack a grassroots base. Moreover, they are likely to disagree on many of the core issues of the day and, as a result, may have difficulty developing a coherent message by which to appeal to the public. Lacking one, the public is likely to be confused by the presence of such different groups in a single party.

Electoral laws can alleviate some of the problems and confusion surrounding these organizational tie-ups. For example, the postreform Italian system offers parties the opportunity to work together as a cartel, forming an official alliance and jointly running a single candidate at the district level while maintaining their own identity in the PR section of the ballot. As a result, Italian parties are able to reap the benefits of allying with other parties without the organizational difficulties that would accompany an official merger, and voters are able to retain a clearer picture of each individual party. Without electoral laws of this kind, new parties formed out of a top-down/merger process face difficulties in their ability to work together. And even in the Italian case, it was not always clear what each *alliance* advocated.

THE MODEL IN BRIEF: CLIENTELISM, FINANCIAL CENTRALIZATION, AND "INSTITUTIONAL PROTECTION"

In sum, I am suggesting a model of opposition failure that is founded on clientelism. Throughout this book, I argue that the combination of clientelism and two other factors – fiscal centralization and institutional protections for clientelist "clienteles" – is sufficient to explain opposition failure because of the following problems it causes.

1. *Candidacy difficulties and weak local foundations.* Clientelism combined with financial centralization, in which localities are financially dependent on the central government, will tend to make party success at the local level difficult to achieve without high levels of strength at the national level. Parties that are weak at the subnational level will have weak local bases and face difficulty generating a pool of strong

candidates for national level races, thereby damaging their chances of winning national parliamentary seats.[19]

2. *Limited geographic zones of competition.* Few systems are founded solely on clientelism. As long as less productive "clienteles" of the state do not cause a serious drain on the resources of the productive sectors of the economy, both sectors can coexist. When productive sectors are hurt by the continued existence of the clientelist state, opposition parties may be able to use the rift that develops to their advantage. However, where regions of the country that are particularly supportive of clientelism have sufficient institutional protection – in particular, in the apportionment of seats to their areas – parties seeking to challenge the clientelist structure will tend to be limited in the number of geographical areas and electoral districts in which they can realistically compete.[20]

3. *Party organization and coherence.* The combination of clientelism and centralized government structure makes new party development difficult to achieve from the ground up. In such systems, with the exception of regional parties, new party growth will tend to be top-down. Where party development requires politicians from a variety of parties to join together under a single new banner, (a) it will usually be difficult for politicians from different preexisting parties to work together for the new party, and (b) the sitting politicians who unite to create the new party will be unlikely (or perceived as unlikely) to agree on a number of different issues, thereby making it more difficult to know what the new party truly stands for.

Ultimately, the first two of these problems – weak local foundations/ candidacy difficulties and limited geographic zones of competition – are sufficient explanations for the failure of Japan's opposition. The third – the problems of party organization and coherence – serves to exacerbate the other obstacles the opposition faces.

INEVITABILITY OF PARTY COMPETITION FAILURE? THE IMPACT OF NATIONAL POLITICIANS

Although the constraints on opposition party success are considerable in Japan, party competition in countries like Japan is not impossible. Structures and institutions can create strong incentives for certain types of behavior, but few such structures are wholly deterministic in their effects. The structures I discuss create incentives that powerfully disadvantage opposition parties, but

---

[19] This would be much less of a disadvantage in party generated, PR-list systems.
[20] Knowing this, the dominant party will be careful in any electoral reform, even one undertaken to assuage hostile public opinion, to make sure this distortion is not completely eliminated.

even within these structures there is room for party competition. However, as long as the constraints I list in Figure 1.1 exist, national-level politician behavior will usually be the key to such party competition.

These structures greatly constrain the likelihood of a grassroots movement that can bring about party competition. In programmatic, party-centered, presidential systems, it is far easier for voters to cast out an unpopular party: Voters are likely to cast ballots for an opposition party presenting a platform that is more popular than that of the ruling party. Voters are less concerned with specific, often advantageous, elements of the incumbent party, such as the personal popularity of many of its candidates. Voters across the country can give an opposition party control of the government by electing a single member – the presidential candidate – of the party and need not coordinate several hundred legislative elections across the country. In contrast, in clientelist, candidate-centered, parliamentary systems, it is much less likely that voters will bring an opposition to power. Many voters support the ruling party simply because it provides them clientelist benefits. No opposition party can appeal to them. Many other voters may have reasons to support an opposition party but will not because of the presence of ruling party candidates with personal qualities that are appealing. Finally, in parliamentary systems – particularly ones with small electoral districts – a type of voter coordination is necessary to defeat an incumbent party because voters must elect opposition candidates in multiple districts.

In such systems, the impact of national-level elites is substantial. In clientelist, centralized systems, voters and subnational politicians in large measure take their affiliation cues from national-level politicians and the composition of the national government. Although incumbents usually have weak incentives to leave a ruling party, from time to time they do decide to defect. It is only at such times that party change is likely.

I discuss the impact of national-level elites in greater detail in Chapter 10. It is possible for the structures I discussed in this chapter to become altered, but such changes are difficult and slow to come about. *Given the foundations* described here, the greatest opportunity for party competition must come from national-level politicians leaving the party in power and creating a new force opposing it. The ultimate implication is that, although voters are typically held to be the ultimate sovereign in a democratic system – even democracies in which voters delegate most decision-making power to elected representatives – structures like these make it much harder for voters opposed to the clientelist regime to help bring about party change.

2

Opposition Failure in Japan

Background and Explanations

It looked like the end of business as usual in Japan as the ruling Liberal Democratic Party lost power in 1993. After the Diet, Japan's parliament, passed a no-confidence motion and new elections were held, a coalition of former opposition parties, former LDP members, and new parties entered into the first non-LDP government since the party was created in 1955. However, by summer 1994, the LDP was the leading party in a coalition government. After then, the party continued to be at the center of every government, with only a small party or two joining it in a coalition. As of the early 2000s, the LDP remained the dominant party in Japan, with a substantial advantage over its potential competitors.

The continuation of one-party dominance in Japan went against a worldwide trend. At the same time that former communist and authoritarian regimes were overcoming their nondemocratic legacies, one-party dominant regimes in long-time democracies were undergoing major changes, as their leading parties lost the grip on power they had held for decades. Among the clearest cases of this change was Italy, where the longtime ruling Christian Democratic Party disintegrated and was replaced by new alternatives. Even in Mexico – often left out of discussions of one-party dominance because of questions over the degree to which Mexico had been democratic – the longtime ruling PRI, which dominated politics to a greater degree than any party in Italy or Japan, lost its firm grasp on power. In 1993 and 1994, it seemed that the LDP would go the way of the DC, but by 2003 the LDP was clearly the dominant party in Japan, more powerful and holding substantially more seats than any other party.

Democracy is predicated on competition and, in times of trouble, democracy's competitive impulses are supposed to lead existing parties either to change their appeals or to spur the creation of credible alternatives.

For additional information on the Japanese party system, see the links to the supplementary Web site for this book at *www.ethanscheiner.com*.

Continued one-party dominance in Japan forces us to consider what brings about responsiveness to voter unhappiness in democracies.

The opposition's inability to knock the LDP out of power had been a puzzle for decades, but the lack of a strong, sustained challenge to the LDP was particularly striking in the post-1993 period, a time of great opportunity for the opposition: Japan faced some of its toughest years since the early postwar period and the LDP itself was widely reviled. Why, even in the face of great dissatisfaction with the dominant party, was no opposition party able to offer itself as a credible challenger in Japan?

This chapter opens by laying out in detail the most puzzling of these issues, the failure of the Japanese opposition in the 1990s and early 2000s. Having laid out the starkest of the puzzles, the bulk of the chapter considers the problem more thoroughly by providing general background on postwar Japanese party politics and indicating the shortcomings in previous analyses that attempted to explain away the problem of opposition failure and LDP dominance. The chapter closes by introducing a new approach to understanding the problem of opposition failure in both the pre- and post-1990 period in Japan. As I explain in Chapter 10, it is possible that the opposition will be able to overcome the LDP. But only by recognizing the reasons for past failure can we understand how opposition success can occur.

THE JAPANESE CONTEXT OR WHY PARTY COMPETITION OUGHT TO HAVE EMERGED

The 1990s have been described as *anni horribili* for Japan (Pempel 1998). It should have been clear that things were not to go Japan's way when, in 1992, while on a trip to Tokyo, flu-ridden U.S. President Bush threw up in the lap of Japanese Prime Minister Miyazawa. Although offering less fodder for late night talk shows and *Saturday Night Live*, Japan's economic bust was probably the country's most consequential problem of the decade. The economy sagged throughout the 1990s and into the new millennium. By the end of 2002, unemployment had hit a record 5.5 percent (*Japan Times*, March 1, 2003),[1] and in the late 1990s and early 2000s the Tokyo Stock Exchange fell to its lowest levels in more than a decade and a half (*Asahi Shinbun*). Once seen as invulnerable, many huge firms such as Yamaichi Securities went bankrupt. Indeed, in early 2000, bankruptcies rose 51 percent from the previous year, and numerous major firms such as Nissan, NEC, and Sony "restructured" massively, each laying off more than 10,000 workers (Pempel 2000). By 2001, public sector debt exceeded gross national product (GNP) and, including the balance in the red from the private sector, was more than double Japan's GNP. Ranked the most internationally competitive

---

[1] Unless otherwise noted, all references to newspaper articles in this chapter are to the online editions.

economy in the world in 1990 by the World Economic Forum, by 1997 Japan had fallen to fourteenth (Pempel 1998: 139).

During this period, news of corruption – particularly involving leading LDP politicians – was widespread. In 1988, the Recruit scandal (stocks for political favors) shook the LDP, with most major leaders of the party implicated, and brought down the Takeshita prime ministership in 1989. A similar scandal involving the Sagawa Kyūbin company led to the bribery arrest of LDP kingpin Kanemaru Shin in March 1993. It was common to find media reports revealing scandals surrounding money for favors between business and politicians, illegal ties between brokerages, organized crime and the LDP, huge local governmental expenditures on wining and dining national officials who regulated and funded the localities, and bid rigging of public construction projects. Big business had always been a major ally of the LDP. But in 1993, when Japan's major business association, Keidanren, felt that the longtime ruling party was not going to back reforms to help constrain such excesses, it cut off its automatic contributions to the LDP (Pempel 1998: 140–1).

The public grew outraged over governmental incompetence and impropriety. After a massive earthquake hit the city of Kobe and killed thousands in 1995, a series of governmental gaffes appeared to dramatically slow relief efforts. In the following year, it was revealed that the Health and Welfare ministries had colluded with blood suppliers to cover up supplier negligence in the blood-screening process, leading to the transfusion of HIV-tainted blood to medical patients. With the collapse of the economic bubble, a number of bad loan crises – widely blamed on the Ministries of Finance and Agriculture – developed, requiring huge sums of public money to resolve them. These events only served to further weaken public support for the LDP.[2]

In 2000, the emergence of Mori Yoshirō as prime minister only brought the LDP into further disrepute. Anger began with the backroom deals used to choose Mori as Japan's leader in the wake of a stroke that ultimately took the life of incumbent Prime Minister Obuchi Keizō. The public resented both the closed-door nature of the decision and the clear dissembling of party leaders. Soon after the decisions were made – ostensibly according to Obuchi's hospital-bed "wishes" – it was reported that in fact Obuchi's stroke had been so massive that he most likely could have made no decision whatsoever.

From the late 1980s, LDP cabinets tended to maintain very low public approval ratings: The Obuchi cabinet came into office with only 24.5 percent approval. As part of an outpouring of support for the dying former

---

[2] And none of this even includes the sarin gas attack unleashed by religious zealots at a Tokyo subway station. Even though it did not directly affect trust in the LDP, the event led to a further deterioration of public trust in general.

Prime Minister Obuchi, the Mori cabinet entered office with a much higher support rating of 41.9 percent (*Yomiuri Shinbun*). However, the new prime minister quickly proved incapable of keeping his foot out of his mouth, calling Japan a divine nation (leading many to fear a return to the ideology of the prewar imperial period) and suggesting that it would be best if unaffiliated voters stayed in bed on election day.

By spring 2001, the Mori cabinet's approval rating had plummeted to under 10 percent, with a disapproval rating exceeding 80 percent (*Yomiuri Shinbun*). Another statistic climaxed a trend that had been building for years: The LDP became the overwhelming top choice for most hated party in Japan, with 44.4 percent of the public citing a dislike of the party, far ahead of the 11 percent who despised the Communists (*Asahi Shinbun*, March 13, 2001).

Just when all seemed lost for the LDP, hope emerged in the form of the long- and wavy-haired reformer Koizumi Junichirō. A longtime LDP maverick from an urban district in Kanagawa Prefecture, Koizumi was given little chance of winning the party presidency. However, a shift in party rules gave subnational branches of the party greater influence in the leadership primary process, and Koizumi was swept into power. As president of the LDP, Koizumi became Japan's prime minister in April 2001. An advocate of "structural reforms without sanctuary," Koizumi sought to shake up the LDP. Threatening to dissolve the parliament and possibly the LDP itself if his reforms were not approved, he sought to transform the Japanese economy through a cleanup of bad bank loans, privatization, deregulation and administrative reform. Koizumi's words and style instantly struck a chord with the Japanese people. His cabinet came into office with a public approval rating of 78 percent, the highest in Japanese history (*Asahi Shinbun*, April 30, 2001), and Koizumi himself received support ratings of higher than 85 percent, with only 5.7 percent demonstrating disapproval (*Yomiuri Shinbun*, May 29, 2001). A record 78 percent of respondents to a national survey indicated an interest in national politics, and 76 percent predicted a bright political future (*Yomiuri Shinbun*, June 13, 2001). Particularly noteworthy, young people – typically the most cynical, pessimistic, and apathetic group in Japan – were the most optimistic of all, as 81 percent of surveyed 20-somethings expressed a belief that politics were improving (*Yomiuri Shinbun*, July 12, 2002). Riding the Koizumi boom, the LDP had its most successful election in more than ten years in the 2001 House of Councillors race.

However, the Koizumi phenomenon did not prove to be the panacea many in the LDP hoped for. Frequently criticized for presenting vague plans with no concrete proposals, Koizumi did not appear to put forth as active a reform campaign as many had hoped. More problematic, Koizumi's plans regularly ran into obstacles placed by LDP bigwigs who sought to avoid major change, in particular relating to key LDP support groups such as the postal system and road construction companies. Koizumi's popularity continued to outstrip the LDP's, but his personal support ratings and those of his cabinet declined over time. By June 2002, cabinet disapproval (47 percent) was greater than approval (37 percent in one poll and 42 percent in another), and 65 percent of survey respondents felt it was unlikely or impossible that Koizumi would achieve his reform aims, as compared to 32 percent who thought he would be successful (*Asahi Shinbun*, June 24, 2002; *Yomiuri Shinbun*, June 25, 2002). In a summer 2002 public opinion survey, only 39 percent of respondents felt Japanese politics were heading in a positive direction, as opposed to 51 percent, a record worst, who felt politics were getting worse. In contrast to a year before, 34 percent of those in their 20s felt politics were improving. Finally, 82 percent cited a lack of trust of politicians and political parties, up nearly 20 percentage points from a year earlier (*Yomiuri Shinbun*, July 12, 2002). Koizumi's leadership at various points, such as the aftermath of revelations that North Korea had kidnapped Japanese citizens in the past, briefly helped his administration's popularity, but that popularity was hardly stable. In July 2004, in the wake of parliamentary moves that were deemed by many to be dictatorial and underhanded on issues relating to pension reform and the sending of troops to Iraq, Koizumi's poll numbers reached a new low, as his cabinet's approval rating hit 35.7 percent (*Yomiuri Shinbun*, July 4, 2004).

In short, there was substantial voter anger in Japan. A desire to create a system where parties would alternate in power fueled much of the vote for new parties in 1993 (Kabashima 1994; Reed 1997). The LDP's once massive societal base of support had shrunk. The combination of the preceding factors and the Japan Socialist Party's[3] willingness to abandon its traditional appeals and join a coalition government with the LDP, its longtime enemy, led to a great distrust of Japan's primary postwar parties. Complaints about the two parties grew louder and more urgent in the latter years of the twentieth century, but their reputations had declined steadily since the 1960s. In 1958, the JSP had the support of nearly 25 percent of the total electorate (i.e., not just those who voted). In the first two elections under Japan's new mixed electoral system in 1996 and 2000, the party received 2–3 percent of votes cast for candidates in single member districts and 6–9 percent of the total party vote, leaving it with support from around 1–5 percent of the total electorate. In the 1958 election, the LDP was supported by nearly 45 percent of the electorate, but this dropped to under 20 percent for the party from 1996 on.

Japanese voters were interested in issues, yet turned off by politics, and this dissatisfaction reached new heights in the 1990s (Pharr 2000). Voter turnout dropped, and independence rose: Prior to the 1990s, roughly 70 percent of eligible voters cast ballots in HR elections. This dropped to roughly

---

[3] The party called itself the JSP until January 1996, when it renamed itself the Social Democratic Party. I will denote the Socialists as the JSP until Chapter 8, when I focus my analysis on the party (by then called SDP) around the 1996 election.

60 percent in HR elections after 1990 and even lower in other elections in Japan. Throughout the 1970s and 1980s, the percentage of the population reporting itself to be independent – that is, supporting no party whatsoever – hovered between 20 and 30 percent, but in the 1990s it rose to between 40 and 50 percent (Tanaka and Nishizawa 1997).

Nevertheless, no serious challenger moved in to mobilize this increasing discontent for more than brief periods. How is this possible?

SOME PERSPECTIVE ON JAPANESE OPPOSITION FAILURE

The failure of the opposition in Japan contrasts with examples of party competition success in the other country cases noted in Chapter 1. By 2003, the DC had long been dead in Italy, and political competition had focused on nothing but new alternatives for a decade. In Sweden, the Social Democratic Party certainly remained Sweden's strongest party, but periods of greater SAP unpopularity had led to electoral losses for the party and a number of years where other parties controlled the government. In Austria, Freedom Party success in the 1999 election helped knock the Social Democratic Party out of government for the first time since 1970,[4] and Austrian People's Party success in the 2002 election left the SPÖ short of a plurality in seats and votes for the first time since 1966. In Mexico, the six-year term won by PAN president Fox ensured that the longtime ruling PRI would be out of executive power for a substantial period.

In contrast, after 50 years since the LDP's birth, the opposition had kept the LDP out of the Japanese government for a mere ten months and 20 days (from August 9, 1993, until June 30, 1994). Moreover, the eleven months of governmental feast were followed yet again by famine. Beginning in the late 1980s, the Japanese public appeared eager to latch on to new party alternatives, but even though new party threats were quick to emerge, they did not find a way to maintain voter allegiance, and, as of 2004, the LDP was yet to face a serious, sustained challenge.

I have attributed success to Italy's new parties because Italian politics came to involve very serious competition, with no party firmly ensconced in power. It might be argued, then, that I am understating the progress of the Japanese opposition and/or that I have lowered the bar too low in evaluating the success of parties in countries like Italy. Unlike the LDP, Italy's formerly dominant DC imploded, leaving a political vacuum to be filled. Moreover, in terms of the number of seats it held, no Italian party was any stronger than the opposition in Japan. Clearly part of the problem for the opposition in Japan was the fact that, from the beginning, it faced a single dominant party. In contrast, Italy's parties entered into a markedly more fragmented

---

[4] Throughout the postwar until 1999, except for 1966–1970, the SPÖ was never out of power.

party arena, which allowed a party to become competitive with a smaller seat share than parties in Japan.

Nevertheless, in Italy and other countries, parties found ways to work within the system's competitive structure and set of rules to overcome an unpopular ruling party. Even the DC could not have been completely toppled if alternatives had not been able to move in and attract voter support that had belonged to the longtime ruling party. Despite the LDP's apparent strength, there was a base of Japanese voters who did not support the LDP, but no one found a way to channel this lack of support into a lasting challenge.

How could such intense displeasure with the status quo exist without any party developing a capability to offer itself as a viable alternative to the LDP? The Japanese system raises critically important questions about representative democracy. In times of citizen anger, voters in a democratic society are supposed to be able to remove the object of their displeasure (at least the object that is up for reelection).

JAPAN'S POSTWAR PARTY SYSTEM AND THE FAILURE OF THE OPPOSITION

The opposition's ineffectiveness during the 1993–2003 period is all the more stunning because it came after decades of opposition failure, which apparently taught the parties relatively little about how to end the LDP's stranglehold on power.

One-and-a-Half Party System

With the exception of the brief inclusion of the Socialists in a coalition government in 1947–8, conservatives – in particular, the Liberal and Democratic (or Progressive) Parties – dominated coalition governments of the first decade after the war. In 1955, the Left and Right Socialist Parties in Japan joined together for electoral purposes to form the Japanese Socialist Party. The Liberals and the Democrats soon followed suit, uniting to form the Liberal Democratic Party. The JSP's base of support was labor (in particular, the public sector union Sōhyō), and the party consistently made its electoral appeals along class lines, taking a confrontational approach to "monopoly capital." The LDP was by and large conservative and represented agriculture, and small and big business. The LDP would come to dominate Japanese politics for the remainder of the twentieth century and, except for the 1993–4 period, was the central player in the government throughout. Until 1994, the JSP was consistently the voters' second choice. Because of the general weakness of the opposition, the system was dubbed a one-and-a-half party system.

In 1960, the JSP led the opposition to renewing the U.S.-Japan Security Treaty. Renewal was unpopular in Japan at the time, and LDP Prime Minister Kishi added fuel to the fire as he rammed the treaty through the Diet using questionable parliamentary tactics. The result was widespread protest in the streets, which led to Kishi's resignation. There was hope on the left that opposition to the treaty would lead to an electorally successful Socialist Party. Instead, it was the LDP that was successful, changing the terms of the debate to focus on economic growth and Prime Minister Ikeda's "Income Doubling Plan." The plan appeared to bear fruit: The 1960s were a time of unprecedented economic success in the country. Japan's "miracle" economy saw huge annual growth rates of 9.7 percent over the first half of the decade, which jumped to 12.2 percent over the second half (Kosai 1986).

In part because of the support it drummed up through its economic growth policies, the LDP remained the dominant party in Japan from that point on. With the exception of a small number of elections for the less important House of Councillors (the Upper House of Japan's national parliament), the party was the leading vote winner in every election in its existence. In addition, the LDP and conservative, independent affiliates formed a majority in the House of Representatives (Lower House) in every year until 1993.[5]

However, despite besting Japan's other parties, the LDP never won a majority of the HR vote after 1963. (See Table 2.1.) At the same time, the JSP's ideological appeals – especially its continued call for dictatorship of the proletariat – were seen as anachronistic at a time in which most Japanese, workers as well as executives, were benefiting from Japan's economic growth. The JSP peaked in 1958, with 33 percent of the vote and 36 percent of the seats in the House of Representatives. While the party made a dramatic run, winning the aberrant 1989 Upper House election, after 1967 the JSP never won more than 24 percent of the vote and 27 percent of the seats in the Lower House.

Other parties began gaining pockets of the support formerly given to the LDP and JSP. In most urban areas, the party system grew very competitive, as alternatives to the LDP and JSP gained significant electoral strength there. But none of the new alternatives grew particularly powerful. Rounding out the parties of the 1950s was the Japan Communist Party, which found little success in the 1950s and 1960s, but gained strength in the 1970s. Even then, the party won no more than 11 percent of the vote and 8 percent of the seats. Centrist parties also emerged. First, in 1959, moderate elements within the JSP split off to form the Democratic Socialist Party, founded in particular on private sector union support. But the centrist party never won more than 8.8 percent of the vote and 7.4 percent of the Lower House seats.

---

[5] The party did not always win a majority of seats in the election itself, but a number of conservative independents would join the LDP after each election, thereby giving the LDP a post-election majority. After the 1983 election, the LDP, which had won 48.9 percent of the total seats, formed a coalition with the New Liberal Club, which held 1.6 percent of the seats. But the LDP did not form the coalition to gain a majority. After nine conservative independents joined the LDP – thereby giving it a majority – the ruling party formed a coalition with the NLC to obtain greater numbers for the sake of managing the Diet more effectively (Hrebenar 1992: 8).

TABLE 2.1 *Percentage of HR Votes (bold) and Seats (parentheses) Won by Japan's Major Parties: 1958–93*

	1958	1960	1963	1967	1969	1972	1976	1979	1980	1983	1986	1990	1993
LDP	57.8	57.6	54.7	48.8	47.6	46.9	41.8	44.6	47.9	45.8	49.4	46.1	36.6
	(61.5)	(63.3)	(60.6)	(57.0)	(59.2)	(55.2)	(48.7)	(48.5)	(56.0)	(48.9)	(58.6)	(53.7)	(43.6)
NLC							4.2	3.0	3.0	2.3	1.8		
							(3.3)	(0.8)	(2.3)	(1.6)	(1.2)		
DSP		8.8	7.4	7.4	7.7	7.0	6.3	6.8	6.6	7.3	6.4	4.8	3.5
		(3.6)	(4.9)	(6.2)	(6.4)	(3.9)	(5.7)	(6.8)	(6.3)	(7.4)	(5.1)	(2.7)	(2.9)
Kōmeitō				5.4	10.9	8.5	10.9	9.8	9.0	10.1	9.4	8.0	8.1
				(5.1)	(9.7)	(5.9)	(10.8)	(11.2)	(6.5)	(11.4)	(10.9)	(8.8)	(10.0)
JSP	32.8	27.6	29.0	27.9	21.4	21.9	20.7	19.7	19.3	19.5	17.2	24.4	15.4
	(35.5)	(31.0)	(30.8)	(28.8)	(18.5)	(24.0)	(24.1)	(20.9)	(20.9)	(21.9)	(16.6)	(26.6)	(13.7)
JCP	2.5	2.9	4.0	4.8	6.8	10.5	10.4	10.4	9.8	9.3	8.8	8.0	7.7
	(0.2)	(0.6)	(1.1)	(1.0)	(2.9)	(7.7)	(3.3)	(7.6)	(5.7)	(5.1)	(5.1)	(3.1)	(2.9)
Shinsei													10.1
													(10.8)
Sakigake													2.6
													(2.5)
JNP													8.0
													(6.8)

Note: All figures do not add up to 100 percent because of rounding and the presence of minor party and independent candidates (not listed here).
Source: Asah. Shinbun and Curtis (1988, 1999).

39

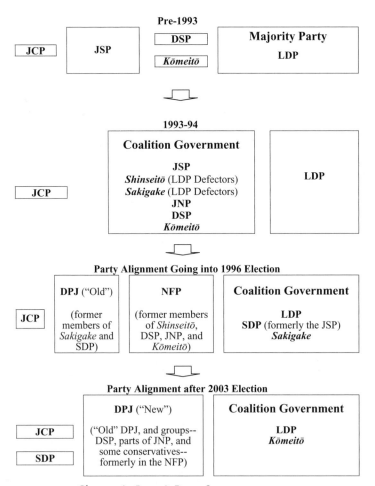

FIGURE 2.1 Changes in Japan's Party System

Second, the Clean Government Party, or *Kōmeitō* – the political wing of *Sōka Gakkai* (a lay Buddhist organization) – formed in 1964 and began contesting national HR elections in 1967. The party immediately drew support from many lower-middle-income urban groups. The party won, at its most popular, 11 percent of the votes and seats. (For a simple picture of the pre-1993 party system, see the top section of Figure 2.1.)

In 1976, a seemingly more serious threat to the LDP appeared in the form of the New Liberal Club. Composed primarily of defectors from the LDP who were fed up with a series of corruption scandals, the NLC appealed to voters who wanted cleaner politics. NLC candidates were extremely popular and did very well in their individual races. However, the party was unable to run many candidates and peaked with 4 percent of the vote and 3 percent of the seats in its initial campaign. In 1983, it joined the LDP in a coalition government. After the 1986 election, it simply died out and was reabsorbed into the LDP.

As I discuss in Chapter 5, the LDP was usually even more dominant in subnational elections, winning on average an even larger seat share than it did at the national level. In contrast, the opposition did *markedly* worse at the subnational level. However, the opposition gained substantially greater popularity and a larger number of seats at the local level in the late 1960s and early 1970s in the wake of deadly pollution crises. These victories, combined with the declining national popularity of the LDP, led many observers to predict the end of Japanese one-party dominance at all levels. But, by the end of the 1970s, the local opposition movement had lost its momentum. Although a number of urban areas continued to maintain substantial opposition strength, in general after the late 1970s the LDP remained dominant at the local level.

Big Changes

In the late 1980s, another potential threat to the LDP emerged. The JSP defeated the LDP for the first time ever in the 1989 Upper House race, fueled by public outrage over a new consumption tax leveled by the LDP and the rise of the extremely popular Doi Takako, the new female leader of the Socialists.[6] However, voter support for the JSP proved temporary. In the more important Lower House race the following year, the LDP skewered the JSP (albeit by less than in many years past), with a winning vote margin of greater than 20 percentage points and took a majority of the seats.

As the economy soured and corruption scandals erupted with increasing regularity, voter anger grew, and new parties emerged hoping to benefit. The first, the Japan New Party, was a new creation. It entered the Japanese political scene in 1992, winning four seats in the House of Councillors election. In 1993, the JNP was quite successful in the more important House of Representatives election. Running mostly in urban districts in which, the party took seats in 35 out of the 57 districts in which it ran candidates.[7]

In 1993, partly inspired by the JNP's initial success, sitting LDP incumbents split from the party to form two new ones, the 35-member *Shinsei* party, and the smaller and more liberal *Sakigake*. Their defection was in large part a response to the Miyazawa government's failure to pass campaign and electoral reform measures. Reform-minded voters were particularly supportive of the defectors, and new party candidates were extremely successful in the

---

[6] The JSP won a plurality of the votes and seats. Nevertheless, only half of the HC runs for election at any given time. Therefore, despite its victory, the JSP did not control the Upper House. For a full explanation of the HC electoral system, see footnote 3 in Chapter 6.

[7] There were 129 districts with a total of 511 seats in 1993.

1993 HR election. On one hand, this was not a complete backlash against the LDP: If we combine the total votes won by LDP candidates and the parties led by LDP defectors, this conservative bloc won roughly a majority of the vote in the election. On the other hand, if we count only the LDP, the party received its worst beating ever, taking only 36.6 percent of the vote (although converted into 43.6 percent of seats).

Together with the entire non-Communist traditional opposition (JSP, Kōmeitō, and DSP) and the JNP, the defectors were able to form a new, non-LDP coalition government (see Figure 2.1). The government's most noted achievement was changing the HR electoral law from the long-derided single nontransferable vote in multimember district system into a mixed-member system with 200 proportional representation seats and 300 single member districts.[8] Under the system, each voter casts one ballot for a party in PR (where parties receive a proportion of seats roughly equal to their proportion of the vote) and one ballot for a candidate in an SMD (where, in each district, the single seat is taken by the candidate with the most votes).

However, marital bliss was brief; in 1994, internal coalition difficulties led the JSP and *Sakigake* to leave the coalition and join the LDP in a new government. The move by the JSP to join in a coalition government with its longtime enemy was shocking. The JSP did so partly because of its poor treatment by the LDP defectors who led the coalition and partly to have its own leader, Murayama Tomiichi, named prime minister. But, in linking up with the LDP, the JSP abandoned the bulk of the major issue positions on which it had fought with the LDP and staked its identity. As prime minister, Murayama "declared the self-defense forces to be constitutional, the U.S.-Japan security treaty to be indispensable, the national anthem Kimigayo and the Hinomaru national flag to be legitimate, nuclear-energy plans in Japan to be necessary, and an increase in the consumption tax to be unavoidable" (Curtis 1999: 198). In short, the old political order was no more.

LDP Versus NFP

The remaining members of the short-lived, non-LDP coalition government joined together to form the New Frontier Party. (See Figure 2.1.) Even without control of the government, with 178 HR members the party was in a solid position to build a challenge to the LDP, which held little more than 200. However, the NFP never grew much larger. The party did extremely well in the 1995 Upper House election, in particular in PR balloting, but was less successful in the 1996 HR election. In 1996, the LDP won only 38.6 percent of the total SMD vote and 32.8 percent of the total PR vote. Nevertheless, despite falling short of the LDP by only five percentage points

---

[8] Prior to the 2000 election, the PR component was reduced to 180 seats. The PR seats are divided into 11 regional blocs.

and winning only ten fewer seats than the LDP in the PR portion of the 1996 Lower House election, the NFP won 73 fewer single member districts (out of 300) than the LDP, leaving it well behind in the final total. (See Table 2.2.) In addition, the NFP scarcely developed at all at the local level, winning only 141 out of 2,927 prefectural assembly seats contested in 1995.

Additional new party formation continued. Not long before the 1996 election, moderate Socialist Party members joined together with a small group of new party members to form the Democratic Party of Japan, which found moderate success in the election (see Figure 2.1). With the Socialist Party's principles ripped apart by its leaders, Socialist supporters felt betrayed and left the party in droves. That fact, combined with the defection of many of its moderates to the DPJ, led the Socialists to verge of extinction in 1996. The Socialists won only 2 percent of the candidate vote, 6 percent of the party vote, and 15 total seats (or 3 percent of the total).

LDP Versus DPJ

Split by internal bickering, the NFP by 1998 disbanded into an array of small splinter parties, ushering in yet another phase in the 1990s' pattern of introducing new parties that confused the Japanese public.[9] The DPJ was seen as the primary opposition hope. In 1998, the DPJ joined with splinter groups that had spun off from the NFP to re-found itself as the centrist, new Democratic Party of Japan. Early signs suggested that the party might develop credibility earlier ones had lacked.

The DPJ surpassed expectations in the 1998 HC election. The Upper House uses a combination of PR and candidate-centered district races. The DPJ won only two fewer PR seats (12 to 14) than the LDP, but the LDP won twice as many (30 to 15) district seats. Like the NFP, the DPJ was even weaker at the local level, winning only 170 out of 2,668 prefectural assembly seats up for election in 1999. The DPJ found greater success in the June 2000 HR election. (See Table 2.2.) The LDP won 41 percent of the SMD vote and 28 percent of the PR vote. The DPJ finished only three percentage points behind the LDP in the PR portion of the ballot and won 47 PR seats to the LDP's 56. But the DPJ could find viable candidates to run in only 242 of the 300 SMDs, and won only 80, a far cry from the LDP's 177. The DPJ increased its seat total substantially, but altogether still only won 127 (out of 480) seats to the LDP's 233. An LDP-led coalition that included the much smaller Conservative Party and *Kōmeitō* – the LDP's coalition partners going into the election – easily continued to control the government.

In important ways, the DPJ made substantial gains in 2003, especially as party consolidation took effect. A former splinter of the NFP, the Liberal

---

[9] For a wonderful, detailed discussion of many of the party movements of the 1990s, see Curtis (1999).

TABLE 2.2 *Percentage of HR Votes (top) and Seats (parentheses): 1996–2003*

	1996			2000			2003		
	PR	SMD	Total Seats %	PR	SMD	Total Seats %	PR	SMD	Total Seats %
LDP	32.8 (35.0)	38.6 (56.3)	47.8	28.3 (31.1)	41.0 (59.0)	48.5	35.0 (38.3)	43.8 (56.0)	49.4
NFP	28.0 (30.0)	28.0 (32.0)	31.2						
DPJ	16.1 (17.5)	10.6 (5.7)	10.4	25.2 (26.1)	27.6 (26.7)	26.5	37.4 (40.0)	36.7 (35.0)	36.9
Kōmeitō				13.0 (13.3)	2.0 (2.3)	6.5	14.8 (13.9)	1.5 (3.0)	7.1
JCP	13.1 (12.0)	12.6 (0.7)	5.2	11.2 (11.1)	12.1 (0.0)	4.2	7.8 (5.0)	8.1 (0.0)	1.9
SDP	6.4 (5.5)	2.2 (1.3)	3.0	9.4 (8.3)	3.8 (1.3)	4.0	5.1 (2.8)	2.9 (0.3)	1.3
Sakigake	1.0 (0.0)	1.3 (0.7)	0.4						
Liberal				11.0 (10.0)	3.4 (1.3)	4.6			
Conservative Party				0.4 (0.0)	2.0 (2.3)	1.5		1.3 (1.3)	0.8
Other	2.6 (0.0)	6.7 (3.3)	2.0	1.5 (0.0)	8.1 (7.0)	4.4		5.7 (4.3)	2.7

Note: Due to rounding, not all figures sum to 100 percent.
Source: Miyagawa (1997, 2000) and *Asahi Shinbun* (various paper editions).

Party (led by Ozawa Ichirō), merged with the DPJ to create a more unified opposition front against the LDP. Meanwhile, the JCP and the Socialists, the two remaining opposition alternatives, each received less than 2 percent of all seats in the 2003 HR election. The result was good for the DPJ, which, with its 37 percent of the PR vote, became the first party in the new HR electoral system to defeat the LDP (35 percent) in PR balloting. Moreover, in terms of seats won, it was the most successful opposition party in postwar Japanese history, with 177 seats (37 percent of the total).

Nevertheless, in many ways, the DPJ's gains were deceptive because there was much to suggest that the LDP remained in a solid position: In 2003, the LDP's coalition partner, *Kōmeitō*, won three more seats (34) than it had in 2000. More striking, the 2003 DPJ gained only half a million votes over the DPJ–Liberal Party total from 2000, while the LDP increased its PR total substantially, winning its largest share ever under the new system. In 2000, the presence of alternative "conservative" Parties – the Liberal and Conservative Parties – and the leadership of Prime Minister Mori reduced the LDP's share of the vote. In 2003, the absence of other conservative parties and the popularity of Prime Minister Koizumi increased the LDP's PR vote share by 7 percentage points. Altogether, the LDP won four more seats (237) than it had in 2000. When combined with the seven politicians (including all four winners from the Conservative Party) who joined the party immediately following the election, the party continued to maintain its majority and held substantially more seats than the DPJ, its top challenger.[10]

DETAILS OF THE JAPANESE PARTY SYSTEM

The preceding discussion, however, offers only a superficial look at party alignments over the postwar period. To get a proper sense of the party system, we need to give attention to three additional features of the system: (1) the major social, economic, and political divisions in Japan; (2) the existence in Japan of what can be called "parallel party systems" and the strength of the opposition in urban areas; and (3) the typically top-down nature of party formation in Japan.

Divisions Within Japan

On what sorts of issues were Japanese divided? Unlike many industrialized democracies, Japan lacked substantial religious and ethnic cleavages, but divisions existed in other areas. Immediately after World War II, Japan was a heavily agricultural society, with many individuals maintaining prewar values that included strong support for the emperor system. This structure

---

[10] Ultimately, the DPJ did win the less important 2004 HC election by one seat over the LDP. I will give this election and its implications greater attention in Chapters 6 and 10.

benefited conservative parties, which represented agricultural interests and sought to revise the American-imposed Constitution – in particular, by rearming Japan.

Over the 1950s, shifts occurred. Education levels rose, and Japan became increasingly urbanized. In 1950, 45.2 percent of the Japanese population worked in agriculture, forestry, and fisheries, but by 1960 this figure had dropped to 30 percent (Watanuki 1991). At the same time, the Korean War boom pushed heavy and chemical industries and led to an increase in white- and blue-collar workers. Sharper cultural and political divisions emerged, seemingly to the advantage of the socialist parties. Whereas in the early 1950s most sociodemographic/economic groups were likely to support conservative parties, by the late 1950s splits between groups were clear. Watanuki (1991: 59–60) argues that the division was largely "cultural," a division between traditional and "modern" values, but the numbers also indicate important differences that fall along more material grounds. The most conspicuous division that emerged was over defense, with younger, more educated voters especially opposed to rearmament and the U.S.–Japan Security Treaty. Japanese under 40 and those with more education were especially likely to support the Socialists, who actively represented workers' rights and protection of the Constitution, in particular the document's restrictions on Japanese remilitarization. Japanese 40 and older and those with less education were more likely to support the LDP. At the same time, splits were clear along occupational lines, suggesting an economic cleavage. Self-employed merchants and manufacturers and farmers were strongly LDP (and LDP-precursor) supporters, but, as might be expected, salaried employees and industrial workers were more likely to support the left (Watanuki 1991: 59–60).

However, in the 1960s, the success of the economy and the decision to downplay the defense issues by the LDP reduced many tensions, such as those between business and labor. Most occupational groups enjoyed the fruits of Japanese economic success. Consensus over economic issues grew, which translated into support for the ruling party. In the 1970s, even though issues such as pollution, welfare, and corruption created more short-term lines of division within society, larger, more long-term cleavages began to diminish. The economy was becoming more diversified, thereby eliminating a clear workers-versus-employers (and farmers) dichotomy. Changes in Japan–China–United States relations reduced the salience of the Japan-U.S. Security Treaty as an issue (Watanuki 1991: 65–6). In turn, social cleavages appeared to play a weaker part in driving the party system. At the same time that the JSP was becoming increasingly a party of white-collar workers, both the LDP and the small opposition parties began to take on a catch-all flavor, appealing to groups of multiple generations and occupational groups. The LDP appealed to voters in nearly every stratum, and not just its historical base of farmers and business. The JCP, DSP, and *Kōmeitō* all appealed to white- and blue-collar workers and self-employed merchants and manufacturers (Watanuki 1991: 64). Although the weakening of social cleavages was important in generating this new, more inclusive party politics, at least as critical was the support that candidates of many parties – especially the LDP – generated through personal and organizational networks that mobilized people of many different social strata.

Nevertheless, substantial socioeconomic changes continued to occur, generating new divisions within Japan. Although nearly half of the Japanese workforce had been employed in farming, fisheries, and forestry in 1950, by 1970 this group represented only 17 percent of the workforce, and by the mid-1990s it was only 6 percent. Similarly, in 1947 employment in family businesses covered about 40 percent of the population, but by 1970 the figure was 16 percent. At the same time, employment in manufacturing went from 22 percent in 1950 to 35 percent in the later decades. Service-sector employment increased from 30 percent in 1950 to 48 percent in 1970 and 60 percent in the 1990s. Finally, employment in firms went from 40 percent in 1947 to 66 percent in 1970 and nearly 80 percent in 1985. (All figures are from Pempel 1998: 171.)

In short, Japan's economy and individuals' places within it had changed dramatically. A divide gradually emerged between those in more efficient, competitive, or productive sectors and those in more inefficient, uncompetitive, or unproductive ones (Pempel 1998; Rosenbluth 1996; Schoppa 2001). During economic success, this divide was not overwhelming because the economy allowed most sectors to profit. However, the cleavage became more problematic beginning in the late 1980s/early 1990s as economic stagnation created a zero-sum climate in which inefficient sectors were seen to be straining the rest of the economy. The inefficient sectors were especially seen as a drag on the economy as the LDP (often with Socialist Party support) sustained them through regular patronage from the state coffers. As a result,

Distributive politics reduced the confidence in government of groups that could not be reached through distributive channels, however. The white-collar middle class, the young, and urban housewives . . . found that no party defended their occupational and residential interests. Thus, clientelism bred growing opposition to such policies and laid the groundwork for conflict between defenders of the status quo and vested interests on the one hand and groups demanding reform of the distributive apparatus (e.g., consumers or taxpayers) on the other. (Otake 2000: 295)

These divisions between economic sectors and concerns surrounding distributive politics offered genuine issues that an opposition party might have been able to take advantage of, and, indeed, Japan's new parties of the post-1993 period did seek to use them to their own benefit. But even though these cleavages divided supporters of and politicians within the LDP – thereby obstructing the ruling party's capacity to respond – more than a decade after the bursting of Japan's economic bubble the opposition had not found a way to use them to knock the LDP out of power.

Parallel Party Systems and Opposition Strength in Japan's Urban Areas

A central trait of Japanese party politics is that the system is less one unified party system and more what I call two *parallel* party system*s*: an LDP-dominated rural party system and a more competitive urban one.

I discuss the LDP-dominated rural system in much greater detail in Chapters 3, 5, and 8, but it can also be described quite simply: The Socialist Party had relative success in rural areas, and in later years rural areas were the location of the largest proportion of Socialist Party supporters. Nevertheless, in large part because of its links to a tightly bound set of rural social networks and its control over government resources that rural areas thoroughly depended upon, by and large the LDP (and its precursors) dominated the countryside.

On the other hand, cleavages of the sort discussed in the previous section played a part in generating much greater success for the opposition in the more urban areas of the country. Japan's opposition party movement always had an urban flavor. For decades, the Japanese urban opposition tended to represent more economically internationalist forces. Even in the 1950s, when separate Right and Left Socialist Parties existed (before they merged to become a single Japan Socialist Party), a clear urban–rural divide existed between the two groups. The Left Socialists were especially representative of public-sector (and less internationally competitive) unions, while the Right Socialists represented unions from the private sector, much of which grew increasingly competitive. In part because of the Right Socialist's more moderate tendencies, but also because of the more competitive enterprises in which its unions sat, the Right Socialist Party was markedly more popular in urban areas (Masumi 1995: 364). The Right Socialists were also the precursors to the Democratic Socialist Party. Not surprising, the DSP, which represented private-sector unions, conducted its electoral challenges in Japan's cities and found its greatest success in urban areas. *Kōmeitō* was founded on an urban lay Buddhist organization; like the DSP, *Kōmeitō*'s strategic emphasis and success came in cities (Scheiner 1999).

In the late 1960s and early to mid-1970s, owing in part to the emergence of *Kōmeitō*, demographic shifts, and additional factors that I discuss in Chapter 5, opposition parties found increasing success in urban areas and cut into the LDP's strength in cities. The success of Japan's economy in the 1980s muted claims that the LDP was on its way out and concerns about an urban opposition were less intense during the decade. Nevertheless, the opposition's base remained in the cities.

As Japan's economic bubble burst and reports of corruption grew more widespread, the LDP was most vulnerable in urban areas. The new party movement was kicked off in 1992 with the emergence of the Japan New Party, which contested a small number of seats in the HC election and called for the reform of Japan's political system. The JNP was an urban party, both focusing its candidacies and winning the bulk of its seats in city districts (Scheiner 1999).

Calls for reform, particularly within the LDP, grew stronger, and there was a clear urban side to support for reform: In late 1992, the LDP's largest faction, the Takeshita faction, divided into two. The split was due in part to a battle over who would lead the faction, but it was instigated by a group led by Ozawa Ichirō and Hata Tsutomu pushing a reform agenda. Within both the Takeshita faction as a whole and the new Ozawa/Hata faction more specifically, urban politicians were more likely to support reform (Reed and Scheiner 2003). Ultimately, this was quite significant, as the Ozawa/Hata group left the faction en bloc in 1992 and made up the largest group of defectors from the LDP in June 1993 when the party failed to make good on its promise to pass electoral reform.

The LDP clearly recognized the problems it faced in urban areas and sought to put on a fresher, hipper face, in the hopes of attracting younger, urban voters. Many of its attempts verged on the comical. As reported by a Japanese weekly, in March 1995 the LDP "re-baptized itself with snazzy English initials – JF – with pick-your-own meanings" (*Nikkei Weekly*, April 17, 1995). I had been skeptical of this report until I came across an actual LDP party handbook from 1995, which detailed the new name. The page was entitled "The Liberal Democratic Party's nickname" [*Jiyūminshutō no aishō*], followed in large, bold letters by "JF." The manual went on to note: "We're spreading a new image, and created a type of nickname... that even young people might find appealing. It's a short, easy-to-say word. Please call us 'JF.'" The manual explained that JF did not stand for any one thing (although it was to signify a new politics); however, it did suggest some possibilities. Written in both English and Japanese (but with the JF usually representing English-language words), the possibilities included "JF = Justice + Freedom," "JF = Joyful + Future," "JF = Japan + Family, Friend, Face," and "JF = Jump + Fresh."

Later that year, the LDP kicked off its House of Councillors election campaign with a big bash that included many of the party's leaders walking onto a stage, followed by young Japanese who proceeded to play "hip" music and rap about how voters should entrust themselves to the LDP. Following the JF report, the *Nikkei Weekly* noted, "So far, voters have been unimpressed" (April 17, 1995), and the 1995 electoral campaign was among the party's least successful. I saw no serious use of rappers by the LDP after 1995, but the LDP's urban skid continued all the same: In the 1998 HC election, the LDP did even worse. Despite winning the largest overall number of seats, the LDP did not win a single seat in the most metropolitan prefectures in the country. (See Chapter 8 for more on the urban–rural split in Japan.)

Nevertheless, cities made up only one of the two parallel party systems existing in Japan. Without greater success in the uncompetitive rural system, the opposition was not able to channel its victories in the competitive urban system into control of the national parliament.

Top-Down Party Formation

Major new party formation in Japan tended to be top-down, in particular based on the defections of individuals from a single party or the merger of existing parties into an entirely new one. The fact that ruling party formation occurred through the behavior of national level elites, rather than a grassroots movement, reinforced the tendency of politicians to utilize government resources heavily as an electoral strategy. Top-down formation did not shape opposition party strategy in the same way because those out of the government of course cannot use state resources similarly. However, it did force the opposition to focus its strategies on the cues and behavior of elites and weakened their capacity to develop at the grassroots level.

The most important party mergers in Japan occurred in 1955 as the Left and Right Socialist Parties combined to form the unified Japan Socialist Party and, soon afterward, the Liberal and Democratic Parties created the Liberal Democratic Party. In 1960, defections by the more conservative members in the JSP led to the formation of the Democratic Socialist Party.

In Japan, the clearest case of Shefter's (1994) externally mobilized party – that is, a party formed by groups in society who are seeking a voice in government (similar to Duverger's "extra-parliamentary" party formation) – was *Kōmeitō* in the mid-1960s. *Kōmeitō* did not form out of splits or mergers of other parties but rather emerged as the political wing of a lay Buddhist organization. However, *Kōmeitō* was clearly an exception to the general rule. Based on members of the *Sōka Gakkai* sect and voters within urban lower economic classes, *Kōmeitō* entered the electoral arena representing a previously unrepresented group.[11] The difference between *Kōmeitō* and other new party formation makes sense in light of the apparent goals of the different parties. Most other new parties focused their efforts on building teams of elites – Diet members who shifted alliances usually in an effort to alter the shape of Japanese politics. The new parties of the 1990s sought to replace the LDP as the governing party. In contrast, *Kōmeitō*'s goals appeared less broadly ambitious. Unlike the DSP, which tried to become a large party quickly, *Kōmeitō* recognized the limits of its base of support and never ran many candidates. It focused instead on finding ways to influence legislation in key areas of interest to the party. Its decision to become a member of the New Frontier Party in the House of Representatives in 1994 was in large part due to its recognition that, as a small party, it would face great trouble in the

---

[11] As Watanuki (1991: 65) points out, in 1967 and 1969 half of *Kōmeitō* supporters had been nonvoters in previous elections.

new single member districts.[12] And the party's decision to link up with the anti-LDP coalition in the first place and then later to join the LDP coalition government in 1999 was due to its desire to be an influential "pivot" party whenever possible.

But *Kōmeitō* was the exception rather than the rule. In the 1970s, new party formation followed the top-down pattern. In 1976, for example, a small group of young Diet members defected from the LDP to form the New Liberal Club. In 1977, an equally small group of moderate politicians left the JSP to form the Social Democratic League.

The most dramatic new party formation occurred in the 1990s. First, the Japan New Party, led by LDP politician Hosokawa Morihiro, began contesting elections with a number of political newcomers in 1992 and found moderate success in the 1993 HR election. In 1993, two groups of defectors from within the LDP formed two additional new parties – *Shinseitō*, led by Ozawa Ichirō and Hata Tsutomu, and *Sakigake*, led by Takemura Masayoshi. These two parties also found moderate success in the 1993 election and, along with the former non-Communist opposition and the JNP, coalesced into the anti-LDP government (see Figure 2.1).

After the JSP and *Sakigake* left the coalition, the remaining groups formed the New Frontier Party in 1994. The NFP therefore included conservative former LDP members, JNP members, union-based Democratic Socialist members, and *Kōmeitō*, the representative of a religious organization.[13] In addition, not long before the 1996 HR election, a substantial set of moderates from the Socialist Party, the bulk of the younger members of *Sakigake* – especially Kan Naoto and Hatoyama Yukio – and the NFP's Hatoyama Kunio (Yukio's brother) formed the Democratic Party of Japan.[14] (see Figure 2.1).

With its defeat in the 1996 election and dissatisfaction within the party over the heavy-handed tactics of its de facto head Ozawa Ichirō, the NFP gradually unraveled. Little by little, individuals and small groups splintered off, and, by the start of 1998, the party had disintegrated. In its place, there was a set of small, "new" parties, not unlike those that existed before the birth of the NFP. In particular, the *Kōmei* group and the Democratic Socialist group each emerged from the NFP once again as autonomous blocs. Perhaps the most interesting and pivotal new splinters from the NFP were two groups made up of former LDP members: the Liberal Party, led by Ozawa Ichirō, and *Minsei*, led by Hata Tsutomu.

---

[12] Interview with *Kōmeitō* HR representative, March 2, 1999.

[13] In reality, only the HR members of *Kōmeitō* joined the NFP. At the local level and in the HC, the party remained its own, separate body, to hedge its bets in the event that the NFP did not survive (interview with *Kōmeitō* HR representative, March 2, 1999).

[14] In 1999, Hatoyama Kunio gave up his seat to run for Governor of Tokyo, which he then lost to populist Ishihara Shintarō. Hatoyama then rejoined the LDP and was reelected to the HR from the second spot on the LDP's Tokyo PR list.

In April 1998 the "old" DPJ merged with the old Democratic Socialist group and the *Minsei* group of former LDP members (the DSP and *Minsei* were of course both previously in the NFP) to form the new DPJ. In short, the new DPJ was composed of moderate former Socialists, former Democratic Socialists, former *Sakigake* members (the more "liberal" group of former LDP defectors), and former *Shinsei* members (the more "conservative" group of LDP defectors). The DPJ took an additional consolidation step in the fall of 2003 when it absorbed Ozawa's Liberal Party to form a larger DPJ. (See Figure 2.1.)

Even putting aside the general poor state of the Japanese economy, there appeared to be no shortage of opportunities for the opposition to succeed in Japan, and it seemed that the opposition's chances continued to improve over the 1990s and early 2000s: There was substantial public anger, especially in more urban areas, toward the LDP-maintained clientelist system. This issue, combined with increasing urbanization, appeared to improve the opposition's chances of success. And success was made more likely as elite-level consolidation created a more unified opposition force.

For these reasons, as of 2004, the opposition had a number of reasons to believe that its fortunes would improve. Nevertheless, what was more striking than the seeming potential for opposition success was that even more than a decade after the bursting of Japan's economic bubble and over ten years after the LDP split of 1993, the opposition had not found a way to remove the LDP's grip on power. What can explain such failure?

STATE OF THE LITERATURE: EXPLANATIONS
FOR OPPOSITION FAILURE IN JAPAN

Various explanations have been offered for one-party dominance and the failure of the opposition in Japan. Most arguments focus on the pre-1993 period, but many extend to the post-LDP split period as well.

Support for Parties

The first set of explanations involves the reasons for high support for the LDP and insufficient support for the opposition.

The most obvious explanation is simply the miracle economy: Much of LDP dominance was founded on Japan's tremendous economic growth. The economy did slow at points in the 1970s with the oil shocks, but in many ways Japan emerged more unscathed than many other advanced industrial countries, especially after the second oil shock. In the 1980s, the strong economy continued, and Japan became an economic superpower. As long as the economy was strong, voters had much less incentive to cast votes against the LDP, the party associated with economic growth.

Numerous other scholars – working from the tradition of, in particular, Nakane (1967), Doi (1971), and Ishida (1971) – have argued that Japanese political culture led to weak partisan ties throughout much of the electorate. Voters, they argue, tend to base their voting decisions on cues from local notables and appeals to traditional Japanese values. Some scholars point to the essentially conservative, change-resistant culture of the Japanese electorate as a factor in maintaining the LDP's hegemony (Hrebenar 1992). Others note that the LDP's appeals to traditional symbols and its promotion of distributive policies allowed the party to create in the voters a sense of indebtedness and obligation (Richardson and Flanagan 1984).

Others explain that the LDP maintained its support through the policies it enacted. Pempel (1990) argues that one-party dominance continued largely because of the ability of the ruling party to create a "virtuous cycle of dominance": Dominant parties gain power through the support of socioeconomic groups. The parties in turn use their public policy agenda to benefit these groups and isolate the opposition. In turn, this further strengthens their electoral position, which allows for greater utilization of the public policy agenda, and so on. Similarly, others suggest that opposition failure has been due to the tremendous policy flexibility of the LDP. That is, the LDP has been able to respond to public sentiment in whatever way was sufficient to maintain its position in office.

Ultimately, however, arguments of these kinds run into difficulty. Although their announced focus is on explaining the continued strong base of voter support for the LDP, in reality in elections after 1963 the LDP won a majority of the seats, but *not a majority of the votes* of Japan's citizens.

Japan's strong economy undoubtedly gave voters greater incentive to vote for the LDP, but a majority did not do so. Making things even more puzzling, even after the late 1980s, a lengthy period of *economic failure*, the opposition was unable to make serious inroads.[15] While cultural arguments emphasize voters' sense of obligation to the LDP, in reality only about 20 percent of the total eligible electorate cast ballots for the LDP. Moreover, cultural arguments cannot satisfactorily explain the early postwar period of multiparty competition, or the shifting nature over time of the LDP's electoral base. Culture cannot explain the increase in LDP support during the 1980s when urban voters were becoming increasingly displaced from the influence of the LDP's traditional appeals and voter organization networks (Kohno 1997).

An explanation similar to those just discussed is the notion that voters simply find the opposition incompetent and, therefore, a risk if it ever were allowed to control the government. There are, no doubt, many voters who feel this way. However, this argument, too, cannot explain the fact that, since

---

[15] Magaloni (1997) suggests that a ruling party can continue to ride the wave of its past economic success for some years after economic failure sets it. However, it would seem that Japan's economic funk was too long for the LDP to continue to reap many of the benefits of past economic success. Indeed, it is quite clear that Japanese grew extremely upset with the LDP over the state of the economy.

1963, a majority of votes go to non-LDP parties. In particular, in the 1996, 2000, and 2003 HR elections, roughly 70 percent of all party ballots were cast for parties other than the LDP.

Pempel's argument about "virtuous cycles," whereby ruling parties' policy profiles and bases of support reinforce each other, has considerable explanatory power. Nevertheless, Pempel himself notes that his analysis is based more on a discussion of "commonalities" among one-party dominant systems and less on the causes of dominance. Analyses based on "virtuous cycles" are not fully able to show why some countries' governing parties can create such cycles and others do not. Moreover, arguments focusing on such cycles can only go so far in explaining LDP success: In an era when more voters cast ballots against than for the LDP, new parties ought to be able to channel the high levels of voter discontent to break the "virtuous cycle."

What about the argument that the LDP is able to maintain support through its own flexibility? LDP flexibility can only be successful when it is combined with opposition policy inflexibility. The argument suggests that if opposition parties were less rigid in their stances, they would have been able to take winning positions on a number of major issues. Instead, the LDP was eventually able to co-opt a number of major issues, such as welfare and pollution in the 1970s, after the opposition parties were slow to respond at the national level. There are two problems with arguments of this kind. First, like the other explanations I discussed, it ignores the fact that the LDP did not win a majority of the vote. Second, opposition inflexibility can hardly be blamed on LDP flexibility. This point is critical in that it indicates the important role opposition party failure has played in LDP success. Opposition rigidity clearly created a large acceptable issue space within which the LDP could work. In this way, opposition failure helped lead to one-party dominance, rather than the other way around. That is, by focusing on the LDP and not paying attention to the failings of the opposition, many past analyses have missed an element critical to explaining one-party dominance.

Others have addressed the issue of Socialist Party inflexibility, arguing that rigid, leftist ideology was to blame for much of its failures. Numerous scholars such as Otake (1990) argue that the Socialist Party, the leading opposition party throughout the bulk of the postwar period, damned itself to eternal opposition status through its radical, leftist appeals.

Although not usually couched in these terms, analysis of this sort fits into Downs' (1957) theories of spatial positioning, which suppose that the winning party will be the one that can capture the vote of the median voter. In order to win this voter's support, parties ought to stake out centrist ideological positions. However, Downs' own analysis, as well as much work since, has questioned the necessity of a centrist voter strategy, especially in multiparty settings where parties' positions in issue space can be more differentiated and the vote therefore is more divided. More recent analysis counterposes a "directional" theory, which holds that voters will be more likely to support parties that stake out an intense policy alternative (Rabinowitz and Macdonald 1989). According to this theory, voters and parties need not occupy the same spot on the ideological spectrum; they need merely be located in the same direction of policy space. Empirical evidence supports the directional theory over the classical spatial theory (Rabinowitz, Macdonald, and Listaug 1991; Iversen 1994). In this light, perhaps the Socialist Party had nothing to gain from moving its appeals to the center, as voters would be attracted by its noncentrist position.

To this it would be reasonable to respond that perhaps the median Japanese voter has had conservative leanings that a party making leftist appeals, such as the JSP, would be unable to tap into or that the Socialists were simply *too* leftist to appeal to those on the center-left of the ideological spectrum. If this is the case, what constrained the JSP from developing a more centrist set of appeals?

Explanations for party rigidity of this type tend to focus on problems of individual party organization. For example, many blame the Italian DC's decline on its highly entrenched organization, which prevented the party from bringing about the institutional reform it needed to retain its legitimacy in the eyes of the Italian public (Wertman 1993; Furlong 1996).[16] Similarly, many scholars have sought to blame party organization for opposition party unresponsiveness in Japan. With the exception of the Japan Communist Party, Japanese parties lack what is usually considered standard in party systems elsewhere – a deep local substructure of party regulars down to precinct workers. A few parties have had strong ties to their voters through Buddhist organizations or unions, but even they have tended to lack strong *party* organizational substructures. In a similar vein, it is frequently argued that the JSP was constrained by a radical organization that would not allow the party to moderate its platform (e.g., Curtis 1988; Stockwin 1992). Yet democratic theory tells us that thirty-odd years of ineffective competition should have led the Socialists to alter their organizational base.

Even though radical ideology might help explain some of the failings of the *Socialists*, it is insufficient to explain *overall* opposition failure. Just as with the other explanations discussed in this chapter, explanations focusing on the positions of Japan's voters and parties in issue space also tend to ignore the submajority of the vote the LDP managed to win in elections after 1963.

---

[16] A similar case is made about the decline of the longtime ruling SAP in Sweden. Over the 1980s, organizational entrenchment in the SAP outstripped its leaders' ability to be strategically flexible, and the party could not respond coherently to challenges from the left and right (Kitschelt 1994a), thereby helping to precipitate its fall from power in 1991. However, suboptimal organization is not sufficient to explain the decline of one-party dominance in Italy and Sweden: The decline of a dominant party for internal organizational reasons cannot topple the ruling regime if opposition parties do not mobilize the disenchanted.

Even though the JSP was seen perhaps as too radical for the relatively conservative Japanese public, other opposition parties were not. Over the years a number of parties such as the DSP, NLC, SDL, and Kōmeitō appeared to hold issue positions that matched those held by the median Japanese voter. Nevertheless, none of these parties found great success. Perhaps more striking, Japan's post-1993 new parties totally avoided leftist radicalism, tending to run from just left of center to neoconservative. Even though this new pragmatism seemed to match the distribution of beliefs among Japanese voters, it did not end the LDP's grip on power.

In sum, many of the leading explanations for one-party dominance and opposition failure in Japan are flawed because they rely on the *seat* majority won by the LDP and pay insufficient attention to the fact that the LDP has not won a majority of the *vote* since 1963. Greater attention must be paid to the opposition's inability to channel the non-LDP vote – a majority of all votes cast – into a non-LDP government.

Electoral Institutions

Scholars of Japan's electoral system have made serious efforts to deal with this problem. Much literature explains one-party dominance and opposition failure by focusing on the now-defunct single nontransferable vote in multi-member district system, which helped fragment the opposition and protected the LDP remarkably well. The process underlying SNTV/MMD is actually quite simple. Each voter could cast one vote for a candidate. The vote had to go only to that candidate and could not be transferred to her party or to a specified alternative candidate. Each district held between two and six seats (with three-, four-, and five-seat districts being the norm throughout the postwar period). Let M stand for the district magnitude (number of seats in the district). The top M vote getters each won a seat: For example, in a three-seat district, the three candidates who received the largest number of votes won seats.

Under this system, parties were likely to make any of three types of "errors," preventing them from winning as many seats as they would have under a perfectly designed strategy. Given a situation in which they had enough votes to elect x candidates, they might (1) nominate too many people (i.e., more than x candidates) and spread their votes too thinly (overnomination); (2) nominate too few (i.e., fewer than x candidates) (undernomination); or (3) nominate x candidates, but divide the vote so unevenly that fewer than x would win (vote division failure). Running only one candidate would of course be a party's simplest strategy. However, with roughly 500 seats, but under 130 districts, a party hoping to win a majority needed to win about two seats per district and therefore needed to run on average at least two candidates per district. As a result, the risks of errors in nominating and vote-dividing strategies were always present, and large parties and parties that hoped to become large faced numerous dilemmas in their nomination and election strategies.

There is no question that the LDP received some benefit from Japan's electoral system. The system offered a greater advantage (a higher percentage of seats than votes) for the LDP than the party probably would have had under a pure PR system. Given that the LDP did not win a majority of the vote after 1963, but typically held a majority of seats, the electoral system clearly helped manufacture parliamentary majorities that the LDP would not have held under a perfectly proportional PR system. To be sure, with only a small percent of the vote needed to win a seat, the system kept the opposition fragmented and less likely to present one consolidated opposition force. Also, Cox (1996, 1997) argues that much of the LDP's advantage over the opposition under the system was attributable to the ruling party's ability to allocate state resources in the form of patronage to divide the vote efficiently. Reed and Bolland (1999) demonstrate one example of the disadvantage the opposition appeared to face under the system: Despite having sufficient votes to run two candidates in many districts, the JSP typically ran only one in order to protect sitting incumbents. Had the Socialists developed a reliable vote-division method, they might not have been left making strategic "errors" that impeded their ability to run a number of candidates sufficient to challenge the LDP.

However, SNTV/MMD is not sufficient to explain opposition failure. To begin with, Japan utilized the SNTV/MMD system at various points in the prewar era, a time in which party competition was the norm. Moreover, Christensen (2000) argues that because the LDP was unable to restrain independent conservative candidates from running regularly, it too was unable to carry out a perfectly "efficient" nomination strategy. Christensen offers convincing evidence that the opposition was, if anything, more efficient than the LDP in its ability to nominate an optimal number of candidates and divide the vote evenly. Similarly, Baker and Scheiner (2004, ND) develop a simulation of party strategy and success in postwar Japan that suggests that, on the whole, the opposition was no more harmed by strategic errors than the LDP was.

On the other hand, the apportionment of seats in the electoral system, combined with the geographic distribution of votes, certainly favored the LDP and harmed overall opposition party seat fortunes. Japan's SNTV/MMD electoral system was malapportioned, so that rural areas – where the LDP maintained its greatest support – received more seats per capita than urban areas did. The ability to win more seats with fewer votes gave the ruling party a significant electoral advantage. Under a correctly apportioned system, there would have been fewer seats in the countryside and more in the city. Presumably, in this correctly apportioned system, vote percentages equal to what they received in the real, malapportioned world would have netted the LDP fewer seats in rural areas and the opposition more seats in urban areas. In this way, malapportionment probably even allowed the LDP to win a majority of seats in years when a correctly apportioned system would not have.

But malapportionment/geographic distribution of votes is insufficient to explain opposition failure. Only in a limited number of elections were malapportionment effects alone sufficient to explain the LDP's ability to channel a submajority of the vote into a majority of the seats (Baker and Scheiner ND; Christensen and Johnson 1995). Even though the LDP was the party best able to benefit from the fact that its votes were in the overly represented rural areas, the Socialists also had some support in rural areas.

Perhaps more important, focusing on mechanical electoral effects leaves unanswered why opposition parties could not gain more strength in rural areas that offered more seats per vote. Also, focusing on mechanical effects and malapportionment issues leaves unexplained the puzzle of why the opposition did so much worse in subnational elections, which also utilized SNTV/MMD.

And focusing too closely on the effects of SNTV/MMD leaves us ignoring the fact that opposition failure continued after 1994, when a different system was in place. With the birth of a new electoral system, we must look elsewhere for an explanation. Some might argue that not enough time elapsed between 1994 and 2003 for the effects of the new electoral system to kick in fully. There is some merit to this argument, as it took time under the new system for the opposition to consolidate most of its forces into one party, the DPJ. Certainly, offering a single alternative to the LDP provided an important advantage not held by the opposition for decades. Nevertheless, it is striking that between 1996 and 2003, even as the opposition became consolidated into a single party, overall the opposition did not cut into the LDP's seat advantage in the House of Representatives. (See Table 2.2.)

Another possible explanation for opposition failure is the opposition's inability in the post-1993 world to coordinate its seats as a national-level coalition. To some extent this argument holds water. The failure of the new-party-led anti-LDP government to maintain a coalition with the Socialists in 1994 led to its breakdown and the return of the LDP to power. Even the LDP needed to govern by means of a coalition in the bulk of the years that followed (because of its submajority in the *Upper* House). However, given that the LDP held a majority of HR seats throughout most of the postwar, and even in the post-1993 years had a majority or near majority of HR seats, opposition coordination would have had to be perfect in order to defeat the LDP. Indeed, even perfect coordination among the principal opposition parties might not have been sufficient: The near majority of seats held by the LDP was actually close to being a de facto majority because of the general unwillingness of many parties to work with the Communist Party.

Perhaps the opposition's problem in the post-1993 years, then, was that in many districts the opposition vote was divided among multiple candidates, allowing the LDP to capture the government with less than a majority of the vote. The fact that the LDP won large numbers of SMDs with well under 50 percent of the total national SMD vote gives this argument credibility.

Admittedly, this problem was prevalent in 1996 when the opposition contained two fairly large parties, the NFP and DPJ, which often refused to compromise on jointly endorsed candidates. This caused problems for the opposition in districts where voters sought to cast a strategic vote against the LDP but were uncertain around whom to unify the vote. Also, 1996 was the first election under the new system, so parties and voters did not yet have sufficient information to work out an effective strategy.

However, this explanation can only take us so far, as the 2000 election presents quite a different case. While the LDP was able to take 59 percent of all SMDs (177 out of 300) with only 41 percent of the vote that year, its success was not due primarily to opposition parties' failure to coordinate. In this election, the second under the new electoral system, the DPJ was the opposition's overwhelmingly leading party; in any given SMD, the opposition camp was less likely to put up multiple candidates who would split the vote and lead to opposition failure when it had enough votes to find success. Indeed, out of the 177 LDP victories, perfect cooperation among the non-Communist opposition would have cost the LDP only 29 districts (at most), still leaving the opposition well behind the LDP (and its mates in the government) in terms of seats.[17]

Perhaps more important, the leading opposition party, the DPJ, did not even have sufficient candidates to contest elections in many SMDs – it ran no candidate in 58 districts in 2000. In 2003, it did show improvement, but still lacked candidates in 33 districts. Many of the candidates it did find were, even according to DPJ leaders, political novices who only ran because no one else was available. There were relatively few strong non-LDP candidates at all in Japan's rural districts.[18] Before focusing on coordination problems, we need to understand new parties' inability to get any votes at all in many districts.

The Puzzle

As the preceding discussion suggests, analyses currently used to explain postwar LDP dominance remain insufficient and opposition failure in the pre-1990s era remains a puzzle.

The post-1990 era is an even greater puzzle. Between 1993 and 2003, Japan's economy stagnated, and government corruption disgusted anyone

---

[17] Chapter 6 also offers district-level analysis that refutes the coordination failure argument.

[18] When I refer to rural areas, I primarily mean agricultural communities, with lower proportions of secondary and tertiary industries. However, my operational definition is based on population density. Rural areas have fewer residents per square kilometer than urban areas do.

paying attention to the news. The opposition did not need to create hostility to the LDP or generate a market for anti-LDP appeals – such hostility and such a market already existed. In addition, the post-1993 opposition was pragmatic and centrist. It was no longer hamstrung by ideological issues or rigidity that forced it to make policy appeals that were outside of the mainstream of the Japanese voting public. Moreover, the new electoral system ought to have reduced many of the problems that the opposition had faced under the old system. *And* the opposition had 50 years of failure to learn from.

Despite *all* this, Japan's opposition continued to fail.

THE IMPACT OF CLIENTELISM ON OPPOSITION FAILURE

This book offers a different take on the problem and argues that Japan's clientelist system is the key to understanding the weakness of party competition in Japan, especially when it was combined with a centralized governmental fiscal structure and electoral arrangements that helped protect regions that benefited from and supported the clientelist system. These factors were important both prior to and after 1990. During the pre-1990 period, they often played a supplemental role, adding on to the effects of a strong economy, but they also provided an extra cushion during times when the economy was less robust. During the post-1990 period, they were central to the continued success of the LDP and the failure of the opposition.

As I researched the explanatory power of the preexisting arguments on opposition failure and one-party dominance, I spoke to a number of Japanese politicians, journalists, and voters. In the early interviews, I tried to determine which explanations held water for my interviewees, but I also asked what problems *they* thought were preventing greater opposition success, especially in the 1990s. These interviews consistently turned up three responses.

The first was the lack of attractive candidates. As Jacobson (1990) shows for the American congressional context, finding strong candidates to run for office is critical to the success of political parties in elections. In Japan, the strength of LDP candidates and the weakness of those running for the opposition played a significant part in the LDP's ability to win a majority of seats with a submajority of the vote. Christensen's analysis indicates that, even though the opposition was at least as efficient as the LDP in terms of nomination strategy, the LDP won more "winnable" seats than the opposition because the LDP won more votes per candidate (or per "winnable seat"), on average, than the opposition did. What kept the Japanese opposition from finding good candidates? DPJ politicians and staff members who were involved in the party's electoral planning explained that the ideal candidates had substantial experience in politics, especially if this experience gave them an established base of voter support. It became clear that the opposition simply did not have many people who fit that description. Jacobson's analysis focuses on parties running candidates in congressional races who had held state-level office, but the opposition in Japan typically held very few seats in elected subnational offices (see Chapter 5).

The question then becomes why the opposition did not hold more subnational office seats.[19] Few public opinion polls provide systematic information on why voters cast ballots for the parties they do at the subnational level, but there is another way to gain leverage over the problem of opposition success at the local level: examining the reasons subnational politicians from the LDP were or were not willing to join the opposition during the opposition's brief period of national level success in 1993–4. At the national level, much of the strength of Japan's new parties in the 1990s came about because sitting politicians defected from the LDP and created the new parties. Indeed, these new parties led the brief anti-LDP coalition government in 1993–4. Yet new parties gained only around 5 percent of all prefectural (Japan's largest administrative subunit) assembly seats.

In general, the only subnational politicians willing to defect from the LDP and join the new parties were from localities represented by national politicians – and especially their own Diet patron – who also defected from the LDP (Kataoka 1997). Given that Japanese local politicians frequently describe their national LDP patron as the pipeline to central governmental resources, this suggests that subnational politicians only defected when not doing so threatened their ability to draw subsidies from the central government.

This also suggests that two characteristics of Japanese politics were critical in shaping party defection (and party affiliation in general – see Chapters 4 and 5) at the subnational level. First, local politicians' relationships with politicians in the central government influenced their decision to defect or not from the LDP. In general, such relationships ought to carry this kind of weight only in a system where localities rely heavily on the central government. Therefore, it seems reasonable to conclude that Japan's high level of financial centralization, in which subnational governments rely heavily upon the central government for funding, was important to local party defection.

Second, if local politicians' decision to defect from the LDP at the local level stemmed from their concern with maintaining a pipeline to the central government, this suggests that they were driven, not by ideological concerns, but rather by their need to deliver goods to their constituents. In general, concerns of this kind only play such a critical role in systems that emphasize politicians' ability to act as benefit providers. Therefore, it also seems reasonable to conclude the central role of benefit delivery (e.g., patronage) in Japanese politics played an important role in local party defection. Thus, it

---

[19] Throughout this book, I use the terms "subnational" and "local" interchangeably. When I seek to distinguish between different levels, I refer to the official administrative titles (e.g., "prefecture" or "city").

appears that the combination of Japan's centralized fiscal structure and its heavy emphasis on patronage gave local politicians a particularly strong incentive to affiliate with the LDP – or any other party that could be relied upon to control the central government's purse strings, resources, and regulatory controls – and not to affiliate with other party options.

The second problem regularly mentioned in the interviews regarding opposition party efforts to challenge the LDP was the ruling party's massive use of government resources, such as pork barrel to attract supporters. That is, Japanese politicians, voters, and journalists argued that the LDP was able to maintain the support of a specific set of constituents who relied greatly on the subsidies it provided. With little access to such resources, the opposition could not hope to attract such groups. On the other hand, many Japanese expressed antagonism toward the LDP's heavy use of pork. What prevented the opposition from channeling this antagonism into opposition party success? It is in large part because the primary areas benefiting from such resources were the ones delivering a very large chunk of the seats that the LDP needed to maintain its dominant position.

Much of the opposition's inability to take greater advantage of antagonism toward the patronage system was tied into the third problem mentioned regularly in the interviews: People did not yet really know what these new parties were. That is, there was substantial uncertainty among voters and elites alike about just what these new parties stood for.

The natural question, then, is why the opposition did not make greater efforts to clarify its principles for the public. It is true that in some cases not enough time had elapsed for parties to have had a full opportunity to make their platforms clear. To make matters worse, the first large new party, the NFP, fell apart after only a few years. It is also true that Japanese campaign laws are extremely restrictive, severely limiting parties' use of television, radio, and print advertising. But it was also confusing for the public that these new parties were combinations of former antagonists from different preexisting parties.

We must ask, then, why Japan's new parties tended to form out of such mergers rather than from some sort of bottom-up movement. Aside from *Kōmeitō*, which never had any illusions about its capacity to win a very large number of seats, there was little grassroots creation of major parties in Japan. The opposition's inability to gain defectors from the LDP at the subnational level offers a clue as to why. If politicians at the subnational level need to affiliate with parties that can provide them with ties to the central government, there will be little incentive for parties to develop from the bottom up. Because such parties would have much greater difficulty developing the necessary links to the central government, new parties need to develop first at the national level. However, any party that is created out of defections from a single preexisting party will inevitably be small. In order for a *large*, new party to develop from the top down, politicians from multiple preexisting parties must merge to create it.

In this light, the three recurring complaints/problems faced by Japan's new opposition parties appear to have a unifying thread running throughout them: the important role of clientelism.

Japan's clientelist structure provided the basis for the LDP's use of pork and patronage. The combination of clientelism and financial centralization made it hard for the opposition to gain subnational office, and therefore hampered its ability to build a local base and find strong candidates for national office. Clientelist arrangements were valuable in linking the LDP to a huge constituency in the earlier decades of the postwar when so much of Japan was heavily rural. As much of Japan urbanized and two parallel party systems emerged, the LDP was able to maintain its most loyal and valuable base of support in the countryside through the patronage-based, clientelist arrangements that governed their relationship. These factors no doubt put the opposition at a massive disadvantage throughout the postwar period and remained a constant even when so much else had changed in the 1990s and early 2000s.

Finally, the combination of clientelism and financial centralization created incentives for parties to develop from the top down and, therefore, led new parties to form by merging old ones. The most likely result was new parties in the more recent period made up of seemingly incompatible parts and public confusion about what principles unite them. Under such conditions, it was even more difficult for these new parties to develop a support base founded on policy programs because observers were likely to view them as simply a collection of power-seeking elites rather than the representatives of a new policy vision.

3

Clientelism and Its Determinants

Clientelism refers to the exchange of benefits (by the government, parties, and/or politicians) for voter or organization support. Clientelist benefits are those awarded to people who support a specific party or candidate and withheld from those who do not (Chapter 1). *Clientelism plays front and center in the Japanese political system, and clientelism lies at the core of Japanese opposition failure.*

In Japan, clientelist mechanisms work through organizations and (especially local) politicians who are able to deliver a substantial number of votes to the ruling LDP. This "organized vote" is achieved by the party monitoring and enforcing a number of exchange practices that are often attributed to the electoral system. Japan's long-used and derided single nontransferable vote in multimember district electoral system is utilized by a very small number of polities. Nevertheless, it has received a large amount of attention, in part because of its perceived effect on clientelism.

In Japan, SNTV/MMD certainly played an important role in *reinforcing* clientelist linkages, but, as I explain in this chapter, clientelism was originally a result of other factors, especially the internal mobilization of the country's first parties and the organization of (especially rural) landholding. In the postwar era, SNTV/MMD contributed substantially to new political arrangements that held clientelism at their core, but electoral system arguments are not sufficient to explain Japanese clientelism. The electoral system was utilized throughout the country, but the levels of clientelism varied widely, according to social structure, local financial dependence on the central government, and political economy.

For additional discussion on the topics here, including the electoral system and SNTV/MMD literature, responses to potential counterarguments (including arguments related to international political economy), and additional comparative discussion, see the links to this book at *www.ethanscheiner.com.*

CITIZEN–POLITICIAN LINKAGES: PROGRAMMATIC
AND CLIENTELIST POLITICS

The conventional view of parties is based on the Western European model, which holds that party competition is founded on cleavage-based programmatism. The model holds that citizen–politician linkages – that is, the relationships between voters and politicians or parties – are indirect, as parties provide collective (i.e., nonexcludable and nonexhaustible) benefits that are not directly contingent on individual voting choices. Cleavages are based on durable differences in interests and specific life experience (e.g., a cleavage might be based on the difference between blue- and white-collar work/life experience). In studying party competition in developed countries, scholars often speak of social cleavages (these are prepolitical and feature different tastes of people and associational affiliations) as well as cleavages that are dimensions of party competition (issues dividing voters that parties are capable of taking advantage of). Theories of spatial voting are driven by the idea that parties compete on issues and programmatic platforms, which are typically assumed to be based on the cleavages defining party competition.

However, programmatic parties based on existing or past cleavages are not always easy to achieve. That is, to the extent that programs matter in a party system, they demand that voters have the capacity to determine which party's programs best match their individual political philosophy, as well as the extent to which they personally will be likely to benefit from complicated policies with uncertain political outcomes.

In contrast to programmatic competition, personal and clientelistic forms of citizen–politician (or party) linkage require fewer of these sorts of demands on voters (Kitschelt 2000). Electoral competition will often be founded on the personal appeal of individual candidates, but the appeal of individual charisma by itself can last only so long. Clientelism is different. Under clientelism, politicians create direct bonds, usually through material side-payments (usually by providing funding), a pattern that can easily become institutionalized for the long term. For this reason, clientelist parties have to make an investment in organization and constantly need to provide funding or goods to valued constituencies.

Clientelist parties may avoid the difficult coordination and consensus building of programmatic policy, which mobilizes *both* party activists and a mass following to work for the party's electoral success. Because it involves fewer coordination costs, politicians may be drawn to clientelism as a more effective and simpler mode of appeal in the short run (Kitschelt 1995b: 449). Where there are large state-owned sectors and heavily regulated business activities, clientelism may be a fairly simple method of ensuring the discipline of supporters, although monitoring them is a potential problem. Sometimes monitoring is simple, as in the Chapter 1 example of nineteenth-century

American parties escorting supporters to the polls and handing them ballots that were distinguishable from those that would be cast for candidates of other parties. However, where individual monitoring is more difficult, parties have other options. The most straightforward is collective monitoring and enforcement, whereby a party monitors the support of an entire region. The party then rewards regions that provide it with vote support and punishes those that do not (Chapter 1).

Many observers of Japanese party politics posit that with its heavy emphasis on clientelism rather than ideology or "issues," the LDP in Japan is not a "real" party. In the world's newest democracies, programmatic party competition appears to be far from the norm (see Kitschelt 1995b; Evans and Whitefield 1993), but even among established democracies, clientelism is hardly unique to Japan. Any text on Italian politics pays great attention to the central role of patronage in its system, especially how it rewards supporters. Austria is also extremely clientelistic. Although founded at first on programmatic politics, Austria's leading parties' use of public-sector patronage, public housing, and industrial protection in exchange for support has come to dominate the system (Kitschelt 1994b).

THEORIES OF CITIZEN–POLITICIAN LINKAGES

Explanations for citizen–politician linkage patterns take many forms.

For years, scholars used sociological and cultural arguments, attributing clientelism to the presence of immigrants and peasants, as well as programmatic competition attributable to the presence of a middle/industrial working class (see, e.g., Banfield and Wilson 1963). However, as Shefter (1994) indicates, most of this analysis ignored empirical counterexamples. Other early explanations for linkage patterns were based on historical institutionalism. Epstein (1967), for example, argues that where civil service is introduced after the franchise, a party system is likely to be more clientelistic, as parties seek to award civil service jobs to win voter favor. However, Epstein's thesis does not fully hold empirically. Clientelistic parties emerged even in systems whose franchise emerged after the introduction of a civil service system, as the leading political elites found ways to get around existing civil service laws in order to dispense patronage jobs themselves (e.g., the DC in postwar Italy and the Chicago party machine).

Shefter (1994) offers a more convincing historical-institutional account: "Timing" matters, but most important is whether a given party enjoyed access to patronage when it first undertook to mobilize a popular base. Shefter (1994) argues that internally mobilized parties – parties created by elites who held positions within the prevailing regime – are most likely to develop a patronage orientation because they already hold ties to the state coffers and civil service. In contrast, externally mobilized parties (created by the "outs") organize a mass following to gain entry into or overthrow the system and – because they lack access to patronage – emphasize programmatic appeals.

Today, much analysis indicates the significance of electoral arrangements in shaping the level of party-oriented political behavior (e.g., Carey and Shugart 1995). Closed-list proportional representation systems – where parties control the placement of the candidates on their PR lists – tend to depersonalize political behavior and make programmatic competition over collective goods more likely. Where party-oriented behavior is discouraged by the electoral system, nonprogrammatic competition is more likely.

Where institutions encourage personalistic competition, coherent and complex programmatic parties are slow to develop because of the differing individual, personal agendas of their members. In addition, in systems where emphasis is placed on personal characteristics over programmatic party behavior, incumbent politicians are apt to use patronage as a "cheap" way to attract voters. In such cases, there is a greater likelihood that parties will become institutionalized along clientelistic than along programmatic lines. This is particularly true in systems where voters are asked to choose between multiple candidates from the same party, such as the open-list PR system used in Brazil (and formerly in Italy) or Japan's SNTV/MMD system (used in the Lower House until 1994).[1] In such systems, candidates from the same party lose credibility (and confuse voters) if they attempt to distinguish themselves from other members of the party on programmatic issues. These systems provide strong incentives for candidates to make personalistic appeals, including using pork and other selective incentives to differentiate themselves from other candidates in their party.

Nevertheless, electoral institutions are far from a sufficient explanation for different kinds of voting behavior or party–voter relationships. Austria, for example has maintained a clientelist party system for years, despite the presence of a closed-list PR electoral system.[2] In addition, theories of institutional effects overstate the impact of institutions on the shape of party competition if they fail to examine the causes of these institutional arrangements. An understanding of the origins of the institutions is necessary to explain fully party behavior in a country's (nonequilibrium) transition period. Also, the omission of origins ignores the fact that the choices of institutions are to

---

[1] Under an open-list PR system, voters cast ballots for individual candidates (although in some cases, they have the option of voting for either a candidate or a party and, in some variants of the system, cast a ballot for a party, but also express a preference for particular candidates within the party). The votes for all candidates of a given party (along with any votes cast simply for that party) are summed to determine the party's vote total. Each party then receives a proportion of total seats roughly equivalent to its share of the vote. The rank ordering of the candidates on the party list is determined by the number of votes they each personally received. For example, a party that wins three seats allots its seats to its three candidates with the largest number of votes. I explain SNTV/MMD in Chapter 2 and later in this chapter.

[2] See footnote 9 of Chapter 1 for an explanation of closed-list PR.

a large degree based on the balance of power at the time of the framing of the institutions and the social cleavages that emerged in the pre–democratic period, all of which have an impact on party competition.

In the end, there is no clear consensus on what precisely determines the shape of citizen–politician linkages. It appears that a wide variety of factors – extending even beyond formal institutions – can affect whether a system will become clientelistic.[3] Kitschelt sums up this point nicely with the following laundry list:

> [T]he choice of linkage mechanisms is not just predicated on formal democratic institutions but also on substantive economic and political power relations that manifest themselves in socioeconomic development, patterns of state formation and democratic suffrage diffusion, and the control of the political economy by markets or political-regulatory mechanisms. Furthermore, the institutional mechanisms that promote clientelist or programmatic linkage strategies may be at least in part endogenous to such power relations. Nevertheless, when institutions remain stable over extended periods and there are no significant external economic, political, or cultural shocks, they induce voters and politicians to adjust their political strategies, even when noninstitutional variables may provide different cues. (2000: 872)

CLIENTELISM IN JAPAN

Voting in Japan

Japanese parties are not wholly candidate- or clientelism-oriented. Partisanship is at its most important in urban areas where voters are less tied into social networks and pork barrel benefits that may link them to individual candidates (Richardson 1974). Also, issues do play a role in Japanese voting behavior: For example, Flanagan (1991) indicates that voters who stopped supporting the ruling LDP in the late 1980s and early 1990s tended to be more concerned with issues, and to the left of loyal LDP supporters. However, the bulk of voting in Japan is along personalistic and clientelistic lines.

Japan has one of the lowest proportions of strong partisans in the industrialized world (Flanagan et al. 1991). From the 1970s, the number of independent voters grew dramatically so that, from the mid 1990s, approximately 50 percent of the electorate claimed to prefer no party at all (Tanaka and Nishizawa 1997). Candidate-specific factors tend to outweigh issues in Japanese voting (Flanagan et al. 1991).

Many voters support particular candidates because of "personal" factors – personal connections, warmth, and loyalty to the candidate – but candidates' capacity to deliver material benefits is also critical. Curtis (1992)

---

[3] See the links to the supplementary Web site for this book at *www.ethanscheiner.com* for brief discussions of the impact on citizen–politician linkage of factors such as presidentialism, the relative timing of different elections, and historical legacy of a country's pre–democratic era.

notes that candidates' focus in Japanese electoral campaigns is on developing their own local organizations and securing the backing of powerful district interest groups: "In working toward these goals, the stress is on constituency service to convince voters that the candidate has the clout in Tokyo to bring the district new roads and bridges, industrial development, and higher living standards" (228). Indeed, as Fukui and Fukai (1996) write, "Japanese voters are mobilized at election time mainly by the lure of pork barrel, only marginally by policy issues, and even less by ideals and visions" (268–9).

Japanese Clientelism

The classic depiction of Japanese politics shows politicians spending countless hours attending weddings, funerals, and meetings with members of their district, passing out cash gifts as they go. Voters develop a close personal relationship with their representatives and are made aware of the material benefits that will follow from their support for specific politicians (Curtis 1971). This behavior might be seen as clientelistic, but it is often not so much an exchange of a gift for a vote, as a gesture to make voters feel a welcome link between themselves and their candidates.

Japanese clientelism assumes many less symbolic forms. Woodall describes Japanese clientelism as "selective allocation of distributive policy benefits by public-sector elites in exchange for the promise of solidarity and mutually beneficial inputs from favored private-sector interests. This exchange may involve government subsidies, official price supports and import quotas, targeted tax breaks, regulatory favors in the allocation of trucking routes, and other policy benefits" (1996: 9–10). In many cases, the exchange has little to do with voters, the clearest case being *amakudari* (descent from heaven), whereby retired bureaucrats are given high-paying, low-pressure second careers at companies they regulated during their first careers.

For elected officials, Richardson (1997) describes Japan as a "party clientelistic state" in which the government acts as a caretaker for the groups that are its clients (260). Pempel nicely outlines the system of side-payments linking the longtime-ruling LDP to its clients – in particular rice farmers, the small-business sector, geographical regions lacking high-growth industries, and industries in decline – with policies having more to do with politics than economic planning (1998: 63–5). These groups all strongly supported the LDP, especially at the ballot booth and, in turn, "were amply rewarded from the public coffers" (Pempel 1998: 63), especially in times of electoral crisis (Calder 1988). Support for these groups came in numerous forms. For example, to small and medium-sized business, the LDP grants lenient tax provisions, ignores large-scale tax evasion, and provides no-collateral, low-interest loans (Okimoto 1989: 187).

This system is not merely founded on spending but also works through the regulatory state: Economic protectionism and state regulations allowed the government to inoculate many of its favored groups, such as farmers and small and medium-sized business (who in turn strongly support the LDP), against more efficient foreign producers.

That said, distributive goods are at the core of Japanese clientelism. Even viewed from a comparative perspective, Japan's policy is heavily distributive. Calder writes that, in fact, "Japan's emphasis on public works and agricultural spending has rarely been matched internationally since the New Deal" (1988: 156). In particular, the government uses public works to fund two of its most important clients: construction industries that carry out projects and farmers who act as part-time construction workers. In 1996, public works spending in Japan amounted to 8.7 percent of the country's GDP, in contrast to figures of 3.2 percent in France, 2.3 percent in Canada, 2.2 percent in Germany, 2.2 percent in Italy, 1.7 percent in the United States, and 1.4 percent in England (Ogawa 2004; Seaman 2003). In many cases, public works projects appeared to have no other de facto goal than funneling money to clients, such as construction companies. For example, the Japanese government regularly seeks to pave its rivers with cement under the questionable auspices of "flood control." Richardson makes clear the real purpose of such policy: "Much of the domestic policy agenda was affected by the needs of political clients" (1997: 233). Ultimately, such policy is a part of many voters' expectations. As Reed (1986) writes: "Each area prefers a representative who can deliver a bigger share of the benefits being distributed to one who represents them on the issues of the day" (35).[4]

In the sense that they involve an apparent exchange, these practices all appear clientelist, but insofar as they are universally distributed, many of these features do not fit neatly into Kitschelt's procedural definition of clientelism (see my Chapter 1). This is clearest in the case of agriculture. The LDP has long allocated huge subsidies to Japanese farming interests; in return, farmers have been some of the LDP's strongest supporters. Nevertheless, even farmers who do not support LDP candidates can benefit easily from the LDP's agricultural policies, and agricultural groups cannot always reliably deliver votes to the LDP.

Mechanisms of Clientelist Exchange in Japan

Precisely what form does clientelist exchange take in Japan? It is first and foremost candidate- or politician-based. Unlike systems such as Austria's, where parties deliver patronage directly, individual politicians are the main link to societal groups in Japan.

Monitoring is critical to clientelism. Without it, parties and candidates cannot know if the groups they are rewarding with benefits are giving

---

[4] Naturally, not *all* voters prefer such a representative: Some voters do not benefit from the distribution of such benefits; some oppose "wasteful" spending of this kind; and some simply have ideological preferences for other parties.

politicians the support that makes the exchange complete. Close monitoring is clearly illegal and usually impractical, so it usually makes more sense to talk about "collective" monitoring, with benefits less tightly targeted and parties monitoring the extent to which particular interest groups or geographic regions support them through donations, campaigning, political quiescence, or a substantial number of votes. Although the discretionary provision of benefits is often not targeted as tightly as is necessary to ensure that the correct group is receiving them, collective monitoring can be quite precise.

It might be argued that some practices and relationships – such as those between agriculture and small and medium-sized business as interest groups on one side and the LDP on the other – walk a fine line between universalistic and clientelist arrangements, but others fall without a doubt into the clientelist camp. In Japan, candidates' relationships with many groups are clearly clientelist, but two especially stand out: *kōenkai* and construction groups, in particular land improvement districts.

Kōenkai. Most LDP and other conservative national-level politicians in Japan maintain *kōenkai*, or personal support organizations (Curtis 1971). Designed to support the electoral activities of individual candidates, *kōenkai* are organized hierarchically, with national politicians at the top, leading local politicians and local business notables at the intermediate levels, and large numbers of voters at the bottom. The largest *kōenkai* contain many tens of thousands of members. The politician at the top provides the *kōenkai* gifts, puts on parties, and organizes lavish trips, at essentially no cost to the members. It is impossible to separate fully the different reasons for someone to join a particular *kōenkai*. Many who join feel a strong personal bond with the candidate they support, and many seek nothing from the candidate and the organization other than camaraderie (and perhaps a promise to act in the best interests of the constituency). At the same time, the exchange portion of the relationship cannot be ignored. As Curtis explains, members of the *kōenkai* "turn to it for various favors and services much as Americans turned to the urban party machine in its heyday earlier in the century. It is this doing of a great variety of favors for the electorate that imposes the greatest demands on the *kōenkai* staff's time and the politician's purse" (1971: 145). Politicians provide their *kōenkai* members with employment, marital introductions, and school placement for their children. Other favors are even weightier. Politicians, for example, donate multiple bottles of expensive *sake* to local organizations and considerable sums of money to help with small-scale construction projects (e.g., roof replacement costs) being pushed by *kōenkai* members (Curtis 1971: 149–50).

In exchange, *kōenkai* members are expected to vote for the candidate, campaign on the candidate's behalf, and provide the names of additional people whom the *kōenkai* can contact to ask to support the candidate. *Kōenkai* are also useful in helping candidates get around Japanese campaign restrictions. In Japan, door-to-door election canvassing during campaigns is illegal. By using the organization's list of members, campaign workers can justify the visit as part of the *kōenkai* activities, and not campaigning (Christensen 1998: 991).

Public Works and Land Improvement Districts. Government public works spending plays a big role in Japan's political economy, in particular in its focus on construction. Roughly 15 percent of Japan's total gross domestic product (GDP) is invested in construction (Okuda 2001). Construction companies employ roughly 10 percent of the Japanese workforce (Woodall 1996: 83), and probably more in rural areas. The construction industry is one of the LDP's biggest supporters, providing the party with large donations and mobilizing voters for LDP candidates. In return, LDP politicians provide public works contracts to construction companies. Statistical analysis indicates a substantial correlation between the presence of LDP politicians in a given Japanese prefecture and the amount of public works spending in the area (Hori 1996; Okuda 2001).[5]

Much public works spending may not match Kitschelt's procedural definition of clientelism (see Chapter 1) perfectly because even many who do not support the candidate may benefit from the project, but certain types of Japanese construction projects fit the definition very neatly. Because LDP national politicians often control very specifically to what areas or what companies national funds are to be disbursed (Curtis 1988: 108), they can target funding very narrowly. Among the clearest cases are land improvement subsidization (*tochi kairyō jigyō*) and the groups that run the projects, the land improvement districts (*tochi kairyōku*). Typically, land improvement subsidies are given by the national government to fund specific agriculture-related projects, such as controlling and undertaking irrigation and land conservation. Among agricultural interest groups, land improvement groups receive by the far the largest subsidy allocation (George Mulgan 2000: 81).

The funding of such projects is extremely attractive for politicians because of its targetability. They can select specific supporters to funnel money to: LDP politicians agree to support their top local political and construction industry clients in the pursuit of project subsidies and to lobby the central bureaucracies to fund the projects. The local leaders of the municipality being allocated the money ensure that a particular company is given the project. The project itself typically does not cover wide expanses of land, so it is easy to identify the project's beneficiaries. Moreover, the land improvement districts regularly make kickbacks to the Diet members who got the project funded (George Mulgan 2000: 407).

The exchange is also appealing to politicians because land improvement groups actively back LDP politicians. The groups have well-developed

---

[5] However, see footnote 2 of Chapter 5 for issues that deserve greater attention in such analysis.

organizations that specialize in politicians' electoral operations. They are a valuable resource because of their close contact with farmers and others with influence over the farm vote and employ farmers who need part-time construction work to supplement their incomes. And thanks in large part to the government subsidies they receive, the land improvement districts have a good deal of money to spend on mobilizing the vote (George Mulgan 2000: 405–7). Japan's leading agricultural cooperatives are often too diffuse to guarantee the delivery of votes, but land improvement grants are very targeted and thereby increase the vote collection power of the groups (George Mulgan 2000: 515–22).[6]

Monitoring and the Impact of Local Politicians

While *kōenkai* and land improvement grants allow for targeted allocation of goods, there is still the problem of monitoring. It is difficult to tell if voters are behaving as they promise. Here, local politicians are particularly useful. Especially in rural areas, national politicians tend to use local politicians more than any other group to deliver their vote (Curtis 1971; Park 1998a, 1998b). National politicians provide local politicians with funds and lobby the central government for funding on their behalf. In exchange, local politicians mobilize individuals to campaign and voters to cast ballots for the correct candidate. As Curtis notes, "Direct vote-buying is rare in Japan, but paying people who supposedly have the ability to deliver their particular group of supporters is not" (1992: 235). With their close ties to and familiarity with their locality, many local politicians, particularly in rural areas, know the voting habits of a large proportion of their constituents.

Short of actually going into the ballot booth, it is impossible to tell which candidate individual voters cast their ballots for, but politicians can *collectively* monitor the voters' home region to see how many votes were cast and can directly monitor local politicians' effort on their behalf. For elections at the most local level, candidates can get elected with as few as two hundred to three hundred votes. In such areas, candidates are familiar with who their supporters are exactly, and these bases of support tend to be *highly* concentrated geographically (Horiuchi 2001: Chapter 4; Steiner 1965). For example, in his study of one local electoral campaign, Horiuchi finds that nearly all voters within a given village neighborhood tend to support a single candidate; as a result, one campaign was able to predict its final tally within eight votes. In national elections, votes are tallied at the larger regional level so that it is not possible to tell how many votes each candidate receives at the most local levels. Nevertheless, in rural areas, even in national elections, ballots are often tallied at the village level with very small populations, at times with total votes cast in the lower hundreds. (That is, in each district

---

[6] For more on public spending and land improvement projects, see Sakakibara (1991).

throughout the country, votes are tallied and made public at the subdistrict level – at the city, ward, town, or village level – before they are summed together to determine the overall district vote.) Given that it is usually well known which local politicians represent and are responsible for mobilizing voters in each village, observers can see the number of votes won by these local representatives and compare them to the number won by the Diet candidate in the area.

This monitoring capacity plays a critical part in shaping the success of clientelist linkages in Japan. National politicians assume that local politicians' support can be transferred to them and that "most of the votes come from countable sources. The two conditions of transferability and countability made it possible to maintain a mutual aid system based on vertical alignment between a Dietman and local politicians" (Park 1998a: 184). Local politicians are therefore held responsible for the full mobilization of voters in the areas.[7] Diet members make it clear to local politicians that they are aware of the number of votes available to be won in their areas, offer future electoral support and funding from the central government as rewards for delivering these votes, and threaten to punish failure by isolating them from future support. In turn, local politicians tend to be quite responsive (Park 1998a).[8]

Monitoring and the Organized Vote

The preceding examples indicate the important role of the "organized vote" in Japan's clientelist system. Japanese campaign laws are extremely restrictive, severely limiting candidates' ability to make mass appeals. Therefore, to attract support, candidates tend to work through organizations, such as *kōenkai*, businesses, unions, and various industrial and occupational associations that can more easily and directly mobilize voter support.

At times, the LDP punishes regions that do not support it (e.g., by withholding funds), but there are risks to such a strategy. By punishing a given region, LDP incumbents who worked hard on behalf of the party will also be punished. Thus, it makes particularly good sense to focus monitoring and enforcement on the organizations and individual politicians who have influence over votes (and campaign funds) in their given areas. For example, when primary elections decided the LDP presidency in the early 1980s, some Japanese firms actually took physical possession of employees' ballots before their votes had been cast (Fukushima 1989: 265), no doubt fearing punishment if they did not deliver a specific number of votes for the correct

---

[7] Such collective monitoring occurs also in more urban areas (Park 1998a), but it is less accurate.

[8] The importance of local politicians to clientelist modes of exchange that link localities to national level politicians is hardly unique to Japan. Ames (1994: 95) notes similar relationships in Colombia, Mexico, Venezuela, and Italy.

candidates. In addition, during the prewar period, landlords who controlled the ballots of their tenants were the key to vote collection and clientelist exchange (Curtis 1971: 41–2). In the postwar period, monitoring and exchange typically focused on the organized vote provided by private organizations – such as construction companies and land improvement groups – *kōenkai*, and local politicians.

"Personal" voting often becomes intertwined with this organized vote. Many voters cast ballots for politicians because of their personal characteristics (even beyond issue stances). But in many cases, the personal draw of candidates has less to do with their individual qualities and more to do with the personal pull of the local politicians and organizational representatives campaigning on behalf of the candidates.

THE FACTORS SHAPING CLIENTELISM IN JAPAN

What explains the high level of clientelism in Japan?

Electoral system arguments are insufficient to explain Japan's clientelism. The origins of clientelism in Japan are due in greater measure to the control particular elites had over state resources and to the organization of Japanese landholding. The SNTV/MMD electoral system reinforced clientelist linkage patterns in the postwar period, but the fact that clientelist patterns varied both across the country and over time in Japan suggests that other factors – in particular, social structure, centralization of financial resources, and political economy – played a larger role in determining the shape of such patterns.

SNTV/MMD as an Explanation

Japan's electoral system is often held responsible for the country's personalistic and clientelistic campaigning, voting, and parties. And SNTV/MMD clearly does influence party and candidate behavior in key ways.

Under SNTV/MMD, each voter casts one ballot for a candidate. Votes cannot be transferred to the candidate's party or to a specified alternative candidate. As I explain in Chapter 2, under Japanese SNTV/MMD in the House of Representatives, each district typically held between three and five seats; if M stands for the district magnitude (number of seats in the district), the top M vote getters each won a seat. Because there were (in the last SNTV election in 1993) only 129 districts, but 511 seats, a party had to win an average of approximately two seats per district in order to control a majority of HR seats, and the LDP therefore tended to run at least two candidates per district. The result was that, despite sharing party affiliation, these candidates were rivals. Because under this system campaigns based on intraparty competition over issues would have proven counterproductive, the system's incentives made SNTV/MMD the most personalistic of any in use throughout the world in recent years (Carey and Shugart 1995).

SNTV/MMD offers incentives to emphasize patronage-based campaigns as a rational vote-division strategy. McCubbins and Rosenbluth (1995) argue that LDP candidates differentiated themselves functionally from one another by having each represent a different organized interest. The LDP then allowed its candidates access to government resources that they could use to win over these interests. Tatebayashi and McKean (2002) find evidence of such a strategy, but also the simultaneous presence of another strategy, whereby LDP candidates differentiated themselves by targeting different geographical regions with particularistic goods, that is benefits provided at the government's discretion to specific, targeted constituencies.[9] The small vote percentage needed to win a seat under SNTV/MMD also increased the incentives for clientelist arrangements, as candidates could target particular groups rather than making broad appeals.

Origins of Japanese Clientelism – Resource Control and Socioeconomic Organization

The argument linking SNTV/MMD to clientelist practices is compelling, as the system offered politicians clear incentives to distribute specific goods in a targeted way to its supporters. By breaking down districts into more specific geographical or functional bases of support, collective monitoring was easier than under systems where candidates had to compete for broader scale interests. Nevertheless, although the system reinforced clientelism, SNTV/MMD does not appear to have been the progenitor of Japanese clientelism.

Resource Based Explanation for Clientelism. Given that Japan's first parties were hatched by government elites who controlled government resources that they could use to their political advantage, it should not be surprising that early Japanese parties emphasized the distribution of particularistic goods. Early parties' role in actual governing was limited. Electoral politics were highly personalized, and parties' main job was to create links to society and channel citizen support into the system, which made the distribution of goods a sensible party strategy.

Ramseyer and Rosenbluth (1995) argue that the SNTV/MMD system introduced in 1925 increased the emphasis on "money" politics in Japanese electoral politics.[10] They are certainly correct that money politics became more intense and widespread under the 1925 electoral system, but vote

---

[9] However, some candidates – particularly those with constituents who are either less interested in such goods or less able to be targeted effectively – would be less likely to pursue such a strategy.

[10] Prewar Japanese elections utilized a variety of SNTV that involved different district magnitudes. Most arguments on the effect of SNTV on clientelism, candidate-centered voting, and factionalism focus on the three to five seats per district system introduced in 1925.

buying was common well before, beginning around 1905 after the Russo-Japan War. The electoral system probably had some impact prior to 1925 when Japan utilized an SNTV/MMD system with between 1 and 13 seats per district (Scalapino 1953).

That said, even from the first Japanese democratic elections in the late nineteenth and early twentieth centuries, huge sums of money were poured into campaigns, irrespective of the electoral system used (Scalapino 1953). Early Japanese parties acted out of a need to create links to society without stepping on the more programmatic concerns of the political elite and bureaucracy. Seeking to create links to various rural agricultural and urban commercial interests, parties focused on providing patronage benefits to their electoral districts (Pempel 1978). Japan's early party organization followed Shefter's (1994) notion of internal mobilization (elites in the government seeking to create a space of power for themselves within the government by creating linkages to society), tending toward patronage-oriented politics because of elites' access to state resources.[11] Early leader Itō Hirobumi, for example, took over the leadership of the Liberal Party (*Jiyūtō*) and reorganized it as *Seiyūkai* in 1900 to create party support within the Diet for his government.

In the early 1910s, civil service laws were changed to give *Seiyūkai* greater opportunity to use patronage, and ties between the parties and ruling oligarchy grew fairly close (Berger 1977). Well-known public servants became party members, and the parties' ties to the bureaucracy grew more pronounced. *Seiyūkai* sought to institutionalize itself and stabilize its electoral base by means of patronage. From that time, Japanese parties were heavily involved in pork distribution (Allinson 1993: 39), creating a link between agricultural interests, which provided votes for the conservative parties, and business, which paid for the parties' operating expenses. As time passed and parties gained greater control over the budget, they increased their ability to dish out pork, their means to cater to local economic interests.

In light of Shefter's (1994) observation that, once established, parties' linkage forms tend to remain fairly constant, much of Japanese clientelistic politics can be explained by pointing to a path-dependent evolution from the prewar period. Even though most accounts of party politics in Japan begin with the postwar period, Pempel (1978) notes the continuity between the pre- and postwar periods, in particular the fact that the main bases of rural conservatism remained intact and loyal to their prewar politicians. Prewar party behavior was reinforced in the early postwar period as the clientelistic prewar parties were reborn as first the Liberals and the Progressives (who became the Democrats) and then the LDP. The fact that the LDP was formed

---

[11] We should be careful with the analogy to internally mobilized parties because the strict civil service laws in the early twentieth-century Japan kept the bureaucracy insulated from party control.

at the top, rather than through a grassroots movement, further encouraged the already clientelist tendencies of its politicians.[12] At first made up in large part by former bureaucrats, the LDP had strong ties to the bureaucracy, thereby giving the party exceptional resources that it could use to reinforce clientelist linkages.

Socioeconomic Organization. While parties' control over state resources played a critical role in shaping early patronage practices, the great power of landlords in the prewar period cemented clientelist linkages. Universal male suffrage was introduced in 1925, and one feature of Japan's socioeconomics made clientelist politics especially effective in this context. Prewar Japan was heavily rural, and because of the great power rural landlords held over their tenants, most voters had little choice but to follow the voting instructions of their landlords. This enabled rural landlords to play a central part in electoral politics (Curtis 1971: 41–2) and made clientelist linkages simple to execute: Politicians channeled government resources to individual landlords; in exchange, landlords made sure all their tenants voted for specified politicians. Given prewar landlords' capacity to deliver votes, this socioeconomic organization would have given politicians under any electoral system an incentive to push targeted goods for clientelist exchange with such power brokers.

Institutional Explanations for Japanese Clientelism

SNTV/MMD as Reinforcement. Nevertheless, there is cross-national evidence that clientelistic politics are common to SNTV electoral systems (Grofman 1999). In Japan, specifically, SNTV/MMD reinforced clientelist tendencies created by the internal mobilization of parties and socioeconomic organization. In the prewar, targeting landlords with direct subsidies had to have been especially attractive to politicians in the SNTV/MMD system, where building a base of concentrated votes was probably the most efficient path to election.

In the postwar, a change in Japan's socioeconomic organization made SNTV/MMD a more potent influence in shaping Japan's clientelist linkages. During the early postwar occupation, the United States imposed a wide-ranging series of reforms on Japan. Land reform was a central platform, and land ownership in a small number of concentrated hands was no longer permitted. Politicians could no longer rely on landlords to deliver the vote, but with their control over government resources, (usually conservative) politicians had incentives to continue to pursue clientelist linkages.

---

[12] It may be tempting to hold the general pattern of top-down party formation as responsible for reinforcing clientelism in Japan, but the bulk of party formation in the postwar period involved *opposition* parties, which did not have the governmental links necessary to push clientelist strategies credibly.

SNTV/MMD was most likely a major influence on the clientelist arrangements that ensued. In theory, the decline in landlord power could have led politicians toward more programmatically oriented behavior in order to generate support. However, because SNTV/MMD created incentives for candidates to avoid program-based appeals and differentiate themselves (whether functionally or geographically) from fellow partisans, and because they needed only a small percentage of the vote to win office, Japanese politicians also had great incentive to pursue narrowly targeted reliable bases of support. In this way, SNTV/MMD promoted the change in candidate strategy that took place in the early postwar period, whereby, in place of local landlords, Japanese national politicians turned increasingly to local politicians and *kōenkai* to deliver votes for them (Curtis 1971: 42–3). As indicated earlier, clientelism was at the heart of these relationships.

Evidence of the Impact of SNTV/MMD. In light of Kitschelt's procedural definition (see my Chapter 1), we should expect clientelist linkages to be most effective when narrowly targeted, where politicians tightly control the receipt of benefits and monitoring is effective. And it is here that the impact of the SNTV/MMD system can clearly be seen.

In 1994, Japan eliminated SNTV/MMD in the HR and replaced it with a mixed-member system combining 300 SMDs and 200 PR seats.[13] Carey and Shugart (1995) argue that, in the form utilized in Japan (no primary elections necessary for a party nomination), SMDs encourage more party-oriented political behavior, in large part because of the control the system gives to parties in the nomination process. Also, most observers hold that, in order to win a plurality of the district vote, candidates under SMD need to develop broad bases of support within a district, and not just focus on specific, tiny constituencies. PR systems are widely hailed as leading to more party-oriented and programmatic behavior. As a result, many early observers predicted that the new electoral system would lead to a decline in clientelistic behavior (see, for example, Ramseyer and Rosenbluth 1993).

Indeed, Hirano (2002) indicates that votes for LDP incumbents were more geographically concentrated under SNTV/MMD than they were in succeeding SMD elections and that the allocation of central government subsidies was more concentrated around LDP incumbents' home offices before reform than after. The implication is that SNTV/MMD gave politicians incentives to target benefits more narrowly, so as to exchange directly government subsidies for votes and find greater ease in monitoring the exchange. Hirano's evidence does not preclude continued clientelist behavior under SMDs, but it does suggest that it is less likely, as clientelist arrangements would be less narrowly targeted and therefore much more costly at a time when funds are in shorter supply than in the past, and possibly harder to monitor.

[13] Total PR seats were reduced to 180 before the 2000 HR election.

Continued Clientelism Even After SNTV/MMD. That said, there is reason to believe that institutional incentives for particularistic behavior, which
makes clientelism more likely, continue under Japan's new system. In the new
system, many SMD candidates simultaneously run as equally ranked candidates on PR lists as well. For example, multiple candidates on a given party's
PR list are all ranked at the same spot on the list. Those who lose in the
SMD race remain on the PR list, and their ranking on the list is determined
by their success vis-à-vis the winner in their respective SMDs. Candidates
who lose "best" (e.g., a candidate whose vote total is nearly identical to
the total won by the winner in his SMD) are placed at a higher spot on
the PR list than other equally ranked "dual" candidates who did not win
as many votes relative to their respective SMD winners. If equally ranked
with other dual candidates at the second spot on the list, the candidate who
loses best will receive the number two ranking; the candidate who loses
second best receives the number three ranking; and so on. SMDs and PR
appear less personalistic than SNTV/MMD. But, even though SMD and PR
rules often encourage programmatic, less-localistic behavior, Japan's mixed-
member system encourages continued localistic orientation on the part of
candidates, including many PR victors, because they need to focus on their
specific district's needs (McKean and Scheiner 2000).

In addition, the PR voting affects only the *PR* component of House of
Representatives elections. In "linked" systems such as Germany's, the percentage of the vote a party wins in PR determines the total number of seats
allotted to it. The seats it wins in SMDs are simply subtracted from this total,
with the remainder allotted to the party in PR. Therefore, the incentive in
such systems is to emphasize programmatic behavior that helps the overall
reputation of the party. In contrast, in "unlinked" systems such as Japan's,
the party's vote in PR balloting only determines the number of seats it wins
in the PR tier. To determine the total number of seats a party has won, these
PR seats are added to the SMDs the party won. Therefore, in Japan, parties and candidates both have an incentive to emphasize the more numerous
SMD races, making more particularistic behavior more likely (McKean and
Scheiner 2000; Moser and Scheiner 2004, in press).

Many observers also predicted that party platforms would become more
important under the new system as party leaders would be better able to control party nominations (see, for example, Ramseyer and Rosenbluth 1993).
In part, this did occur with the increased use of national party manifestos
in 2003. However, the importance of party platforms did not seem to be
wholly borne out in practice, in part because the introduction of SMDs gave
local mayors greater weight in candidate nomination and local party organization.[14] As a result, candidates who gave greater consideration to local

---

[14] Interview with a Democratic Party of Japan election bureau staff member (December 18,
    1998).

matters – and, hence, targeted goods to the locality – gained a better chance of winning party nominations. There is evidence of SMD candidates under Japan's new system focusing campaign appeals more on big regional development projects and less on allocations that would help specific groups (Park 1998a: 296). However, the meaning of such evidence is inconclusive because many candidates also made broader appeals under the SNTV/MMD system and, as in the example just noted, were most likely to do so in urban areas.

Moreover, there are features of SMDs that facilitate clientelist exchange *better* than SNTV/MMD. The introduction of SMDs helped collective monitoring in a number of ways. As the sole representatives of their specific districts, LDP candidates under SMDs became responsible for the success of the *party* in PR races in the region, not only in Lower House races but in Upper House ones as well.[15] In many cases, candidates were warned that a failure to bring in a quota of party votes would lead to a decline in their influence within the party. Probably more important is the impact of the SMD system on local politicians. According to Yamada (1998), the SMD system helped make local politicians' behavior more transparent, thereby improving the monitoring that is necessary for the functioning of clientelist exchange. Under SNTV/MMD, local politicians sometimes avoided linking up with particular LDP politicians out of fear that these national politicians' intraparty rivals within the district would punish them for their choice. Under the SMD system, because only one LDP politician runs in each district's HR race, local LDP politicians are obliged to create tight links with that Diet candidate (Otake 1998; Yamada 1998). The result, one campaign manager noted, was that among local politicians "double-dealing has disappeared" (Yamada 1998: 55): Local politicians worked actively on behalf of national LDP politicians. Such tight links were much more prevalent in poorer rural areas, which depend more on the goods the LDP helps transfer from the central to the local governments (Yamada 1998: 55). And because national politicians knew clearly which local politicians were working on their behalf, they could monitor the outcome in specific regions (Otake 1998: 15) and reward or punish local politicians accordingly.

Even with the elimination of SNTV/MMD, two pieces of institutional continuity remain: the rules governing vote-tallying regions and the core components of Japanese campaign law. First, a unique aspect of Japan's vote tallying makes monitoring efforts easier. Votes are first tallied and reported at subdistrict municipality levels – city, ward, town, or village levels – before being compiled into the district's overall vote. This means that collective monitoring and monitoring of local politicians' campaign activity on behalf of national candidates is relatively easy in rural villages, which contain small numbers of residents. Second, Japanese campaign laws offer candidates and parties only limited access to television, radio, and print as a way

---

[15] Steven R. Reed, personal communication.

to appeal to voters. As a result, it is difficult for candidates and parties to campaign on broad-based, mass appeals (Christensen 1998). Without mass appeal methods open to them, candidates have substantial incentives to target their appeals narrowly. These laws no doubt combined with SNTV/MMD to push candidates toward more targeted appeals, but their continued presence makes the maintenance of clientelist linkages likely.

Indeed, in a study of campaign practices in 1996 under Japan's new system, Christensen (1998: 1003) finds no evidence of a change in campaign style. In the one campaign he followed that emphasized mass appeals to the voters rather than *kōenkai*, the candidate lost, blamed the defeat on moving away from more tried-and-true methods of campaigning, and planned to emphasize more *kōenkai*-based campaigning in the following election. Krauss and Pekkanen's (2004) close analysis of political behavior under Japan's new system indicates that, if anything, the use of *kōenkai* perhaps grew even more important.

Impact of Social Structure, Financial Centralization, and Political Economy

Even under SNTV/MMD, there was substantial variation in the level of clientelism, suggesting strongly the insufficiency of the electoral system argument. SNTV/MMD was utilized throughout the country, but the use of and support for patronage and clientelist practices varied over time and cross-regionally. In short, even though SNTV/MMD undoubtedly reinforced clientelism, other features were more important in shaping the level of clientelism.

Over time, especially in the late 1990s and early 2000s, Japanese railed increasingly against the corruption and waste in the clientelist system. Japan's new opposition parties of the post-1993 period were founded in part on anti-clientelist appeals, and many voters responded to such appeals (Chapter 8). The ascent in 2001 of "maverick" LDP politician Junichirō Koizumi to the post of prime minister indicated the growing appeal of anti-clientelism groups.

Moreover, clientelist practices were still more prevalent and more favorably received in rural areas. As noted previously, pork barrel is not equivalent to clientelism: Because targeting of pork is often not perfect, even those who do not support the politicians involved will often be able to benefit from the allocation of the funds. Nevertheless, pork barrel is a useful "tracer" of clientelism, which shows substantial differences in urban and rural areas.

In 1993, the Japan Election Studies II (JES-II) public opinion survey asked respondents, (a) if there was in their district a "candidate who has done something special for the people of this area such as improving roads or acquiring government grants" and (b) all else equal, if they would be more likely to cast a ballot for a candidate who dedicates himself primarily to national and foreign affairs or one who devotes himself "to activities involving the

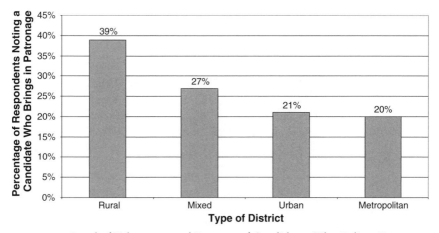

FIGURE 3.1 Level of Urban-ness and Presence of Candidates Who Deliver Patronage (*Source:* JES-II public opinion survey)

protection of local interests." Question (a) provides a useful proxy for the level of clientelist behavior: Where voters more often cite the presence of candidates who provide patronage benefits, clientelist practices are likely to be more common. Given that protection of specifically local interests often involves clientelist favors, Question (b) represents a reasonable approximation of respondents' support for clientelism.

The responses to the questions varied substantially by region. As Figure 3.1 indicates, patronage-oriented behavior was more widespread in rural areas. And, as Figure 3.2 shows, respondents in rural areas were markedly more likely to support politicians with a local orientation than were those in urban areas.[16]

Three principal factors explain these differences: social structure, centralization of government financing, and political economy.

Social Structure. Pork-based clientelistic behavior by politicians is more efficient in rural areas: In cities, public works projects usually influence innumerable people – many who vote in another district – which makes it more difficult for parties to use the projects to target specific groups of voters. In rural areas, it is easier to target specific, geographically concentrated groups and claim credit for spending because a larger proportion of beneficiaries live and vote in the area. For this reason, it should not be surprising that rural candidates' bases of voter support tend to be more geographically concentrated than those of urban candidates.

Social networks are important as well. Rural residents tend to hold closer community ties and links to their local political leaders, making it easier for

---

[16] Level of urban-ness is determined by the population density of each locality.

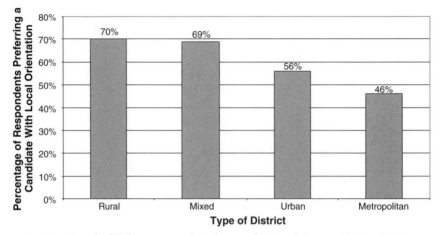

FIGURE 3.2 Level of Urban-ness and Preference for Candidates with Local Orientation (*Source:* JES-II public opinion survey)

local leaders to mobilize groups of voters and more effective for national politicians to channel particularistic goods through these leaders to appeal to voters. Rural social networks and the incentives created by SNTV/MMD reinforced one another because the networks gave rural politicians a greater capacity to develop geographically targeted bases of support that, under SNTV/MMD, made individual candidate success more likely and offered, as Tatebayashi and McKean (2002) suggest, an efficient vote-division strategy. In contrast, urban residents are less well tied together, and therefore urban politicians are more inclined to appeal to them through voluntary organizations and direct appeals to the electorate (Curtis 1971: 252). Analysis of urban campaigning indicates a greater emphasis in cities on appeals designed for the district as whole and not just specific groups within it (Park 1998a).

Social structural factors also played a role in the clamor for the elimination of many of Japan's clientelist practices that grew over the late 1990s and early 2000s. Over the years, demographics of the average Japanese changed to favor less clientelism. Local communities were more tightly knit in the early postwar period, and political and social networks were especially close in rural areas. However, Japan has grown – and is continuing to grow – more urban with large proportions of Japanese living in cities (see Chapter 8 and Figure 8.1). With the increasing flight of voters from the countryside, these community links loosened for many (George Mulgan 2000: 382–3), making it far more difficult to keep many voters in the clientelist networks.

Centralization of Government Financing. The Japanese central government is the leading financer of local governmental expenditures in most of the country's municipalities but the central government avoids funding local governments' wide-sweeping public goods types of projects (Reed 1986). As a result, in much of the country, even when voters might approve of a more public-goods-oriented policy, they have less incentive to cast ballots for candidates who espouse them because these policies will be less likely to get funded by the central government. Similarly, Japanese urban areas usually maintain greater wealth than rural ones, rely less upon the central government for funding, and can safely ignore the center's policy "recommendations." Not surprising therefore, urban areas consistently have a greater "programmatic" orientation to their policymaking. (See Chapter 5.) As a result, even though centralization does not generate clientelistic behavior, a centralized funding structure helps maintain it.

Political Economy

VARIATION IN SUPPORT FOR CLIENTELISM OVER TIME. The LDP has found great electoral success by supporting a variety of groups, especially large firms, professionals, small subcontractors and distributors, and farmers. Particularly key was its relationship with groups that depended on governmental subsidization, such as farmers, small and medium-sized businesses, and construction interests. These relations do not always fit perfectly into Kitschelt's definition of clientelism. Nevertheless, there is very often an approximation, as the relationships were usually built very much on exchange: Politicians provided individuals and groups in such industries with substantial targeted favors in return for support, which the politicians then monitored either through locally based elites or through collective monitoring practices.

In the early postwar decades, even as many larger firms grew internationally competitive, tremendous growth created a positive sum economy in which it was possible – and politically advantageous – for the LDP to continue to support all of its major constituents. But the party's ability to maintain the support of such disparate groups depended on the insulation of the Japanese market and high economic growth. These factors could not be sustained, and, by the 1990s, Japan's economy slowed dramatically.

Over time, various pressures brought about changes in Japan. Foreign countries and firms lobbied Japan to open its economy, and the country responded by liberalizing some of its markets. Slowed economic growth increased the need for trade-offs between the different groups supporting the LDP. Although Rosenbluth emphasizes the role of Japan's internationally competitive firms fearing a backlash in a world of increased capital exposure and global economy (1996: 148), domestic distributive struggles (which Rosenbluth also notes) appear to have played the key role in generating a backlash against clientelism within Japan. Over the postwar period, Japan shifted from a highly rural society to a much more urban one (see Chapter 8). Urban consumers and efficient businesses grew increasingly tired of government pork barrel practices, targeted favors for LDP clients and the accompanying corruption, which were straining Japan's economy and their own pocketbooks. Decrying LDP clientelism, leading business associations supported anti-LDP alternatives in the early 1990s, and urban voters consistently did so as well throughout the decade.

Despite some changes, the LDP continued to channel goods to its inefficient, but still politically supportive, clienteles. After holding roughly steady for about a decade, central governmental public works spending more than doubled in the early 1990s and, while jumping up and down dramatically from year to year, remained high throughout the decade (Ōkurashō 2001). In the 1960s, Japanese public works spending – perhaps the best tracer of clientelist behavior – was roughly twice the average in other major industrial countries. Such spending in 1997 was roughly three to four times the percentage of GDP that is spent in the major economies of Europe (OECD 1998; Seaman 2003). Pempel notes that many fiscal packages were passed between 1992 and 2000. Worth over $1 trillion, these packages were made up in large part by pork barrel construction projects and assistance for small and medium-sized firms (Pempel 2000).

In the face of such "wasteful" spending and economic failure, public outrage against clientelism grew and led to the prime ministership of Koizumi, who promised the elimination of such practices. As of the writing of this book, the outcome of Koizumi's efforts appeared mixed. On one hand, clientelist interests and Diet members looking to protect such interests continued to hold a strong position within the LDP, frequently blocking attacks on the clientelist system. On the other, the combination of Koizumi's efforts and the decline in governmental resources – very much a result of Japan's weakened economy – led to a reduction in funding for many clientelist practices such as public works.[17]

REGIONAL VARIATION IN SUPPORT FOR CLIENTELISM. Individual socioeconomic self-interest plays a substantial role in shaping voters' receptiveness to clientelism. In times of economic downturn, where clientelism is perceived as a drag on the economy, voters' willingness to support the practice is likely to be based on the extent to which they benefit from clientelist exchange. Rural residents have socioeconomic characteristics that make them more likely to depend on and benefit from these exchanges.

The JES-II public opinion survey's question on voters' support for candidates with a localistic orientation is useful in determining what shaped Japanese citizens' support for clientelist practices in Japan in the early 1990s because the protection of local interests typically involved clientelist favors like targeted subsidies and protection of local business. Based on statistical analysis of the factors shaping voters' support for locally oriented candidates, it appears that rural voters were more likely to support localistic and

---

[17] See the *Japan Statistical Yearbook* and *www.mof.go.jp* for statistics that indicate the drop in public works funding, in terms of both raw numbers and percentage of the total budget.

presumably clientelistic practices (see Scheiner ND). But even controlling for urban-ness, Japanese facing particular sociodemographic/economic conditions were still more likely to support such localistic behavior: Individuals whose household head was employed in farming, forestry, fisheries, mining, or transportation, which were especially dependent upon the benefits of clientelism, and people working in small businesses, which also depended greatly on governmental regulations and protections, were more likely to have a clientelist orientation.

Because older citizens and those with less education have less labor flexibility, they ought to be more supportive of clientelism, given the importance of clientelist practices to protecting their jobs in the face of growing pressures to become more "efficient." Indeed, the greatest impact on support for clientelist practices was education, with less-educated voters markedly more likely to support localistic behavior. The average Japanese with only grade school education had a 76 percent probability of supporting localistic behavior, as compared to a 32 percent probability for those with college and graduate school experience. Similarly, older Japanese were more likely to have localistic tendencies, but older Japanese with high levels of education preferred more "issue"-oriented politics.

And the average residents of rural areas displayed socioeconomic or demographic characteristics that made them more likely to support localistic and clientelistic politics than residents of more urban areas. Rural Japanese were older, less-educated, more likely to be employed in clientelism-related professions, and work in a smaller workplace than urban Japanese (Table 3.1).

TABLE 3.1 *Socioeconomic/Demographic Means by Type of District*

	Rural	Mixed	Urban	Metropolitan
Age	0.48	0.39	0.36	0.30
Education	1.79	2.10	2.19	2.50
Clientelist occupation	0.17	0.10	0.05	0.02
Household head in clientelist occupation	0.14	0.07	0.04	0.03
Work size	2.36	2.50	2.75	2.87

Key:
Age: Proportion of the respondents 55 years of age or older.
Education: Education level (4-point scale). 1, Primary or lower secondary; 2, high school; 3, jr. college/trade school; 4, university and grad school.
Clientelist occupation: Proportion of the respondents working in farming, forestry, fisheries, mining or transportation.
Household head in clientelist occupation: Proportion of the respondents whose head of household works in farming, forestry, fisheries, mining or transportation.
Work size: Number of people who work in the respondent's place of employment (5-point scale). 1, 1–4 people; 2, 5–29 people; 3, 30–299 people; 4, 300–999 people; 5, 1,000 people or more.
Source: JES-II public opinion survey results.

IMPORTANCE OF ELECTORAL INSTITUTIONS: PROTECTING
CLIENTELISM BY CHANNELING PREFERENCES

I have downplayed the impact of institutions, but electoral institutions can in fact neutralize the impact of political economy, insofar as the political expression of such interests must be filtered through them. In Japan, the regions most supportive of the clientelist state have sufficient political clout to prevent greater success by anti-clientelist parties, and the LDP in turn has had incentives to protect clientelist arrangements.

Japan's new parties of the 1990s were founded to a large degree on a voter backlash against clientelism (Chapter 8). Urban voters were quite antagonistic to Japan's clientelist system, and the backing of these voters led new parties to substantial success in urban areas. However, many rural voters supported and even depended on Japan's clientelist system. Their support for clientelism was highly correlated with support for the LDP and its candidates.

Largely because of this support, the LDP dominated SMD races in rural areas but did much less well in the remainder of the country. The candidate-centered small-district (SMD) electoral system was critical here as it allowed the LDP to channel only 50 percent of the rural SMD vote into 75 percent of its SMDs, almost one third of all the seats needed for a majority (Chapter 8). In short, the LDP relied for the largest part of its support on a part of the population that for socioeconomic reasons will continue to be a huge booster of clientelism, thereby making it extremely difficult for the party to dismantle that system.

CONCLUSION

Japan's electoral institutions certainly play an important role in protecting the clientelist system. Even in clientelist systems, there are voters who oppose clientelist practices, but still others – those that benefit from the system – remain very supportive. Electoral institutions play a major part in determining the extent to which these clientelist-supporting areas are sufficient to protect the regime that maintains clientelism. Japan's long-used SNTV/MMD electoral system certainly promoted clientelist practices, as did other institutional arrangements such as campaign laws, fiscal centralization, and vote tallying precinct size in rural areas.

Nevertheless, other factors were responsible for the original sprouting of Japanese clientelist practices, and given that the level of clientelist practices varied over time and across the country, the electoral system is an insufficient explanation for their continuation.[18]

---

[18] Ultimately, too, one-party dominance probably helped maintain clientelism. With little real party competition, the LDP could worry less about forging programmatic appeals to distinguish itself from the opposition.

Nonelectoral system forces – especially differences between urban and rural areas and voters – are responsible for this variation. Anti-clientelist positions and characteristics consistent with such positions grow stronger with each level of urban-ness in Japan (Table 3.1). In Italy and Austria, increasing urbanization helped increase the antagonism toward the clientelist system, which in turn exacted political costs on their ruling regimes (see Chapter 7). Continued urbanization may also undercut the Japanese clientelist system.

Like Shefter (1994) and Verdier (1995), this analysis emphasizes the "supply side," where strategies of politicians determine the type of citizen–politician linkage. But it would be a mistake to ignore the analysis of Piattoni (2001: 194), who notes that in the long term the "demand side" can have an impact on linkage as well. Japan's great wealth could limit the Japanese government's capacity to maintain its clientelist system. With increased wealth comes a sense that the benefits won from additional public works projects simply do not matter enough. And in times of economic weakness, such as those faced by Japan in the 1990s and early 2000s, many opposed spending money on arguably unnecessary infrastructure. These views are particularly strong in areas – such as cities – that benefit less from clientelist projects. In this way, popular opinion may overcome the power of institutions to uphold the clientelist system.

4

The Impact of Clientelism and Centralized Government Financial Structure

Comparative Analysis

A defining feature of Japanese politics is the combination of clientelism and a centralized financial structure. Where a political system is clientelist and centralized – where local politicians must rely on the financial graces of the central government to do their job – parties that are not strong at the national level will have difficulty winning subnational office, and national ruling parties will hold a near monopoly on local power across most of the country. To investigate the *combined* impact of clientelism and centralization, this chapter examines different combinations of citizen–politician linkage and financial centralization in a number of countries outside Japan.

The combination of clientelism and local dependence on the center creates very strong incentives for (1) ambitious *local* politicians – who rely on the image of being able to pull in money and projects from the center – to ally with the party controlling the purse strings at the national level (the ruling party) and (2) voters to cast ballots in local elections for such candidates. Here I am pointing to "ambition" in Schlesinger's (1966) sense of politicians who want a long and productive career in politics. I am not suggesting that politicians who affiliate with non-ruling parties are somehow *un*ambitious, and I am certainly not ignoring the fact that many candidates will choose non-ruling parties for other reasons, such as ideology. But, in general, politicians who wish to increase their probability of winning an election and win higher office in the future will have greater incentive to affiliate with the national ruling party. Similarly, I am not suggesting that voters cast ballots only for local candidates affiliated with the ruling party. Many voters have personal, ideological, or policy-based reasons for supporting other parties. However, where voters have reason to value political connections to the central government, in general they will have a greater incentive to vote for politicians affiliated with the national ruling party.

The national ruling party can use its resource edge to attract strong candidates for local office and substantial numbers of voters even when the party itself is not the most sincerely preferred option. In Clientelist/

Financially Centralized systems, opposition parties find great difficulty attracting candidates and voters for local office. And where they hold little strength at the local level, parties have difficulty building local party foundations and getting their message out. They are left with a dearth of strong candidates to run in national-level races, causing much greater difficulty in winning national-level seats (see Chapter 6).

The argument here is not simply that politicians develop a core of loyal voters through constituency service and that members of a ruling party are advantaged because of the party's access to state resources. Rather, it is that the impact of access to resources varies dramatically depending on the type of system. In programmatic systems, the impact is weaker. In Clientelist/Financially Decentralized cases, where access to subnational funding is important, local party power will vary widely across the country. However, in Clientelist/Financially Centralized cases, the national ruling party is not simply advantaged by its access to state resources, it is also able to use this access to gain a near-monopoly on local power throughout the country.[1]

FISCAL CENTRALIZATION + CLIENTELISM = LOCAL OPPOSITION FAILURE

Two interactive factors – the degree of financial centralization and the type of citizen–politician linkage – play a critical role in the success of parties in the subnational level.

Financial Centralization

In many systems, the central government gives subnational governments the power to find their own local financial support for locally devised programs. (Examples would be extensive freedom in revenue collection and subnational policy innovation.) Because they are not dependent solely on the center for financial transfers to fund local programs, financially autonomous subnational governments cannot be readily punished by a national government governed by a party different from that governing the locality.[2]

Where localities depend heavily upon the central government for funding, voters' and candidates' decisions to ally with particular parties will tend to be based very much on the state of politics at the national level. In contrast, where localities are financially independent, party affiliation may have little to do with national parties. For example, Sellers (1998) indicates that decentralized policymaking helped create significant local strongholds for the

---

[1] The primary exceptions would be the few localities that do not rely heavily on funding.

[2] It is important to emphasize *financial* decentralization. Some systems (e.g., Austria and Mexico) are formally federal bodies where subnational units have various administrative powers, but they are also heavily dependent on the central government for their funding.

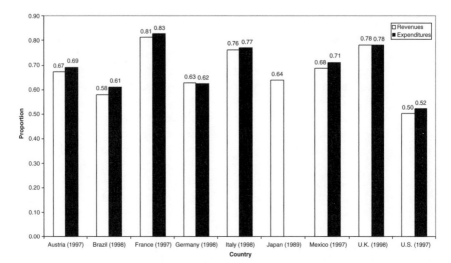

FIGURE 4.1 Central Government Revenues and Expenditures as a Proportion of Total
Calculated by dividing central government revenues (or expenditures) by the sum of central government and subnational government revenues (or expenditures).
Source: Data from IMF (1999, 2002). Note that the source only provides data for Japan up to 1989 and only on revenues (not expenditures). For more on centralization in Japan, see Chapter 5.

Greens in Germany, while centrally led expansion retarded Green growth in France. Studies of Italy (Hine 1993), Mexico (Diaz-Cayeros et al. 2000), and Japan (Curtis 1971) suggest that in centralized systems local candidates and/or voters tend to affiliate with a national government party to have a better chance of gaining central funding. That country experts on three different centralized cases reach such similar conclusions is compelling.

Figure 4.1 illustrates the proportion of total governmental revenues and expenditures made up by the central government in a number of different countries.[3] In Figure 4.1, higher values imply greater centralization. In reality, though, the numbers it provides can only tell us a limited amount about who has budgetary power. As Tarrow notes:

The problem with using measures of financial subsidization of local government as an indicator of centralization is to know what political meaning to give to them . . . in the

---

[3] Unfortunately, the IMF data on Japan is limited. For consistency's sake, I provide what information the IMF source does have. Given my argument about Japan being fiscally centralized, the relatively low levels of central governmental revenue collection may surprise the reader. However, as I note here, the proportions in the figure are meant to be illustrative, but not definitive, of central governmental fiscal power. Most important, the Japanese central government exerts great influence on both general policymaking and fiscal issues in local governments (see Chapter 5).

absence of independent measures of the centralization of government decision making and the political influence of local elites and the mass public, the centralization of expenditures is a totally neutral indicator with respect to who has power over whom. (1978: 12)

But there are also reasons to think that centralization is an insufficient explanation. In some systems (such as France), transfers to subnational governments are determined according to a depoliticized formula, and connections to the central government will be less likely to affect a locality's chances of receiving funding. However, where the central government has discretion over distribution of much subnational government funding, transfers take on a political form that encourages localities to find better connections to the center. In short, for it to have the effect I have attributed to it, centralized funding must also be distributed at the *discretion* of the central government.[4]

Citizen–Politician Linkage

In addition, even in centralized systems, it does not always make sense for local politicians or voters to affiliate with a party simply because it controls the central government. In the highly centralized United Kingdom, local party fortunes fluctuate with little clear relationship to the makeup of the central parliament. In countries where ideology and/or issues are more important than simple allocation of goods, services, or funds, local politicians and voters affiliate with parties according to their policy stances.

In other words, citizen–politician linkage is of great importance in determining the impact of national-level politics on local partisan electoral outcomes. In systems where strong programmatic links bind voters and parties, subnational party success is based on the extent to which voters approve of parties' messages. Where linkages are clientelist, subnational party success tends to be based on voters' impressions of which parties' candidates will be best able to provide goods and services.

Of course not all parties and voters in a country are driven by the same motivations. Even in clientelist systems, many voters and parties may act according to ideology rather than clientelist concerns. There is programmatic and ideological behavior in clientelist systems, and substantial clientelistic behavior in programmatic ones. The typology is based on ideal types. Nevertheless, what I describe in this chapter for each country case is the general pattern used to describe citizen–politician linkages within it.

In combination, these two factors – citizen–politician linkages and financial centralization – have a substantial effect on parties' local success. Table 4.1 provides a typology and set of predictions about the combined impacts of citizen–politician linkage types and degree of financial centralization.

[4] Thanks to Sidney Tarrow for this insight.

TABLE 4.1 *Typology and Predictions for Local Party Success*

Citizen–Politician Linkages	Level of Governmental Financial Centralization	
	Decentralized	Centralized
Programmatic	Prediction • Within each region, a given party will receive roughly equal numbers of votes in both local and national level elections. • Within a given region, small parties may even do better in local level races than in national level ones. Cases • Germany	Prediction • A party's success in local-level elections will be highly correlated with its general level of party support within the region at the time. Cases • United Kingdom
Clientelist	Prediction • Local- and national-level party success within each region will tend to be idiosyncratic. • *Exception*: Where a subnational executive dominates resources, there will be substantial affiliation with the party of the executive. Cases • United States, Brazil	Prediction • Parties that sit in the government at the national level will dominate local-level elections. • *Exception*: Other parties may find success in areas that do not rely heavily on central governmental funding. Cases • Italy, Austria, Mexico, Japan

The predictions made in the table appear well borne out by comparative analysis.

PROGRAMMATIC/FINANCIALLY DECENTRALIZED

In Programmatic/Financially Decentralized systems, localities are financially independent, and voters and candidates take cues from programmatic parties. Partisan ties and programmatic similarities between local and national parties link individual voters to the same parties at both levels, and local fiscal autonomy offers parties that are small at the national level the ability to exert substantial influence at the local level. Therefore, voters and candidates in such systems have greater incentives to cast ballots for and affiliate with small parties (or parties that are weak at the national level) in local-level elections. Within a given region, (1) any given party ought to receive roughly equal numbers of votes in both local- and national-level elections, and (2) small parties may even do better in local-level races than in national-level ones.[5]

Germany is an ideal Programmatic/Financially Decentralized type. Its parties tend to focus on universally distributed, collective goods programs, and Germany's strong federal system gives the *Länder* (states) great freedom to raise and spend money as they wish. First-cut analysis of election results from the late 1990s suggests that in nearly every region, each major German party receives a proportion of the national-level vote[6] roughly equal to that which it wins in the local contest.[7] This result is even more striking given that elections that are held nonconcurrently – as German elections are – tend to generate greater differences in party vote totals (Jones 1997; Shugart 1995).

In certain regions, small parties like the Green Party are noticeably more successful in local elections than in national ones. The Greens, which held only about 7 percent of all Bundestag seats after the 1998 election, held anywhere from 0 to 17 percent of seats in the *Länder* at the same time.[8] In the 1997 Hamburg *Land* election, the Greens received nearly 115,000 votes out of approximately 850,000. In contrast, despite total turnout for the national Bundestag election of 1998 that was nearly 150,000 votes greater, the Greens received 10,000 fewer votes in Hamburg than they had in the local contest. In Hamburg, the Greens had more local than national support from the same voters, and were able to develop a strong local base there.

CLIENTELIST/FINANCIALLY DECENTRALIZED

Unlike their programmatic mates, Clientelist/Financially Decentralized systems emphasize representatives as targeted benefit and patronage providers. Individual representatives' capacity to provide services, goods, and especially pork to a locality will often mean more to voters than partisan affiliation. Where strong partisanship develops, it is often founded less on ideology than on a party machine that dominates the services in a given area. In addition,

---

[5] Voters may be more likely to cast local-level ballots for a party that is small at the national level if they wish to "try out" the party at the local level or feel that its policies are better suited for the local-level context.

[6] The German electoral system makes it substantially more difficult to determine the number of seats won for any party outside of the CDU and SPD, which dominate the single member districts, so I rely solely on votes as the measure for comparison. This might make more sense anyway: Given the high correlation between votes in German local and national elections, differences in seat totals will typically be simply due to different electoral arrangements.

[7] A small number of exceptions such as Saxony exist where parties received markedly different proportions of the vote in the national and local elections.

[8] Data compiled from *www.statistik-bund.de/wahlen/e/index_e.htm*.

subnational governments in Clientelist/Financially Decentralized systems do not need to rely primarily on the graces of the central government to carry out their business.

As a result, aside from areas where political machines predominate, there is likely to be a low correlation between party strength at the local and national levels, even within a given locality. In strongly partisan or programmatic systems, voters are apt to vote for the same party in both local and national elections. But, in the Clientelist/Financially Decentralized type, local independence weakens ties to the governing party in the central government, which tends to make voters and ambitious politicians more idiosyncratic in their decisions to support and/or affiliate with specific parties. However, where ties to subnational-level officeholders are important for gaining funding, local voters and politicians will be more likely to affiliate with parties that control local resources.

United States

The United States grants substantial local financial autonomy to its subnational units in many areas of governance, including the levying and spending of tax revenues. Although some might dispute calling the United States clientelist, it is clear that the exchange of selective governmental benefits for political support and campaign contributions has long been central to American politics. Until the 1930s, the U.S. national government focused on distributive politics – defined as patronage (Lowi 1985) – and such politics remain a central focus even today. In the United States, partisan and ideological differences are in fact often put aside for the sake of the locality. See, for example, the close relationship between longtime senators Republican Alphonse D'Amato and Democrat Daniel Patrick Moynihan, who often fought side by side to bring projects to New York. In the Clientelist/Financially Decentralized type, the combination of regional autonomy and quest for pork may allow a single party in the form of a machine to dominate service and goods provision in certain regions. The clearest recent example of this is of course the Daley machine's control of Chicago under the auspices of the Democratic Party.

But such machines do not dominate all parts of the country, and even though there are pockets of strength for each party, there is no direct relationship in most regions between national and local-level party strength. For example, going into the 2000 federal election, in 18 of the 50 U.S. states, the Democratic Party's share of seats in the state House exceeded by more than 20 percentage points the proportion of the national House of Representatives seats going to Democrats from that state.[9] In six states, the Democratic

---

[9] I focus on seat shares here, but there also appears to be a fairly low correlation between vote totals for a given party in both state- and national-level elections.

Party's share of HR seats exceeded its portion of state House seats by more than 20 percentage points. In short, in just under half the U.S. states, there was a marked difference between the proportion of local and national level seats held by each party. From a different angle, in 19 states (38 percent), the Democratic Party held a majority of the legislative seats available for that state at one level of government, but less than a majority at the other level.

Brazil

There is no question about Brazil's clientelist credentials. As Ames writes: "Brazil is unique in the pervasiveness of these exchanges and in their tendency to substitute for broader, more ideologically or programmatically driven policy-making" (2002: 24). Brazil also clearly falls into the financially decentralized category. Since redemocratization began in the early 1980s, states have gained substantially greater political discretion and fiscal autonomy (Samuels and Abrucio 2000: 44). In particular, fiscal decentralization increased dramatically over the 1990s (Garrett and Rodden 2001: Table 1).

The most striking result is the power afforded to mayors and governors. Through their control of clientelist resources, these political executives wield substantial influence over voters in their fiefdoms. In Brazil, there is a "gubernatorial coattails effect," whereby candidates for national deputy (legislature) office seek to align themselves with strong candidates for state governor. Since 1994, national deputy candidates have made a greater effort to align themselves with governors than with presidential candidates because of governors' control of clientelist networks (Samuels 2000a, 2000b). Even though political observers in the United States talk about presidential coattails, subnational executives' power over clientelist networks in Brazil has led to a "reverse coattails effect," whereby presidential candidates rely on city mayors to attract a following (Ames 1994).

Perhaps the clearest indication that the Clientelist/Financially Decentralized system strongly affects Brazilian politics is the desired career path of individual politicians. Because subnational governments control a huge proportion of resources and clientelist networks in Brazil, national legislators tend to act as "ambassadors" of the subnational governments. Holding national deputy office is not a top career aim but rather a stepping stone to a subnational executive office such as city mayor or state governor, where the "real" power is (Samuels 2003).[10]

National governmental control therefore has much less impact on party success in state deputy offices. Brazil's open-list proportional representation electoral system, which is used in both national and state deputy races,

---

[10] Presidents in Brazil must often negotiate with state governors to acquire legislative support.

puts greater emphasis on individuals than parties.[11] Mutual aid agreements (*dobradinha*) link together state and federal deputy candidates usually of the same party,[12] and alliances link these candidates to a candidate for governor (Samuels 2000b). Most likely for this reason, parties often receive in each state roughly equal numbers of votes in federal and state deputy races.[13] Nevertheless, voters also cast ballots for individual candidates with less regard to party because so much of their support is founded on the personal connections individual politicians have with key controllers of resources (especially subnational-level executives).[14] As Samuels notes, the root of these ties lies "in the impact of the institutions of Brazilian federalism on the party system in limiting the linkage between national executive and legislative elections" (2000b: 15).

Because of the weakness of party ties, party switching is very common in Brazil. A desire for access to state government resources greatly influences national deputies' party-switching decisions: It is not at all uncommon for deputies to leave their party and switch to the party of the governor that runs their state (Desposato 2002).

PROGRAMMATIC/FINANCIALLY CENTRALIZED

Localities have little autonomy in the Programmatic/Financially Centralized type, and candidates at all levels are evaluated according to their issue positions and party affiliation. Centralization and strong partisan ties give parties at the national-level the edge in determining party policy and candidacies. Given the heavy hand parties are able to lay on candidacies and the fact that politics are not founded on the distribution of goods and services, local politicians are limited in their ability to act as independent political entrepreneurs. As a result, candidates' incentive is to ally with national-level parties and voters' incentive is to cast votes in local elections for the party they support at the national level. For this reason, there is a high correlation between national-level support for parties and the success of parties in local elections.

Britain clearly fits the Programmatic/Financially Centralized type. Even though such figures must be taken as only partly indicative of central governmental power, the British central government's share of total public spending and expenditures exceeds 78 percent, a portion substantially higher than in

---

[11] For an explanation of open-list PR, see footnote 1 in Chapter 3.
[12] Personal communication with David Samuels.
[13] See Brazilian electoral data in Nicolau (1998). Great thanks to Scott Morgenstern for this source.
[14] Brazilian governors are quite willing to share resources with members of other parties if they form an electoral alliance in the state with the governor's party.

the three cases of financial decentralization discussed here (see Figure 4.1). Indeed, Miller notes that "most analysts of British local government have highlighted its lack of autonomy" (1988: 1).

On the citizen–politician linkage dimension, Britain offers a substantial contrast to the United States and an even starker one to Brazil. Cain, Ferejohn, and Fiorina explain: "In the American context, securing projects and other advantages for the district is the traditional pork barrel function of the congressman, a function that would seem altogether absent in Britain" (1987: 39). Moreover, British politics are typically held to be highly partisan and nationalized. In a thoughtful twist on Mayhew's (1974) famous quote about the U.S. Congress, Cain et al. argue: "[I]f a group of planners sat down and tried to design an institution that magnified the dependence of legislative members on their national parties, they would be hard pressed to improve on what exists in Britain" (1987: 215). As Peterson and Kantor (1977) suggest, subnational issues are subordinated to national ones, and local party policy is largely a reflection of the national platform.

Miller explains that there is little interest in local politics in Britain. This is probably because of the highly centralized nature of politics. Peterson and Kantor explain that raising issues at the local level is difficult, in part because the central government constrains local authorities and British institutional arrangements make it difficult for elected local politicians to exert much influence in the policy process (1977: 213). As a result, not only is local party policy largely determined at the national level, but also local voting largely occurs along the lines of party popularity at the national level. Rallings and Thrasher note that British prime ministers frequently use local elections as a test for the popularity of their governments and to help decide whether or not to hold national-level elections (1997: 50). Miller finds that 84 percent of the electorate votes in local elections in accordance with their national political preferences (1988: 167, 236). And Fletcher (1967, cited in Peterson and Kantor 1977) finds that in the early 1960s, the average swing in local elections was within 1 percentage point of the national swing in attitudes toward the national parties as measured by Gallup Polls.

This correspondence between national and subnational electoral outcomes is different from what I will suggest should happen in the Clientelist/ Financially Centralized type. In the latter, subnational electoral success will not match national *popularity*. Rather, it will be highly skewed at the subnational level in favor of the national *ruling* party because it controls transfers and subsidies to the localities. In Clientelist/Financially Centralized systems, subnational elections are not a popularity contest for the national-level parties, but instead an attempt by voters (and candidates) to win favor with the national ruling party. Voters are not expressing their own support for the parties, but are in a sense voting strategically to get something from the party that controls resources. This may mean that voters whose sympathies lie with the opposition will vote at the subnational level for the ruling party.

In Programmatic/Financially Centralized systems, seats held at the local level have less to do with the breakdown of seats at the national level and more to do with popularity of the national party at the time of the local election. For example, even though Labour held roughly twice as many seats in the House of Commons as all other parties combined in 1999, in the local elections that year Labour lost more than 1,300 seats in local elections, compared to the Conservatives' net gain of more than 1,400.[15] The main difference between national and local outcomes then is a measure of changing sentiment. National and local elections each represent voter sentiment at the time they occur.

CLIENTELIST/FINANCIALLY CENTRALIZED

Except among Clientelist/Financially Centralized countries, there is plenty of room for party success at the local level, irrespective of a party's seat share at the national level. But in Clientelist/Financially Centralized systems, it is difficult for parties to gain substantial local electoral strength unless they also hold great power at the national level.

In Programmatic/Financially Centralized systems, voters cast ballots, and candidates make affiliation decisions according to partisan ties, issues, and ideology. The Clientelist/Financially Centralized type is markedly different. As in the Clientelist/Financially Decentralized type, voters cast their ballots for candidates they judge most capable of delivering goods and services to the locality. However, in the financially Centralized type, local politicians rely heavily on the central government to gain access to these goods and services. For this reason, candidates have incentive to join parties that control the national purse strings. And voters who value the political distribution of private goods have incentive to support local candidates from such parties, especially in times of budgetary belt-tightening.

Bruhn argues that centralization hampers democratic competition by rel-egating opposition parties to marginal offices that "emasculate" them by forcing them to rely on the national government (1997: 228, 310). Even though the British case indicates that local dependence on the center is insuf-ficient to explain this local-level emasculation of opposition parties, Bruhn's point applies well to Clientelist/Financially Centralized systems. In Finan-cially Centralized systems that grant localities only limited autonomy, op-position parties – especially new ones – face greater difficulty building local bases and drawing potentially attractive politicians to join them at the local level.

---

[15] Data from *www.lgcnet.com/*.

It is not simply that ruling parties have an advantage because of their access to pork. Rather, in contrast to other types of systems, in Clientelist/ Financially Centralized systems *national ruling parties will monopolize local power across most of the country.*

Italy

Italy is famous for being among the most clientelistic political systems in the world. Graft of course comes from a variety of different sources, but the political system and the money that flows through it are very centralized in Italy (Koff and Koff 2000). Nearly 80 percent of all public spending and revenues go through the central government (see Figure 4.1). Local fundamental laws or statutes are formed or approved by the central government, and the central government "controls the activities of the [subnational units] even to the point of being able to dismiss their representative organs under specified conditions" (Koff and Koff 2000: 184). As Tarrow explains, Italian local governments simply do not have much autonomy over how they expend their resources (1977: 93).

The influence of national-level party strength on local party power in Italy appears substantial. The link between partisanship and ability to deliver goods to the locality is well established. Writing of Italy, Hine explains: "In a centralized political system the extraction of benefits from the centre is a prime obligation for national representatives and explains why strong local distinctiveness coexists with the dominance of national parties. National representatives are better placed to serve the locality if they are part of the party which is strong (preferably in government) in the centre" (1993: 260). Local office was seen as the first step toward a position as a national representative – most Italian members of parliament began their careers in local government (Hine 1993: 173). Italianists note that a very large number of local executive positions were controlled by the Christian Democrats, the dominant party at the national level: Local politicians' affiliation was seen as important to their political success. Subnational governments were closely linked to the center through vertical personal and party connections (Hine 1993: 260), and membership in the national ruling party was seen as useful for local politicians, helping them fulfill their perceived local political duties. One local politician admitted joining the DC in order "to help me in my activities as mayor" (quoted in Tarrow 1977: 200).

In a system where the primary activity of local office holders was bringing in money from the center, affiliating with national ruling parties was key to gaining access to that money. As Tarrow writes, local Italian politicians were "essentially political entrepreneurs with a wide network of contacts in both local and national political systems who use their party affiliations to open up a network of contacts in seeking resources for their communities" (1977: 19). Local governments led by mayors with high levels of party experience received a larger (per capita) share of their municipal budgets from higher levels of government (Tarrow 1977: 196).

Pointing to this pattern, Allum (1997) notes how power at each level reinforced power at the other levels. In the case of the Christian Democrats, the long-time party of the government, Allum writes: "Their power in Naples secured their power in Rome and their power in Rome strengthened their power in Naples in an ever-wider spiral movement. For the [local] bosses, it was a question of controlling the local party apparatus . . . and of developing privileged relations with the national party leadership" (1997: 34).

To be more definitive, it will be necessary to look at national and local-party success broken down subnationally for each level of election. But getting local-level data for Italian elections is more difficult than for the many other countries I examine here. Fortunately, Zariski (1984) includes the seat totals from "ordinary" regional elections in 1970, 1975, and 1980.[16] First-cut examination offers some meaningful results. First, the DC did extremely well in nearly every region in the local elections. This result might be expected given the DC's control of national governmental resources, but it is also somewhat unexpected given the strongly regional nature of Italian politics. Second, regional government coalition partners for the DC were subject to approval by the central party headquarters, even when local DC members were the primary agents seeking the coalition (Zariski 1984: 419, footnote 25). The center's control over resources appears to have kept local DC party members in line.

Third, the PCI (Communists), the leading party consistently outside of the government, held pockets of regional strength and led the government in a few regions. Nevertheless, the PCI was never content to govern alone in any region and always sought other coalition partners, even when it already held a majority of seats (Zariski 1984: 411). It nearly always sought a partnership with the Socialists (PSI), who usually were part of the national cabinet with the DC. Clearly the PCI's search for greater legitimacy and acceptance were part of this strategy. However, the quest for favors from parties in the national-level government may have contributed as well. Tarrow writes that voters permitted "parties to have interpersonal relations with supporters of other parties, and partisanship is reinforced by policy success. The Italian system appears to encourage instrumental, rather than ideological, mass partisan involvement" (1977: 211).

Finally, even though there is clear regional variation, the similarities between the proportion of seats held by each party at the national level and the regional levels aggregated is striking.[17] This is similar to the Japanese case, but with a significant exception. In Japan, the LDP, the national governing

---

[16] The region is Italy's largest geographical and administrative subunit.

[17] For these results, see Gourevitch (1978: 52), Zariski (1984), and the *www.ethanscheiner.com* links to the supplementary Web site for this book.

party, did extremely well at both levels, but the Japanese opposition did *markedly* worse at the subnational level. In contrast, in Italy, even small parties did roughly as well at the regional level as at the national.

At first blush, this runs counter to my argument, but the patterns actually make sense within the framework here. The predictions of the clientelism/centralization model are founded on the assumption that most parties have little access to central government patronage. In Italy, with a coalition always needed to form a government, even smaller parties joined in government formation and could take home a portion of the spoils to distribute to their supporters.[18] The fact that the PCI could form coalitions with some of these parties at the local level gave the PCI additional access to government resources. Moreover, in the 1970s, the PCI actively lobbied the central government for favors, including pork barrel funding (Tarrow 1977) and appears to have done well in many local elections, in part because of the ruling DC's willingness during that period to share patronage, "if only because any other strategy would have increased polarization and undermined [the DC's] position at the center of the political spectrum" (Tarrow 1990: 319).

Perhaps most important, the PCI's greatest success came in areas such as Emilia Romagna, which, while admittedly also more industrial and hence left-leaning, were among Italy's most autonomous regions. The DC's greatest strength was in the especially dependent south, where the DC often did better in subnational elections than in national. All this said, further analysis of the PCI's strength at the local level is needed to determine whether greater access to pork aided the party during the 1970s.

Austria

Austria offers perhaps a better comparison to Japan because its party system has been less fragmented than Italy's, offering less bargaining power in cabinet formation. Austria is heavily clientelistic, with two leading parties, the Social Democratic Party and the Austrian People's Party, controlling the bulk of patronage (Kitschelt 1994b; Lauber 1996a). Dachs notes that even though Austria is at least formally federal, the central government is much stronger than the *Länder*. With respect to financing, the *Länder* and municipalities are essentially subordinate to and dependent upon the central government (1996a: 235–9).

The result has been remarkably similar to the Japanese case. Unlike Japan, early postwar Austrian leaders consciously sought to avoid domination by a single party in order to hold off a repeat of the authoritarian era (Lauber 1996a). Through the *Proporz* system, most *Länder* governments were forced

---

[18] The omnipresence of nonmajority parties and coalition governments in Italy was no doubt due to its PR electoral system and widely varying distribution of voter sentiment.

to include any party holding seats in the assembly. However, in practice, the majority party in any *Land* holds significantly greater power than any other party, even though all other parties are included in the *Land* government (Dachs 1996: 247). As a result, and as predicted, third and fourth parties had very little influence at the *Land* level. Party competition increased throughout Austria in the 1990s, but there was little variation in Green Party strength of the kind witnessed in Germany, and, unlike Germany, the Green Party was not more successful at the local level than at the national level.[19]

Perhaps even more striking, even though the *Proporz* rule was nominally in effect, in reality from the 1940s to the mid-1980s nearly every *Land* maintained a predominant party system (Dachs 1996: 246). That is, one-party dominance was *the norm* at the state level. Even though the SPÖ and ÖVP (often together) dominated national politics in Austria throughout this era, each one carved out local niches for itself in specific *Länder*, in which that single party dominated regional politics.

In the late 1980s and 1990s, there was a clear increase in the competitiveness of elections at both the national and the *Land* level in Austria, particularly with the rise in popularity of the Austrian Freedom Party. In the 1999 election, for example, the SPÖ, ÖVP, and FPÖ took, respectively, 36, 28, and 28 percent of all seats in the *Nationalrat* and nearly identical numbers in the aggregate in the *Länder*.[20]

However, two points should be made about this shift. First, much of this increased competitiveness can be attributed to a decline in patronage (Dachs 1996: 247; Müller 1996b: 83), which was in large part due to a backlash against clientelism in Austria (see Chapter 6). This backlash generally occurred in areas with younger voters working in more "productive" urban sectors. Urbanization went hand in hand with the shift and was significant in moving the system away from the Clientelist/Financially Centralized type. As a result, the number of parties grew dramatically in cities, especially in city councils (Dachs 1996: 242–8).

Second, the shift to more competitive party politics occurred *first* at the national level – voters and elites at the local level did not give up their distributive gravy train until it was no longer running at the national level. Dachs points out that "[t]he shift from relative contentedness and apathy to more competition and protest observed in the parliamentary elections [of the late 1980s and 90s] is spreading to *Land* politics" (1996: 248).

---

[19] The Austrian Greens won 7.7 percent of the total seats in the 1999 national elections and, at the time, held 4.6 percent of all the *Länder* assembly seats (with a low of zero in one *Land* and a high of 8.3 percent in another). Data compiled from *www-public.rz.uni-duesseldorf.de/~nordsiew/indexe.html*.

[20] Data compiled from *www-public.rz.uni-duesseldorf.de/~nordsiew/indexe.html*. There is significant variation across *Länder*, but, as of the early 2000s, no party held an absolute majority in any single *Land*.

Mexico

Mexico is formally a federal system, but governmental financial power is clearly placed in the central government (especially its presidency), and patronage and targeted favors are widely used to buy support (Bailey 1994; Rodriguez 1997; Ward and Rodriguez 1999). Mexico falls neatly into the Clientelist/Financially Centralized type, and the similarities to Japan are striking. The ruling PRI's political cliques or *camarillas* are in many ways similar to the patron–client relationships between Japanese national- and local-level politicians discussed in Chapter 5 (Camp 1999: 117). The PRI, which dominated politics at the national level, did so at least as strongly at the local level, although this fact must be taken with a grain of salt given that for years the country was low on most scales of democratic-ness.

The reasons for the local-level successes and failures of opposition parties require a more systematic examination than is possible with the data available to me. Nevertheless, three points, consistent with the typology discussed in the book, should be noted. First, national-level politicians played a significant role in the development of opposition local success. Prior to the 1988 Mexican presidential campaign, a group of politicians defected from the PRI along with future presidential candidate Cuauhtemoc Cardenas and formed the PRD. Areas from which such politicians hailed were able to establish fairly strong PRD branches and run their leaders as local candidates. However, where there was no such group of elites, developing the PRD at the local level was more difficult (Bruhn 1997: 123).[21]

Second, the first rise in opposition strength at the local level began in the early 1980s, when decentralization, which occurred gradually after then, began under President de la Madrid (Rodriguez 1997). Real decentralization focused on granting greater power to the states but formally involved the devolution of financial autonomy to the various subnational levels of government. I cannot yet rule out the possibility that increasing opposition success helped bring about decentralization or the possibility that decentralization went hand in hand with a decrease in vote fraud. However, it is consistent with my argument that, as decentralization and local autonomy increase, politicians find it increasingly rewarding to ally with opposition parties and that voters become increasingly willing to vote for opposition parties at the local and national levels.

Third, beginning with the 1988 presidential election in which opposition candidate Cardenas nearly toppled the PRI, both opposition parties (Cardenas' PRD and the PAN under Vicente Fox, who won in the 2000

---

[21] It should be noted, though, that PRD had both top-down (Bruhn 1997) and bottom-up (Greene 2002) dimensions.

presidential election) made strides in the national legislature and increased their numbers in every subsequent local election (Rodriguez 1997: 54). This too is consistent with my argument that in heavily centralized and clientelistic systems, a party's success at the local level will typically only follow what occurs at the national level first (or, as I also argue in this chapter, occurs in more autonomous regions).

Ultimately, though, the patronage-filled Mexican system continues to be centered on the Mexican presidency, which until July 2000 the PRI continued to hold. Not surprising, therefore, the opposition tended to control at best only 20–25 percent of all municipalities, but these included, as my framework would expect, most large and (presumably) more fiscally autonomous areas (Klesner 1997; Rodriguez 1997). Indeed, the bulk of PAN success before Fox's victorious presidential bid was in subnational elections in states that were largely autonomous. Before the opposition began gaining in local elections, most localities received the bulk of their revenue from higher governments, but opposition local governments made great effort to raise more revenue on their own (Diaz-Cayeros et al. 2000; Rodriguez and Ward 1995).

However, changes from the 1980s and 1990s may alter the calculus. The opposition not only found success in the 1988 and 2000 presidential elections but also did extremely well in the 1997 national legislative elections (largely because of the peso crisis). After 1988, it gained local strength, owing in part to decentralization and growing national-level opposition strength. Given the importance of central resources to an opposition's (in)ability to gain local office, presumably the presence of a non-PRI president helps the opposition gain local strength. At the same time, because the Zedillo administration depoliticized center-local transfers in the 1990s (Diaz-Cayeros, Gonzalez, and Rojas 2002), state governors gained greater power over resources (Diaz-Cayeros in press). Therefore, all else being equal, non-PRI candidates should be more likely to win state governorships; however, at the municipal level and in the state legislatures, affiliation with the party of the *governor* may increase (as is predicted for the Clientelist/Financially Decentralized type).

The Importance of National Party Defection in Clientelist/Financially Centralized Systems

Finally, within Clientelist/Financially Centralized systems, there is one way opposition parties can develop locally in dependent regions, even without Italian-type patronage-oriented compromises. To gain more certain access to goods from the center, local politicians in Clientelist/Financially Centralized systems are likely to develop close ties to national politicians. And on occasion, national-level politicians decide to defect from the ruling party and join alternatives (Desposato 2002; Reed and Scheiner 2003). Although such cases create a dilemma for subnational politicians, fear of losing their national-level patron may induce local politicians linked to these politicians to defect as well.

In this way, opposition parties may develop fairly quickly in specific regions, but their development depends on the defection first of national-level leaders representing those localities. This appeared to be the case with the Cardenas movement in Mexico in 1988 and, as I discuss in Chapter 5, in Japan in 1993–4.

5

Local Opposition Failure in Japan

The impact of the combination of clientelism and fiscal centralization is particularly potent in Japan. The Japanese Clientelist/Financially Centralized system has led to overwhelming subnational opposition party failure and LDP dominance.

BACKGROUND

As noted in Chapter 3, the Japanese party system rests on personalistic and clientelistic competition. Even the new, mixed-member electoral system, which includes a PR component, offers significant incentives for personalistic and clientelistic behavior (McKean and Scheiner 2000).

Japanese localities depend financially on the national government, and local officials see central funding as being critical to local viability. The dependence of localities on the center in Japan is captured by the phrase *sanwari jichi*, or 30 percent autonomy. While Japanese localities increased their independence somewhat over time, for years local taxes constituted only about 30 percent of local governmental revenues, while the remaining roughly 70 percent came from other sources, especially the central government. As the Japanese economy grew in the 1980s, local revenues reached as high as 44.3 percent, but with the collapse of the Japanese economic bubble, it dropped back down to the low 30s (Jichishō, *Chihō zaisei tōkei nenkan* and *Chihō zaisei hakusho* various years). All other revenues must come from the central government (Akizuki 1995).

From a comparative perspective, local taxes covering 30–40 percent is at or above the median for major industrialized countries and particularly high for a unitary state (Reed 1986) (i.e., the opposite of a federal system).[1]

For many additional details and responses to potential counterarguments, see the links to the supplementary web site for Chapter 5 at *www.ethanscheiner.com*.

[1] See Figure 4.1 in Chapter 4.

However, as I noted in Chapter 4, unless we have independent measures of the centralization of government decision making and the political influence of local elites and the mass public, knowing the degree to which funding is based in the center or the periphery does not tell us who is actually controlling how the money is spent (Tarrow 1978: 12).

In reality, Japanese local governments lack the flexibility to be able to raise their own sources over the long run to pay for large projects or higher levels of services. The central government's regulation of local taxes is especially restrictive – even when compared to other unitary systems – and grants and loans are typically given solely for purposes defined by the central government (Reed 1986: 27–9). The central government determines how much money each locality needs according to a complex, but fairly politically blind variety of formulae (Ishihara 1986: 139–41; Yonehara 1986: 161–3). According to an index of fiscal capacity, localities are expected to make up a certain proportion of their vital needs through local taxes, and the central government makes up the bulk of the remainder through allocation tax transfers: The central government collects this tax from all regions but then redistributes revenue disproportionately to the poorer ones. Additional funding in the form of central government disbursements (subsidies) is typically determined at the central government's discretion (Ishihara 1986; Yonehara 1986), and the central government can push its own priorities at the local level through its power to provide and deny subsidies.

Incentives to Affiliate with the LDP

The LDP does not simply reward all supporters and punish all opponents (see Reed 2001),[2] but local politicians and voters have good reason to believe that the LDP distributes funding strategically (and even vengefully). The LDP controls the national government and has discretion in deciding which localities get subsidies beyond their basic needs. Subsidies are more likely to be given to poorer localities, but many argue that the central government also uses subsidies politically. For example, Igarashi and Ogawa note cases where the central government halted the disbursement of subsidies when faced with citizen opposition to other planned public works projects in regions heavily dependent on central funding (1997: 92–3). Kobayashi

---

[2] It should not be surprising that Reed's (2001) statistical analysis of central government spending on localities finds no evidence of totally *systematic* carrot/stick behavior by the LDP: The LDP often focuses its spending in areas where its support would be particularly useful from an electoral perspective – such as districts where it is engaged in a close race – not simply where it is strongest. In other words, as Horiuchi and Saito (2003) suggest, the LDP does not simply reward strong supporters but also uses spending to buy off marginal voters, thereby funding regions where the party is *less* strong. Also, at times the LDP funds projects that it simply deems necessary, irrespective of political considerations. Statistical analysis would need to differentiate between these different types of spending to determine accurately the extent of politically motivated spending.

(1999) argues that large numbers of local officials willingly give up much of their own discretion in exchange for greater funding from the center. Frequently, the only other revenue-raising option for localities is borrowing, which the central government has often restrained. As a result, Akizuki writes: "In order to obtain . . . subsidies, local governments have to lobby either directly or through politicians (usually the ruling Liberal Democratic Party's Diet members from the local district)" (1995: 354).

A description of politics in Toyama Prefecture offers a nice example of how this process works. In Toyama, the LDP maintains a branch in every municipality in the prefecture. These party branches collect citizens' concerns and demands and present them to local governments and legislatures (which tend to be dominated by LDP members). If the most local levels of the party approve, then the prefectural LDP consolidates the proposals and presents them to prefectural governments and legislatures. Proposals that receive approval at the party's prefectural level are taken to the appropriate central ministries and agencies, either by the LDP national headquarters or individual LDP Diet members (Fukui and Fukai 1996: 275). My own discussions with politicians in other prefectures suggest that the process in Toyama is the norm. But local politicians' lobbying does not stop at the prefecture's edge. Delegations of local politicians (from all prefectures) constantly visit (*especially LDP*) representatives from their prefecture to arrange introductions to and appointments with the bureaucrats in Tokyo who oversee the process of subsidizing the proposal for which they seek funding (Fukui and Fukai 1996: 278).

The effect is substantial. The LDP controls the national government and has discretion in deciding to which localities it will allocate subsidies beyond the most basic needs. As Curtis explains, LDP national politicians are "often at the center of decisions as to where within the prefecture certain funds should go, or what companies should obtain government construction contracts" (1988: 108). The government does tend to disburse subsidies to those most in need, but because the LDP has been known to halt disbursements for political reasons, it is widely believed that the party is more likely to give subsidies to areas that support it (Igarashi and Ogawa 1997). Such beliefs are further fueled by announcements like the one in a released internal bureaucratic report that cited a leading LDP politician as exclaiming, "We can't allow a new project in an area that didn't vote for the LDP," which was followed by the freezing of projects in particular non-LDP supporting areas (*Asahi Shinbun*, March 6, 2002).[3] It has been suggested, for example, that the weakened infrastructure of Takaoka City – a city in Toyama, a very poor prefecture that is heavily dependent on the central government – was due to the city being led by non-LDP parties and, hence, punished by the central government (Fukui and Fukai 1996: 283).

---

[3] Unless otherwise noted, all newspaper references in this chapter are to the online edition.

LDP politicians have explained that one of the main things their time out of power taught them was that government ministries tend to give far greater attention to requests made by politicians in the government than by those made by opposition parties. Local politicians certainly have this impression: When the non-LDP coalition government formed in 1993, members of the coalition suddenly received a marked increase in the intensity and number of requests from local officials and businesses for help funding local projects (Fukui and Fukai 1996: 283). The general sense that the national ruling party connections are key to gaining resources is made explicit by Fukui and Fukai, who write: "Distribution of resources needed for the development of local and regional economies by pork barrel politics gets inevitably skewed in favor of localities that are politically better connected" (1996: 285).

When facing electoral threats, leaders of the LDP are quick to suggest that victories by non-LDP candidates may lead to the central government cutting off funds to their localities (Scheiner 2003). For example, in Nagano prefecture, LDP leaders made two such threats very publicly in the periods just before the 1999 HC by-election (*Asahi Shinbun*, paper version, October 19, 1999) and just prior to the 2000 gubernatorial election (*Yomiuri Shinbun*, September 19, 2000). In the latter case, Yoshida Hiromi, speaker of the Nagano prefectural assembly, warned the public that the election of an inexperienced, non-LDP-associated candidate to office could have "severe consequences," as "the governor is required to have ... connections with the central government" (*Yomiuri Shinban*, September 19, 2000). Similarly, before the 2000 HR election in the third district in Miyazaki Prefecture, associates close to LDP incumbent Mochinaga Kazumi made it clear that if construction and related businesses in the district did not make a clear show of support for Mochinaga, they could expect construction contracts to disappear in the future (*New York Times*, June 24, 2000).

Such threats and punishments are not merely a recent phenomenon. Using data from the early 1960s, Kuroda finds that the central government regularly used pork barrel to keep local voters in line and ensure that local political leaders would remain with the LDP (1974: 133). Although only 43 percent of the local voting public in the localities Kuroda studied had a genuine preference for the LDP and its principles, 95 percent of local governments' "top leadership" chose the LDP. His argument is similar to mine: Local officials in a fiscally very centralized system do not have enough power to separate themselves from the national party leaders.

Incentives for Organizations, Local Candidates, and Voters to Affiliate with the LDP

From the LDP's perspective, depriving entire regions of funding for failing to support the party can be risky because it punishes LDP supporters and politicians from the region who worked on behalf of the party. To give local politicians and organized interests a good reason to line up with the party, it makes greater sense to reward them for helping the LDP and punish them when they do not deliver. For this reason, a large proportion of electoral behavior in Japan focuses on clientelist exchange between national LDP candidates (and the national LDP government) and groups at the district level that could offer an organized vote.

The "organized vote" is important in Japan. Trying to gain the support of voters who are not a part of existing organizations can be difficult, especially given Japan's restrictions on candidates' ability to advertise themselves directly. Where intermediate organizations exist and work on behalf of candidates, members of the organizations can be mobilized to support them.

Japan's Clientelist/Financially Centralized system creates incentives for three key groups – intermediate organizations, local candidates, and voters – to affiliate with the national ruling LDP. Other factors may also influence their behavior, but the heavily organized vote further encourages local candidates and voters to align with the LDP.

Incentives for Organizations. *Kōenkai* are the most well-known organizations in Japanese politics (see Chapter 3), but numerous seemingly nonpolitical local organizations also play a major role in campaigning in Japan. Included are neighborhood associations, small and medium-sized businesses, local branches of industrial and occupational associations, the chamber of commerce, agricultural cooperatives, and construction firms (Curtis 1971; Park 1998a, 1998b).[4]

Why are organizations so involved in the campaign process? In some cases (e.g., neighborhood associations), they have limited aims: They may seek small material benefits, such as getting traffic ticket fines reduced, or nonmaterial benefits, such as the honor of being central to the election of a candidate and a sense of group solidarity (Curtis 1971: 117; Park 1998a: 243). However, others – in particular, businesses and industrial and occupation organizations – have a much more tangible aim: "Support is contingent on the expectation of specific favors. Also, these groups operate on the basis of organizations rather than personal support. They are trying to represent the group interest in the political arena and are in pursuit of clientelistic ties" (Park 1998a: 244).

Why do local candidates make such organizations central to their campaigns? Monitoring voters directly is difficult, and there are limited resources to use to contact large numbers of voters, but leaders of organized groups can simplify both of these jobs and act as proxies for individual

---

[4] Curtis and Park write about campaigns for national office, but my experience following local campaigns also indicates the same patterns are true.

candidates (Park 1998a: 243). Often, candidates seek the support of particular subleaders within organizations who can mobilize the votes of individuals below them in the organization (Curtis 1971: 208–9). Large companies are not ideal campaign organizations because they tend to be concentrated geographically and frequently have unions that are more inclined to cast ballots against the LDP. In contrast, small and medium-sized companies, where employees often behave as a political bloc, are far more useful for election campaigning (Park 1998b: 83). Industrial and occupational organizations also serve as strong organizers of the vote: Their hierarchical structure helps coordinate mobilization and creates accountability in the process. In addition, such organizations tend to have many branches, spreading out geographically the vote-collection process (Park: 1998a: 244).

It can be difficult to monitor the campaign effort and effect of such organizations, but often there may be less need to do so. Where organizations work to ensure election of a candidate who will maintain their clientelist links, they have strong incentives to campaign hard and mobilize the vote. That said, organizations and their subgroups are often monitored by the "collective" approaches that I discussed in Chapters 1 and 3: Specific organizations and individuals within the organization are held responsible for ensuring that a candidate receives a certain number of votes in a specific area, and candidates threaten to eliminate funding from groups that do not mobilize enough votes (Park 1998a). As a result, different individuals within an organization often compete to be the one who provides the largest number of votes for a candidate. This fits in with the clientelist exchange, whereby individuals believe that greater vote delivery will lead to greater favor with the candidate in power.

For most organizations concerned with gaining material benefits from their mobilization efforts, it is critical that these efforts are made on behalf of LDP candidates. In his research on national elections, Curtis (1971: 180–1) finds that under the multimember district system, many local organizations made a point of endorsing all LDP candidates in the district or none at all. The reasoning here is clear: Under the multimember district system, the organization does not want to alienate itself from any LDP candidate who can hinder the organization's chances of funding from the government. Note that the endorsement focuses on LDP candidates. Local organizations seeking governmental funding are less likely to endorse non-LDP candidates, who have less access to central power.

Incentives for Candidates. Because localities have little autonomy in making real "policies" in Japan's clientelistic system, local politicians are often evaluated on their ability to develop a relationship with national governmental leaders and bring home funding for local projects (Reed 1986: 29). As a result, it is critical for local politicians seeking to provide valuable services to their constituents to develop good relations with a member of the Diet (Curtis 1971: 44–5):

In order to give the project a higher priority, get more subsidies from the central government, and designate a favorable business partner as a caretaker of the project, local politicians have to consult closely with Diet members. In expectation of future benefits like these, local politicians line up with a representative from the local district who serves as a transmission belt to either powerful . . . politicians or individual ministries. (Park 1998a: 209)

At the most local levels in Japan, politicians tend not to affiliate with any party. It is widely viewed that at these levels partisanship gets in the way of distributive politics (Reed 1986: 35–6). The idea is that all politicians at such levels should focus on creating links to the (LDP-led) central government. However, no such nonpartisan ethos exists at the prefectural assembly level – the highest subnational-level legislature – and there most politicians affiliate with a party. Given that members of the ruling LDP most thoroughly control access to funding, ambitious prefectural assembly members have strong incentives to affiliate with the LDP.

In addition, when organizations find a candidate that they would like to run for office, they undoubtedly pressure him to align with the LDP to best serve their distributive needs. Even when the organization's leaders are not acting explicitly on behalf of the organization, they are frequently the heads of candidate *kōenkai* (Park 1998b: 73) and therefore have strong incentives to push their candidate toward the LDP.

The incentives to align with the LDP – while substantial for politicians at either level – are greater for local politicians than for national-level ones. Programmatic-policy debate does not play much role in most prefectural assemblies. Except in prefectures that have greater independent budgetary power, holding a prefectural assembly office involves little more than providing connections, constituent service, and distributive favors. To do well, it is most frequently in a candidate's best interest to affiliate with the LDP. In contrast, Diet members perform a wider array of functions. Delivering pork is certainly one of them, but national Diet members can also advertise and push policy positions. And many run for national office under an opposition banner in order to challenge the LDP and the policies it represents. For a number of reasons – including greater access to central budgeting and greater involvement in government policy making – there appear to be greater incentives for politicians to run under the LDP banner at the national level as well, but because of national politicians' varied roles, these incentives appear to be weaker than at the local level.[5]

---

[5] Voters no doubt also more typically look to local politicians as service providers but expect a wider set of functions performed by their national politicians.

The effect on local politicians in Japan is very clear. As one prefectural assembly member in Tochigi prefecture said, when asked about which party he and his colleagues planned to align with, "It does not matter [which party] wins the election. What matters to us is to stand in line with the ruling party whichever the case is" (*Yomiuri Shinbun*, July 18, 1996, cited in Park 1998a: 214, footnote 39). And the need for local politicians to channel centrally distributed resources to the locality makes it extremely difficult for the opposition to construct local political bases (Park 1998a: 329).

Incentives for Voters. Even voters who personally support the opposition parties – because of the issues or principles they represent – have an incentive to vote for LDP local politicians if they, as voters, also care about procuring benefits for their localities or even private goods for themselves. Even if governmental threats to cut benefits are simply bluffs, the anecdotal evidence of the LDP's withholding funding and the open threats made by LDP leaders appear to have instilled a popular perception that ties to the LDP-led central government are critical for funding. Moreover, as long as the LDP is dominant at the center and has discretion over subsidies, it is easier for areas with a large number of LDP local politicians to lobby the LDP central government for subsidies.

I do not have public opinion data on voting in local elections, but an analysis of vote choice in the 1996 HR election illuminates the important role played by subsidies in the Japanese system and the central part the LDP plays in their distribution. Respondents in the JEDS96 survey were asked to name all the candidates they could remember from their district and describe each. One sixth of all respondents who mentioned an LDP candidate first described the candidate as able to deliver subsidies. And out of 309 respondents who mentioned at least one candidate capable of delivering such subsidies, 211 cited the LDP candidate from their district. The second most-cited party was the NFP, which was mentioned only 58 times. Multivariate analysis indicates that voters citing an LDP candidate's ability to deliver subsidies to the district were markedly more likely to support the LDP than other parties (see Chapter 8), and respondents not citing subsidy delivery ability were more likely than those citing such delivery capacity to support Japan's new opposition parties.

Many voters appear to cast ballots out of such material interests. Indeed, much analysis of voting in Japan points to patronage as the primary factor in voters' decision making (Miyake 1995: Chapter 1; Otake 2000: 295). However, many voters make their voting decisions according to other criteria: Many simply do not see themselves as direct beneficiaries of the distribution of government goods to their district and/or are less concerned with trying to receive such benefits. These voters may cast ballots for more broadly programmatic reasons or based on the personal characteristics of the candidates.

Still others may cast their ballots based on their positions as a members of an organization. Local organizations that seek material benefits from the government have a great deal to gain from the election of their preferred (LDP) candidates and therefore work hard to convince their members to support them. One of the central assumptions of Japanese candidates' organized vote strategy is that many voters feel identity with the interests voiced by the leaders of the organizations to which they belong (Curtis 1971: 180), and many voters therefore cast ballots for their organization's preferred candidates. In fact, there is in Japanese a phrase, *kigyō gurumi*, which refers to the practice whereby everyone employed by a company (often, but not always, a small business) campaigns and votes for a single candidate (Otake 2000: 295). Often, this behavior is not based on material concerns of the voter at all. In many cases, a personal relationship is involved, but rather than direct ties to the candidate, the relationship is with one of the candidate's campaigners, often a leader within the "nonpolitical" organization in which the voter is a part (Curtis 1971: 40).

Of course, the organized vote only applies to voters who are in fact organized in some way. Many voters are not. These voters will cast their ballots for any of a number of reasons, from policy preferences to personal material benefit concerns to simple personal appeal of the candidate. However, even here the LDP is advantaged: Because candidates have a strong incentive to align with the LDP, and organizations have strong incentives to push LDP candidates, the bulk of potentially strong local candidates who run will be LDP candidates. Therefore, even voters who tend to cast ballots based simply on the personal qualities of the candidates will be more likely to vote for an LDP candidate.

Local-Level Failure of Japan's Opposition

It should not be surprising therefore that the LDP has been almost wholly dominant in subnational elections, with its most potent challenge coming from (typically conservative) independent candidates.[6] Naturally, not all voters and subnational regions support the LDP. In many cases, ideological principles or ties to particular unions (which typically maintained specific ideological principles) drive the vote for non-LDP parties. Moreover, the anti-LDP vote is particularly prominent in cities in both national and local elections. In addition to ideological or union-based reasons, four explanations in particular help to explain the lower vote support for the LDP in urban areas. First, close community ties in rural areas facilitate the creation of the personal support organizations that history and large sums of money make particularly available to the LDP. Such ties are less well developed in urban areas. Second, the well-organized farmers groups are among the

---

[6] Many of these local-level independents have close links to national-level LDP politicians.

leading support groups for the LDP and are more powerful in rural areas. Indeed, the LDP used Japan's leading agricultural organization, *Nōkyō*, as a rural vote-gathering machine (George Mulgan 2000).[7]

Third, it is harder to use patronage such as public works projects to attract urban voters. In urban areas, these projects typically influence the lives of countless people – many of whom are not even voters in the area under construction – and it is therefore more difficult for parties to target specific groups and claim credit for the benefits of the projects. Fourth, urban areas are usually better able to cover a larger proportion of their own spending. Urban areas simply depend less on central governmental support, and voters therefore have less incentive to cast ballots for the LDP.[8]

Despite these exceptions, voters and localities support the LDP very strongly in subnational elections. Figures 5.1 and 5.2 show the proportion of the total number of prefectural assembly and national HR seats held by, respectively, the LDP and non-LDP parties over time. Even when the opposition did moderately well at the national level, it could not translate this success into subnational seats. Indeed, even while non-LDP success in national elections fluctuated over time, the number of seats held by non-LDP parties at the local level stayed very low over the entire period. In contrast, the LDP always dominated the prefectural level, in many prefectures and many years exceeding what it held at the national level.[9]

I also examine, for the 1967–91 period, opposition party success with the prefecture as the level of analysis. Even controlling for the number of prefectural-assembly seats allotted to smaller prefectures, the opposition did much worse at the subnational level. The opposition won a larger share of

[7] In exchange, *Nōkyō* influenced LDP spending on its farmers.

[8] These explanations all fit with my larger argument about the impact of clientelism and centralized funding.

[9] As of 1997, roughly one quarter of all of Japan's prefectural assembly members held no party affiliation (*Japan Statistical Yearbook* 1999). If ties to the ruling party were so critical, why were there so many independents? The largest increase in independents occurred in 1995, the first unified local election after the 1993–4 national party realignment. The 1995 election had been preceded by two years of multiple changes in the partisan composition of the national government. Prefectural assembly members with no party affiliation jumped from roughly 15 to 25 percent of the entire pool. In large measure, this was because of concern with the volatile state of politics at the national level. It was one thing to run as an independent, and therefore not openly oppose the ruling party (whichever party that was at the time), but, for many politicians, it was quite another to get caught in the opposing party. A number of prefectural-assembly members had defected from the LDP along with a member of the Diet in 1993–4. At first, many even joined new parties with their patron Diet member. However, because of confusion over who was to control the national government, many became independents right off the bat, and, after the LDP came back into power in 1994, many prefectural-assembly members who had earlier joined new parties dropped their party affiliation (interviews with LDP national Diet defectors, May–July 1999). Increasing voter distrust of parties was important as well and led to more candidates becoming officially independent, while still maintaining close ties to particular LDP Diet members.

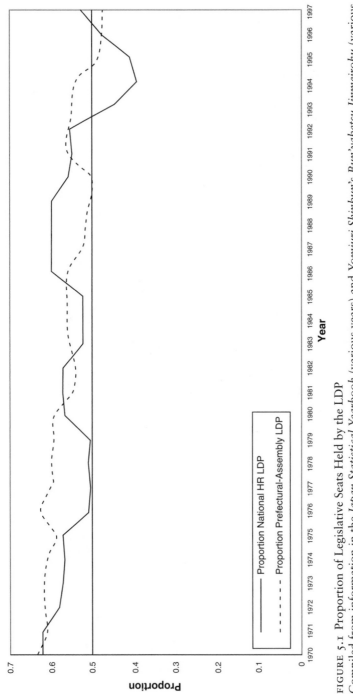

FIGURE 5.1 Proportion of Legislative Seats Held by the LDP Compiled from information in the *Japan Statistical Yearbook* (various years) and *Yomiuri Shinbun's Bun'yabetsu Jinmeiroku* (various years).

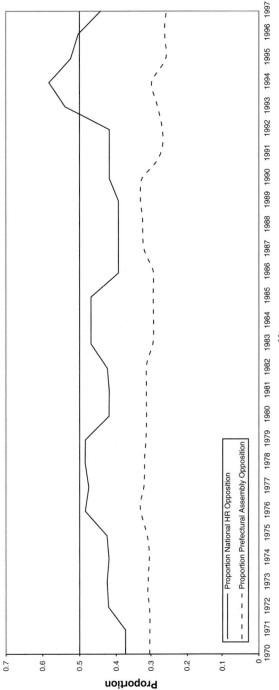

FIGURE 5.2 Proportion of Seats Held by Non-LDP Parties

Note that a number of seat holders remain officially independent; therefore, the totals won by the LDP (Figure 5.1) and non-LDP (Figure 5.2) *parties* sum to less than one.

Compiled from information in the *Japan Statistical Yearbook* (various years) and *Yomiuri Shinbun's Bun'yabetsu Jinmeiroku* (various years).

seats in the national-level race in 83 percent (273 out of 328) of the prefectural cases in the data set. On average within each prefecture, the opposition won 10 percentage points more seats in national races than in prefectural assembly races.

Interviews offer additional support. When asked about the reasons for LDP hegemony at the local level, local opposition leaders from a variety of Japanese prefectures explain that it was because LDP politicians typically are perceived as more capable of acting as a "pipeline" (*paipu*) between the LDP-led central government and the localities.[10]

MEASURES OF LOCAL AUTONOMY AND LOCAL OPPOSITION SUCCESS

Although Japan is heavily centralized, not all subnational units are equally dependent upon the center. The degree of local fiscal autonomy varies with both region and time. Certain areas of the country are more financially autonomous than others, and the country as a whole goes through periods where localities hold greater independence. Moreover, where localities are more independent, politics should be more like the Clientelist/Financially Decentralized type. Under such conditions, candidates and voters need to worry less about affiliating with the national ruling party and can more freely support politicians of their most preferred party.

Local Autonomy Index and Prefectural Assembly Success

Japan is split up into a variety of subdivisions. At the highest level are 47 prefectures, which are smaller geographically than the average administrative subunits in most countries, but about average in terms of population. At the most local level, the country is divided into more than 3,000 cities, towns, and villages, each being a legally distinct category. The largest cities are specially designated as metropolitan zones, and the largest – Tokyo – is coterminous with a prefecture.

Most candidates for prefectural-level assembly office carry the affiliation of one of the major national parties. If local dependence on the center is truly important to local electoral politics, opposition parties should do poorly in highly dependent prefectures and be most successful in autonomous ones. To investigate this, we need a measure of Japanese local governments' fiscal independence.

In Japan, a commonly used index of local fiscal strength (*zaiseiryoku-shisū*), or what I call "Autonomy," is computed by dividing the localities'

---

[10] Interviews conducted by the author with local opposition leaders in Japan from October 1998 through August 1999. For other analysis indicating the importance of such pipelines to local affiliation with the LDP, see Curtis (1971: 11) and Park (1998a: 295).

own revenues (e.g., local taxes)[11] by a measure (computed by the central government according to a complex and fairly politically blind formula) of the localities' expenditure needs. Using this index for each prefecture in the fiscal year directly before the seven local elections held between 1967 and 1991, there is a substantial (.57) correlation between local fiscal strength and the proportion of the prefectural assembly seats held by opposition parties.[12] Figure 5.3 illustrates this relationship. Only in the most autonomous prefectures does the opposition win a large proportion of prefectural assembly seats. Elsewhere (Scheiner in press), I confirm the positive relationship between Autonomy and opposition prefectural assembly success through statistical analysis that controls for a number of other variables.

Comparing public opinion data from urban and rural areas offers additional support. Rural areas tend to be less autonomous than urban ones. Analysis of the 1996 JEDS public opinion survey indicates that even though nearly 30 percent of rural voters noted "ability to bring in subsidies" as a significant characteristic of at least one House of Representatives candidate in their district, little more than 10 percent of urban voters did. Generating financial support from the central government for localities is a more important task for politicians representing rural areas than for those representing cities. Given this and the fact that opposition parties win roughly half as large a proportion of assembly seats in rural as in urban areas (*Japan Statistical Yearbook*, various years), it seems that much of opposition parties' weakness in rural areas stems from voters' perception that they are less able to deliver subsidies.[13] (For more on the urban–rural split, see Chapter 8.)

Slack Resources and the Opposition's Ability to Gain Subnational Executive Office

Acquiring Autonomy measures for multiple years for all 3,000-plus municipalities is difficult, so I cannot be as systematic in examining subnational executive office affiliation. Fortunately, there are other ways to measure Autonomy. Reed provides a useful insight into the relationship between resources and policy freedom: "Local governments with resources will have greater capacity to innovate and to avoid slavishly following the fiscal incentives of central grant programs.... Central policies that affect local budgeting at the margin will be more likely to result in central influence and

---

[11] The central government caps local tax rates fairly uniformly across the country. A locality cannot easily raise its Autonomy score simply by raising taxes.

[12] After 1993, the opposition gained more prefectural assembly members when a number of such politicians defected from the LDP along with their national-level Diet patron. This increase had nothing to do with changes in local autonomy; therefore, including post-1991 elections would misrepresent the correlation between Autonomy and opposition prefectural assembly success that exists in equilibrium.

[13] I explain later why Autonomy is not simply a proxy for urban-ness.

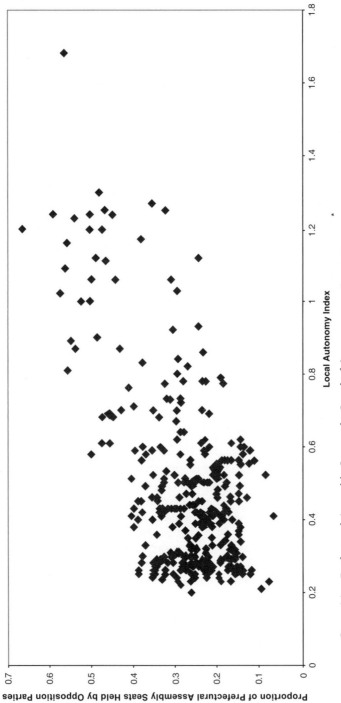

FIGURE 5.3 Opposition Prefectural Assembly Success by Level of Autonomy: 1967–1991.
Source: Jichishō, *Todōfuken Zaiseishisūhyō* (various years).

more likely to inhibit local innovation" (1986: 159). This suggests that sub-national governments with more slack resources – that is, resources that the local governments can spend and use at their own discretion – will exercise greater policy freedom and be less beholden to the central government. Because they are less dependent on the center, localities with large amounts of slack resources ought to be more likely to elect opposition party candidates to subnational office.

It can be difficult to determine under what conditions particular resources are slack, but we can determine proxy measures that signal when local governments have such resources. One such proxy is economic growth. During periods of high economic growth, local governments ought to gain greater slack resources, leading to less reliance on the center. After resting at a fairly low level in the 1950s, local government tax revenues picked up dramatically over the 1960s and first half of the 1970s simply because Japan grew richer. Japanese local tax revenues increased by 1,200 percent over the 1959–74 fiscal years before dropping in 1975 (Jichishō, *Chihō zaisei hakusho* and *Chihō zaisei tōkei nenkan*, various years).[14] This growth in slack resources gave local governments the capacity to pursue new programs, and, indeed, local programmatic innovation and the number of opposition local governmental executives both grew dramatically during this time. Not surprising, during this period, the mean value of the Autonomy index reached its highest point in the entire postwar era.

As just suggested, greater autonomy allowed local governments to offer new policies. Perhaps the most important "innovation" was local government response to the pollution crisis of the time. Various forms of pollution in the 1950s and 1960s in Japan were disfiguring and sometimes even killing its citizens, and at the same time that the central government was slow to respond to the crisis, local governments introduced a series of anti-pollution policies (McKean 1977, 1981). Successful innovation in response to pollution appeared to encourage local governments to pursue other problems as well, in particular social-welfare programs. In 1969, Tokyo's Governor Minobe Ryōkichi had started much of the trend toward progressive local government by pushing spending programs such as free health care for the elderly (Campbell 1979). As Reed (1986) explains, once Tokyo enacted policies of this kind, many other local governments put similar programs into place. Campbell writes: "Minobe's action received extensive national publicity, and the idea of free medical care for the elderly diffused among other local governments with astonishing speed," so that within two and a half years, 44 of Japan's 47 prefectures offered elderly health care support (1979: 333).

---

[14] After a one-year decline, local tax revenues increased until 1991, but not at the same dramatic rate.

My analysis suggests that much of this innovation was attributable to greater local fiscal autonomy, but if budget autonomy was the issue, why did opposition politicians win instead on public goods issues such as the environment during these years? Reed offers a simple answer: "Economic growth provided local governments with slack resources that could be allocated to new programs.... [E]conomic growth and increased revenues were necessary conditions for the spurt of innovative local policymaking, providing local governments with the wherewithal to respond creatively to new needs and demands" (1986: 58–9).

As local governments saw that they could spend more on such programs and put forward their own individual plans and as opposition parties and candidates saw that they could push such measures without serious punishment by the central government, opposition parties and candidates became more likely to run and voters became more likely to support them. Progressive opposition parties made great strides in local executive elections, going from 84 mayoral seats in 1963 to 92 in 1967, to 114 in 1971, and to 122 in 1975 (Zenkoku Kakushin Shichōkai 1990).

Deficit spending can be used as another proxy measure for slack resources and autonomy. For Japanese localities, deficit spending represents money borrowed to cover expenses that go beyond what they are able to raise on their own through local taxes and what they receive from the central government through transfers and subsidies. If deficit spending were a perfect proxy, localities with more deficit spending would be more autonomous than those with less. This is silly as the most autonomous governments are those with sufficient funding of their own so that they do not need to operate at a deficit. Nevertheless, deficit spending might work as a proxy. Insofar as deficit spending serves as a way around some of the constraints placed by the central government, it might represent the assertion of discretion over spending by local governments. That is, when local governments are denied subsidies, oftentimes their best bet for funding is to borrow and run a deficit.

During the high-growth era of the 1960s, there was no clear relationship between the number of localities operating at a deficit and the number of progressive mayors in Japan (Jichishō, *Chihō zaisei tōkei nenkan* and *Chihō zaisei hakusho*, various years). Early in the 1960s, many localities spent more than they took in, but their tax revenue increased because of the country's unprecedented economic growth. By the late 1960s and early 1970s, far fewer were falling into the red. Thanks to growing local innovation, the number of progressive mayors elected in cities during this time increased steadily. With the further increase in local programs in the early 1970s and the first oil shock, however, the number of localities operating at a deficit increased between 1972 and 1975.

Beginning in the latter half of the 1970s, the Ministry of Home Affairs and the Ministry of Finance grew anxious because of lower growth rates that lay ahead and consciously sought to roll back the local programmatic

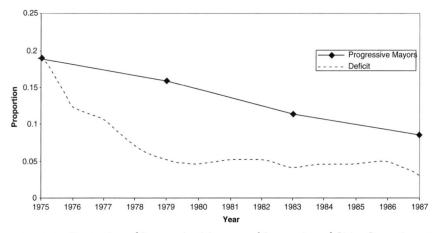

FIGURE 5.4 Proportion of Progressive Mayors and Proportion of Cities Operating at a Deficit
Compiled from information in *Japan Statistical Yearbook* (various years), Jichishō, *Chihō zaisei hakusho* and *Chihō zaisei tōkei nenkan* (various years), Richardson (1997: Table 4.2, p. 87), Zenkoku Kakushin Shichōkai (1990: Appendix, pp. 549–58).

"excesses" of the early 1970s. They initiated a campaign to curb local social welfare programs and to push many localities away from their previous programmatic promises. In particular, their efforts rested on controlling local finances (Reed 1986: 55–6; *Yomiuri Shinbun*, paper version, May 25 and August 6, 1982). The debates surrounding these moves were partly ideological battles over the substance of policy, but they were also very much focused on whether the central government had the right, even the obligation, to maintain control over spending by local governments (Reed 1986).

The central government won, and far fewer localities were permitted to operate at a deficit. By 1979, the number of municipalities operating at a deficit was at its lowest in more than two decades, down to just 5 percent of Japan's municipalities. As Figure 5.4 indicates, the decline in slack resources available to localities was accompanied by a decline in the number of progressive party government executives. As further evidence that the decline in the number of municipalities operating at a deficit was due to central governmental constraints (and not local governmental choice), note that the mean local fiscal strength (Autonomy) index for all localities in the post-1960 period was at its lowest in the latter half of the 1970s.

The local fiscal strength (Autonomy) measure utilized in the analysis of prefectural assembly seat holders reinforces the discussion. Figure 5.5 plots the mean Autonomy measure (for all prefectures) by year and the proportion of local executive office holders who were progressives. I standardize

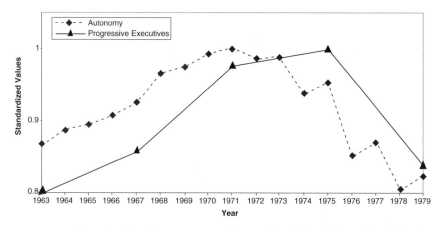

FIGURE 5.5 Mean Levels of Autonomy and Proportion of Local Executives Who Are Progressive
Autonomy refers to the local fiscal strength index averaged across all the prefectures in the year. Note that each of these is standardized, so that each year's value is computed by dividing the actual value of the variable for a given year by the largest value of the variable for all of the years.
Sources: The Local Fiscal Autonomy data were compiled from Jichishō, *Todōfuken Zaiseishisūhyō*. The progressive executive data were compiled from information in *Japan Statistical Yearbook* (various years), Jichishō, *Chihō zaisei hakusho* and *Chihō zaisei tōkei tōkei nenkan* (various years), Richardson (1997: Table 4.2, p. 87), Zenkoku Kakushin Shichōkai (1990: Appendix, p. 549–58).

the measures in order to make their patterns more visually recognizable.[15] Even before standardizing the variables, the correlation between them is an extremely high (.8). That is, Figure 5.5 indicates that as Autonomy increases, so do the proportion of local executive seats won by progressive candidates. And as Autonomy decreases, so does the proportion of local, progressive-held executive seats.

These progressive/non-LDP mayors did not always lose office. In many cases, they actually linked up with the LDP so that they were supported not just by the opposition camp but by the LDP as well. As Figure 5.6 shows, the number of joint LDP–opposition party mayors increased dramatically from 1976, while the number of opposition-only mayors plummeted to around 10 percent of all mayors.[16]

---

[15] I divide the value of each variable by the largest value of that variable across all years.

[16] In the years of confusion following the LDP's split in 1993, many governors were eager to hedge their bets and engage in pan-party coalitions because of their inability to predict which party would control the government at the national level. (Personal communication with Robert Weiner, who is doing work on such pan-party candidates.)

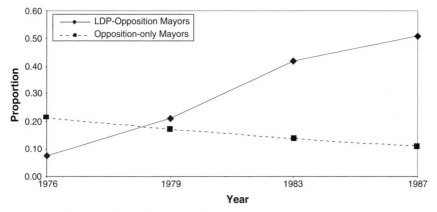

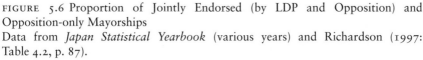

FIGURE 5.6 Proportion of Jointly Endorsed (by LDP and Opposition) and Opposition-only Mayorships
Data from *Japan Statistical Yearbook* (various years) and Richardson (1997: Table 4.2, p. 87).

It is noteworthy that the shift from opposition-only to LDP-linked mayorships occurred in the late 1970s, when the central government tightened the screws on local governments' ability to operate at a deficit and when local governments' ability to generate their own revenues had declined. That is, opposition party local executives developed stronger ties to the LDP at exactly the time when links to the central government appeared more critical to funding local programs. As localities maintained fewer slack resources to pursue their own funding, it is likely that they linked themselves up with the LDP in order to better extract resources from the central government.

TOP-DOWN PARTY DEVELOPMENT AND LOCAL PARTY SWITCHING

The Clientelist/Financially Centralized system shaped the opposition's ability to win office at the subnational level. In particular, the opposition tended to win local office only in regions that were less dependent on the central government. But Japan's Clientelist/Financially Centralized system also shaped the likelihood of sitting subnational LDP politicians defecting from the national ruling party. In particular, Japan's Clientelist/Financially Centralized system gave sitting local politicians little incentive to join new parties, unless doing so was their principal means to maintaining their connection to the central government.

If the argument here is correct, the "pipeline" function, whereby LDP local and national politicians connect the periphery to the center, causes party formation to be from the top down. Even if a new party gains support, local candidates' reliance on national politicians makes them unlikely to join non-LDP parties unless doing so helps maintain their relationship with the center: The conventional wisdom tends to be that joining non-LDP parties harms politicians' ability to attract patronage and therefore creates another obstacle to opposition parties developing a base of local politicians.

Except for *Kōmeitō*, which was founded to represent a preexisting constituency (a lay Buddhist organization), every major Japanese party of the postwar period began at the national level, and most grew out of splits from existing parties. Parties rarely emerge from the grassroots, and local politicians usually affiliate with a party only once it is established at the national level. Japanese local politicians seem to have little desire to affiliate with a party that has no ties to central power, unless their locality has independent sources of revenue.

Japan has *yūryokusha*, or political bosses, running the local political show, much as the Daley machine ran Chicago (Curtis 1971). However, although the mayor was the boss in the Chicago machine, in Japan the Diet member is usually the leader and local politicians follow (Reed 1986). This makes sense because it is the national politician who controls access to central governmental financing. Within Japan, patron–client relationships, called *keiretsu*, link national LDP politicians to local LDP politicians (Inoue 1992).[17] As Kataoka explains, "under LDP rule, its [prefectural and local] assembly members could expect their demands upon the national government to be registered through a connection with their patron LDP Diet member" (1997: 208). To gain national pork, many local politicians join national politicians' *keiretsu*. It is striking that members of Japan's traditional opposition parties typically do not have *keiretsu*, which tend to be tied only to the benefit-providing center of Japan, the LDP-controlled central government.

The impact of the Clientelist/Financially Centralized system on *keiretsu* and local party affiliation patterns can be seen in the party defection patterns of prefectural assembly members. In 1993–4, the national LDP appeared to be a sinking ship. More than 15 percent of LDP Diet members joined the new *Shinsei* (Revival) party, but only around 5 percent of LDP prefectural assembly members switched to the new party. Analyses of the national-level defections indicate that party switching was most likely among two types of politicians: first, reformers who were unhappy with the lack of reform being pushed by the LDP and, second, politicians whose recent electoral fortunes either gave them sufficient security to act with no fear of voter retribution or made them so insecure that they needed to try something radical (Cox and Rosenbluth 1995; Kato 1998; Reed and Scheiner 2003). Yet, no such patterns emerge in analyses of *prefectural* assembly defections (see Desposato and Scheiner ND).

---

[17] *Keiretsu* is commonly used to describe a particular relationship among firms in Japan, but it also has a less well-known meaning, which refers to the political relationship described here.

However, prefecture-level defection was not random. It tended to occur in prefectures where a Diet member had left the LDP. Indeed, numerous national- and subnational-level politicians and local-level reporters explain that in their prefecture, whenever a Diet member defected from the LDP, all the members of his *keiretsu* left the LDP with him and that the only prefectural assembly members to defect from the LDP were those in the *keiretsu* of a Diet member who defected from the LDP as well.[18] It was rare that any prefectural assembly members switched parties in prefectures where no Diet member did, and those few cases were due to highly aberrant circumstances, such as one prefectural-assembly member who defected just before he was to be expelled from the LDP for violating party rules. In a few cases, Diet members defected, but their *keiretsu* members did not, but this was usually because the subnational office holders decided not to join *Shinsei* out of concern that it would hinder their ability to get funding for the prefecture from the national government (Desposato and Scheiner ND).

Shinsei was in the national government in 1993–4, so it might seem odd that LDP prefectural assembly members were wary of switching to it. However, this wariness was due to the sense by many that the non-LDP government was unstable. Party switching at the national level did put *Shinsei* in the government, but the coalition was short lived, holding a Diet majority for only nine months. Given *Shinsei's* brief control of the government, general uncertainty about the stability of the new party system, and local skepticism about the new party's ability to stay in power,[19] it is reasonable to think that many local politicians did not see *Shinsei* as a reliable long-term pipeline to the center.

The fact that most local politicians' party switching occurred in concert with national *keiretsu* leader's party switching indicates the importance of links between the two levels. If all local politicians in the *keiretsu* of LDP Diet party switchers had also left the LDP to join *Shinsei*, we could not tell if they were defecting because of personal loyalty or to maintain their pipeline to the center. However, in general, local politicians did not switch parties unless their national *keiretsu* leader did, and most local politicians switched parties when their *keiretsu* leader did. And some local politicians did not switch parties because they feared losing central governmental funding. This all indicates strong ties between local- and national-level politicians, based in very large part on the ability of national politicians to act as a pipeline for the local politicians' funding needs.

---

[18] Based on interviews and written correspondence, May–August 1999.

[19] Interviews I conducted over May–August 1999 with Diet members from three different parties (the DPJ, *Kōmeitō*, and the LDP) and the DPJ prefectural organization in Hyogo (June 24, 1999) as well as correspondence over the same period with prefectural reporters in Hiroshima and Saga confirmed the uneasiness held by a number of subnational politicians about the stability of the party system and the anti-LDP government.

There is additional evidence that *keiretsu* ties were based in large part on electoral considerations and the desire for patronage, and not just on personal ties and loyalty. When Japan changed its electoral law in 1994, the changes in district lines complicated *keiretsu* links by separating national and local politicians who had represented identical areas in the past: In some cases, the district redrawing meant that a national and local politician pair who had previously both represented a given locality no longer represented the same region as one another. As a result, a number of local politicians sought new national-level patrons, whose shared geographic representation made them better suited for electoral purposes (Kataoka 1997). During that period, the leading opposition party, the NFP, had increasingly gained strength in a number of prefectural assemblies by attracting sitting LDP members, *until the LDP abruptly returned to power* (Kataoka 1997: 210). Subnational LDP members were willing to switch to the party controlling the national government but were unwilling to leave the LDP once it was in power again.

The main point here is: *If Japan's clientelistic and fiscally centralized system prevented defection for even those whose links to national politicians might have given them an incentive to defect, it is no wonder that opposition parties have been able to attract so few potential local politicians,* even in years when such parties had fairly substantial popularity.

One final point hammers home the argument here. After World War II, Occupation authorities, concerned about the role centralized power had played in Japan's prewar imperialism, took steps to increase local autonomy. After the Occupation period ended, however, the central government gradually decreased the amount of autonomy it granted subnational units. During the late 1950s and early 1960s, as local governments lost their independence, several progressive party mayors switched to the LDP to improve their chances of obtaining public works project funding (Reed 1986: 45).

URBAN-NESS, NOT AUTONOMY?

An argument might be made that my findings are based on a spurious correlation: Autonomy and urban-ness are highly correlated, and urban voters have reasons beyond independence from the center for supporting opposition parties. For example, because LDP politicians rely on well-organized networks of voters, these politicians are less able to find success in cities, where voters are less tightly knit. In short, opposition party success at the prefectural level depends on the level of urban-ness and not the level of autonomy.

Arguments of this kind certainly have merit, and networks and the organized vote clearly have greater impact in rural areas, but there are good reasons to believe that the combination of clientelism and fiscal centralization also play a critical role in shaping opposition failure at the subnational level. First, unless we include the impact of clientelism and dependence on the center, focusing on other urban–rural differences cannot offer a sufficient explanation for why the opposition does so much worse in *subnational*-level elections. In contrast, my argument posits that voters and candidates will be especially likely to affiliate with the national ruling party in contests for *subnational*-level office. Second, subnational opposition success is not simply based on urban-ness but has increased and decreased over time as well. These changing levels of opposition success were very much a result of, first, greater overall local governmental financial independence and, second, a return to greater dependence on the central government for funding.

CONCLUSION

My preliminary comparative analysis in Chapter 4 and my more systematic and detailed analysis of the Japanese case here suggest that opposition parties face tremendous obstacles to gaining power at the local level in Clientelist/Financially Centralized systems. Most obvious, the system gives local organizations, politicians, and voters much greater incentive to affiliate with the national ruling party than with the opposition. In the Japanese case, this dramatically helped the LDP.

In short, the combined impact of clientelism and the centralization of governmental resources is at the heart of the opposition's inability to gain a local foothold in Japan. In the next chapter, I discuss the broader implications of this local weakness – the ways in which local failure in turn led to the opposition's inability to succeed at the national level.

6

National-Level Opposition Failure

The Impact of Subnational-Level Weakness

As I showed in the previous chapter, Japan's Clientelist/Financially Centralized system greatly hindered opposition parties' capacity to develop subnational-level strength. In this chapter, I demonstrate how this subnational-level weakness led to opposition party failure at the *national* level.

The 1990s and early 2000s were seen as a period of opportunity for a challenge to the LDP to arise. Voters proved themselves more than willing to support the new opposition of the era. The first new challenger, the New Frontier Party, fell just short of the LDP in proportional representation balloting in the 1996 House of Representatives election. Similarly, the Democratic Party of Japan ran nearly even with the LDP in PR balloting in the 2000 HR race and even won more PR votes than the ruling party in 2003. At the same time, the opposition won far fewer district races and was therefore unable to topple the LDP.

In the 1990s, there were many changes in Japanese politics that ought to have benefited the opposition (see Chapter 2), but there was a clear constant that remained from the pre-1990 era: the Clientelist/Financially Centralized system. In a Clientelist/Financially Centralized system, parties that are not strong at the national level have great difficulty winning local-office. In turn, parties that hold little strength at the local level have weak foundations and face difficulty getting their message out.

Most important, by not holding many local-level offices, Japan's opposition parties had few experienced candidates that they could run for national office: When able to run an experienced candidate, the opposition was at least as successful in national-level races as the LDP. However, because of its failure in subnational races, the opposition had very few such candidates to run, and therefore was typically unable to compete with the LDP.

For more details on the statistical analysis cited in this chapter, see the links to the supplementary Web site at *www.ethanscheiner.com*.

NATIONAL CANDIDACIES

In any country where voters cast ballots for individual candidates, a party's best chance at success hinges on the strength of its candidates. For example, Kornberg and Winsborough (1968), writing about Canada, and Norris and Lovenduski (1993), writing about Britain, demonstrate the importance of candidate background in shaping parties' success. Similarly, Jacobson's (1990) work on congressional elections in the United States argues that the "quality" or experience of candidates is very important to a party's success in winning seats. For Jacobson, quality candidates are those with substantial experience in governmental office. For example, in the United States, high-level state politicians such as state assembly members would be high-quality candidates for congressional races because of the connections they already established to their constituency and because their time in office establishes them as having had sufficient experience to justify voters' faith in them. Even though he is not always explicit in his reasoning behind this, it seems that, for Jacobson, "quality" is shorthand for the talent and resources such candidates are likely to have. In American congressional elections, experienced candidates have a substantial advantage over inexperienced ones. According to Jacobson, experienced candidates challenging incumbents in American congressional races are four times as likely to defeat the incumbent as an inexperienced challenger, and experienced candidates are also more likely to win open seat races. Jacobson argues that for many years in the United States the heart of the Republicans' difficulty in House of Representatives' races was the relatively poor quality of candidates who challenged incumbents and contested open seats under the Republican banner (1990: 61–3).

Aldrich and Griffin's (ND) analysis of the rise of the Republican Party in the U.S. South relates even more directly to the Japanese case. The Democratic Party dominated the American South for roughly a century, and Aldrich and Griffin find that the Republican Party did not make serious gains in Southern congressional races until it picked up a substantial number of seats in state legislative races. Like Jacobson, they find that prior office experience was a key to success among Republican congressional hopefuls.[1] The rise of the Republican Party in the South is of course a fairly recent phenomenon, and Jacobson also notes that in fact the impact of challenger quality has increased in the United States as elections have become more candidate-centered (Jacobson 1990: 51–7).

This is particularly suggestive for Japan, which is firmly founded on candidate-centered politics. Diet candidates' capacity to deliver pork is important, but the personal connection is also significant. All else being equal, voters will be more likely to cast votes for candidates in whom they have

---

[1] As a *decentralized* system, the United States offers fewer incentives for local voters and candidates to affiliate with a party merely because it controls the government at the center.

particularly strong personal confidence or affinity. Many candidates develop this reputation through their prior careers (especially in public service), where they distinguish themselves as particularly capable or personally attractive. Because of the important role of the organized vote in Japan, perhaps the most valuable thing candidates can draw from their prior careers is a strong, organized, and mobilizable base of support.

To succeed in Japan, it is clearly important for any party to find a large number of quality candidates of these kinds. Former bureaucrats make attractive candidates because they hold political experience and important connections to the central government. As the governing party, the LDP has a close relationship with the bureaucracy and therefore ought to have an advantage recruiting bureaucrats. However, given the importance of organized bases of support, local office holders turn out to be ideal quality candidates for national office. Even though bureaucrats made up a particularly large proportion of Diet members at one time, recent national legislators were more likely to have gained experience in local political office.[2]

This suggests a great disadvantage for the opposition, which has done so poorly in local races. After the 1995 local elections, the leading opposition party, the NFP, had representation in only 27 out of the 47 prefectural assemblies, averaging just over five assembly members in the prefectures in which it actually had any representation. This gave the NFP only 4.8 percent (141 out of 2,927) of all of Japan's prefectural assembly members. The party's poor showing is all the more stark when compared to the LDP and its conservative independent allies, who held a majority or near majority in nearly every prefectural assembly. Given its lack of strength at the local level, the NFP could achieve substantial popularity but still have great difficulty seriously challenging the LDP in national elections. In the 1995 House of Councillors election, the NFP outpolled the LDP by 1.5 million votes in the PR section of the ballot and took home three more PR seats than the LDP. However, it won nine fewer seats than the LDP in the candidate-centered races in the prefectural district component of the HC.[3]

---

[2] More than twice as many former local office holders as bureaucrats were elected to the HR in 2000 (based on calculations from Miyagawa 2000).

[3] The HC (the less important branch), like the HR since 1994, is divided into two parts. One is a national PR district, which before 1983 was one large SNTV/MMD district electing 50 winners at a time. From 1983 until 2001, the tier was a straightforward national PR tier, with each voter casting one ballot for a party. As part of a plan to take advantage of the fact that it had a larger number of attractive or, at least, well-established individual candidates, beginning with the 2001 HC election, the LDP enacted reform to make the PR tier of the Upper House an open-list system, so that voters could cast a single ballot for a candidate, but the number of seats awarded to each party is determined by summing the votes awarded to all of the party's candidates (along with votes cast just for the party). The HC's other tier uses SNTV/MMD with the multimember districts coinciding with prefectural boundaries. Only half of the HC stands for reelection every three years, so these multimember districts only put up half their seats for reelection every three years as well. As a result, in any given prefecture, there is between one and four seats available to be contested in a given election.

Similarly, the NFP won nearly as many votes and seats as the LDP in PR balloting in the 1996 HR election, but the party did *markedly* worse than the LDP in the single member district component of the HR race, winning only 96 SMDs to the LDP's 169.

Although the breakup of the NFP led to the creation of a larger, stronger DPJ, the new DPJ suffered from disadvantages much like those of the NFP. The 44 prefectures that held local elections in 1999 had an average of 60 seats per assembly, with the DPJ holding 3.9 seats per assembly. This summed to only 6.4 percent of all prefectural assembly seats in these 44 prefectures, a much smaller percentage than the DPJ's share of votes and seats in national-level elections.[4] The DPJ found great success in the PR bloc of the 1998 HC election, finishing a mere two seats behind the LDP, despite being less than half a year old. However, the DPJ ran candidates in only 20 of the 47 (candidate-centered) district races, and won 15 out of the total 76 prefectural district seats, while the LDP won 31. In the 2000 HR election, the DPJ finished only a few percentage points behind the LDP in PR balloting, but won only 80 SMDs to the LDP's 177.[5] And in the 2003 HR election, the DPJ had the opposition's most successful election ever. It defeated the LDP (37 percent to 35 percent) in PR, but won 63 fewer SMDs (105 to 168) than the LDP.

Without looking at the data, the most convincing potential explanation for this opposition failure in district races would probably be a failure to coordinate. One could speculate that the opposition split its vote among too many different parties. However, while the opposition was harmed some-what by coordination issues that allowed the LDP to win SMDs with fewer votes than the combined non-Communist opposition in 1996, this problem was far less severe in 2000, occurring in only 29 out of the LDP's 177 SMD victories. In short, opposition failure in Japan's mixed SMD/PR system did not appear to be due primarily to a failure of the opposition to cooperate.

My analysis suggests that the opposition's failure had more to do with its difficulty finding experienced candidates. When able to run experienced candidates in prefectural districts in the HC election in 1995, the NFP was extremely successful. It actually won half a million more votes than the LDP throughout the country in the district-level races. Yet the party was able to find suitable candidates to run in HC prefectural districts in only 32 out of the total 47 prefectures, and its candidates won seats in only 22 of these.

---

[4] Compiled from local editions of the *Asahi Shinbun* the day after the April 11, 1999 unified local election.

[5] Another new party, the New Liberal Club faced a similar problem in Japan in the late 1970s and early 80s. The party was never able to pull together a base of more than 39 (approximately 1 percent of the nation's total) prefectural assembly members throughout the country (*Japan Statistical Yearbook* various years), and, despite widespread popularity, it was never able to find many quality candidates to run under its banner at the national level. The Japan New Party in the early 1990s and the Socialists in the late 1980s and early 1990s faced a similar problem finding strong candidates (Otake 2000: 306, footnote 8).

TABLE 6.1 *All Quality Candidates Do Well, but the LDP Has Higher Proportion of Quality Candidates*

	LDP	DPJ
Total candidates	280	242
New candidates	56	139
Percent of new candidates who were quality	59%	18%
Percent of nonquality new candidates who won	22%	12%
Percent of quality new candidates who won	42%	48%

Quality LDP and DPJ candidates in 2000 (300 total single member districts).

In contrast, the LDP took seats in 31 prefectures (*Asahi Shinbun*, July 24, 1995). Similarly, in the 1996 HR election, even as NFP popularity was on the decline, it finished only 4.5 percentage points behind the LDP in PR votes and won only ten fewer (out of 200 total) PR seats than the LDP did. But with its larger pool of incumbents and quality new candidates (e.g., pulled from local politics), the LDP crushed the NFP in SMDs. Out of just over 100 new NFP candidates running in Japan's 300 SMDs, only 20 were victorious in 1996 (McKean and Scheiner 2000). And these 20 included 11 former local politicians, along with 3 central government bureaucrats who had been given field assignments in the prefecture where they ran for the HC, one former television newscaster, and one former baseball star from the region.[6]

More systematic analysis makes the point much more definitively. An analysis of major party (LDP and DPJ), new candidates (i.e., those who had never previously held HR office) from the SMD tier in the June 2000 HR election suggests that quality candidacies are absolutely key to party success. To begin with, simply being a relatively new opposition party is usually a disadvantage, as most candidates of such parties will be challengers. As Table 6.1 indicates, out of 242 DPJ candidates, 139 had never held HR office, in contrast to only 56 newcomers out of nearly 300 candidates for the LDP. Indeed, the head of the DPJ's electoral strategy bureau explained that the DPJ's most substantial obstacle to electoral success was the very small number of potentially strong candidates it could run in SMDs.[7] This lack of national-level political experience was a great disadvantage to the DPJ, as, overall, new candidates showed only limited success, with 26 (18.7 percent) winning for the DPJ and 19 (33.9 percent) for the LDP in 2000.[8]

At least as important though, the LDP was able to run many more quality new candidates. Jacobson's definition of quality focuses on people who have

---

[6] Based on information compiled in Miyagawa (1997).

[7] Interview, December 18, 1998.

[8] Data from the 2000 election were compiled from *www.yomiuri.co.jp/election2000/main.htm* and *www.asahi.com/senkyo2000/index.html*.

held political office. I certainly include this definition, but in the Japanese case I focus on candidates who are likely to have developed a substantial organized base of support: (1) former prefectural governors or assembly members, (2) former city mayors, and (3) former national Upper House members. Such candidates both fit Jacobson's definition and ought to have developed a substantial (and, most likely, organized) base of support. I also add (4) candidates who "inherited" an SMD from a relative. In Japan, the practice of inheriting districts is common, particularly within families of very successful politicians. Inheriting a seat is an incredible advantage, as it provides, in effect, the entire organization of the deceased incumbent. Where the incumbent was strong, inheritance nearly guarantees victory. For example, when Prime Minister Obuchi died in 2000, his 26-year-old daughter inherited his district and won with more than 76 percent of the vote.

In Japanese politics, other types of experience can also make a candidate capable of attracting strong support. For this reason, I expand the definition to include (5) former national-level bureaucrats and (6) former television news reporters. National-level bureaucrats are typically held in high esteem and attract greater support merely on the basis of their bureaucratic reputation. As highly esteemed sons of the community, they maintain connections that facilitate electoral success in their chosen district. Television reporters have instant credibility as candidates because of their exposure and appearance of expertise.[9]

Using this operational definition, the LDP's advantage becomes clearer. In Table 6.1, which uses my operational definition, 33 (58.9 percent) LDP new candidates were quality candidates, compared to 25 (18 percent) DPJ newcomers. In SMD races in which it fielded a nonquality candidate, the DPJ won only 12.3 percent (14 out of 114), not far off from the 21.7 percent (five out of 23) won by the LDP's nonquality candidates. In contrast, the LDP (42 percent) and DPJ (48 percent) each won over 40 percent of races in which it ran a quality new candidate.

My emphasis in this chapter, though, is on the importance of candidates with *local-level* experience. Here, too, the LDP has a major advantage. Only approximately 10 percent of DPJ new candidates had held office either as a city mayor or prefectural assembly member, in contrast to more than a quarter of all LDP new candidates.

Statistical analysis of new candidate success (defined as winning an SMD) in the 2000 HR election confirms that the LDP's advantage is in the quality or experience of its candidates.[10] Three findings stand out. First, even controlling for a number of other variables, quality candidates – and, most

---

[9] See links to the supplementary Web site at *www.ethanscheiner.com* for an explanation of why I do not include other careers in the definition.

[10] For details of the statistics, see links to the supplementary Web site at *www.ethanscheiner.com*.

noteworthy, former local office holders – were more likely to win their SMD than non-quality candidates. Based on the results of the statistical analysis, we can predict the likelihood of a given candidate winning a seat. Controlling for a number of other forces that have an impact on the likelihood of victory, on average, DPJ and LDP new candidates had a 19 percent chance of winning their SMDs, but average former local office holders had a 37 percent chance of winning.[11]

Second, new candidates who ran against strong incumbents were less likely to win their seat, but quality new candidates were more likely to win than non-quality candidates, no matter whom they ran against. Nonquality new candidates who ran against either a DPJ or an LDP incumbent had almost no chance (5.7 percent) of winning. Nonquality candidates running in open races had a moderately good (30.1 percent) chance of victory. However, new candidates who were former local office holders and who faced no incumbent had a very good chance of victory, with a probability of victory near 60 percent.

Third, the statistical analysis provides no support for a number of leading alternative hypotheses for opposition failure and LDP success. One such hypothesis I analyze is coordination failure – that is, whether candidates were harmed by competition from members on their own side. For example, for opposition party candidates, coordination failure exists when, in addition to facing an LDP candidate, they also must run against other opposition candidates. In the end, my statistical analysis shows no discernible effect of coordination problems on new candidate outcomes in 2000.

I also control for campaign expenditures in the analysis.[12] Surprisingly, candidates' campaign spending had no discernible effect on their likelihood of success. To speculate, this result may be due primarily to the important role played by organization. It appears that the advantage held by former local office holders is their well-established and mobilizable base of supporters, a huge proportion of whom will vote and get out the vote for their candidate, irrespective of the amount of money spent during the actual campaign period.

Finally, once we control for other variables – in particular, the level of quality or experience held by the new candidate – it becomes clear that LDP candidates acquired no inherent advantage from their party affiliation. Controlling for other variables, LDP candidates were no more likely to win than DPJ new candidates were. New candidates from the LDP were more successful than new candidates from other parties, not because they were from the LDP, but because they had more experience and were higher quality candidates than those who ran from other parties.

---

[11] In determining the probability, I assume that all other variables are equal to their mean value.
[12] Great thanks to Masahiko Asano for sharing his data on campaign expenditures.

This is important. Many have sought to explain opposition failure by the strength of the economy, impressions of opposition incompetence, or supposed qualities of the LDP such as policy flexibility, capacity to run more efficient nomination strategies, and general popularity (see Chapter 2). However, my findings indicate that much of the LDP's advantage in national races stems from its greater ability to recruit better candidates. In this way, the LDP's success in candidate-based races is not unlike Fenno's (1975) argument about the United States, where many voters hated Congress but loved their individual representative. Extended to the Japanese case, it appears that many voters hate the LDP, but – either because they find the representative personally appealing or are mobilized by an organization to do so – continue to cast ballots for their individual LDP Diet member. The problem for the opposition is therefore clear. It simply does not have a sufficient number of quality candidates, in particular experienced local politicians, to make credible challenges in the bulk of the national district races.[13]

Potential Endogeneity?

Undoubtedly, the opposition faced a problem because in many districts it had to run against powerful incumbents, who scared off additional candidates from running. I am unable to control perfectly for this possibility,[14] and it is certainly clear that the "win-ability" of the race must play some role in shaping the ability of parties to find strong candidates to run. Nevertheless, very good reasons remain to believe that the results are accurate and that candidate quality – most noteworthy, former local office holders as candidates – is important to party success.

Especially persuasive is the lack of a correlation between the presence of local politicians or quality candidates and features that should scare them off from running. I examined the statistical correlation between, on one side, a quality candidate or, more specifically, a former local office holder running in the district and, on the other side, campaign spending by the opponents in the district, the presence of an incumbent or major party incumbent running in the district, and opponent success in the district in the previous election. In each case, the correlation was very low, and for DPJ new candidates,

[13] This suggests an unusual problem of coordination failure. The opposition would like to find strong candidates for national office. Many LDP subnational office holders would like to run for and hold national office seats. However, such subnational office holders could only reasonably risk running for national office under the opposition banner if they knew that sufficiently large numbers of other LDP local politicians would also do so and win enough seats to give the opposition a majority. Great thanks to David Laitin for this observation.

[14] I have run a first-cut, two-stage probit model to deal with this endogeneity problem. Even controlling for the "win-ability" of the race, the first-cut model suggests that former local office holders are more likely than non-quality candidates to win. For information on the two-stage probit model, see links to the supplementary Web site at *www.ethanscheiner.com*.

the correlation was usually very close to zero. The lack of impact of win-ability is probably due in large part to Japan's electoral rules under its new system, which makes running against strong SMD incumbents less risky for candidates. SMD candidates can simultaneously appear on their party's PR list. In this way, parties can offer candidates a safety net: Even if they lose their SMD race, they may still be able to win office via the PR route.

Much of the reason for the apparent lack of impact of win-ability on candidacy choices here is probably the newness of the SMD electoral system in Japan. Cox and Katz (2002: 166–7) find that, in the U.S. case, entry by quality challengers is particularly likely immediately after district reappor-tionment. They see the period as optimal for challengers because it offers the greatest amount of time until the next reapportionment (Cox and Katz 2002: 163), but presumably the incumbent's relative lack of established base in the new district in its entirety is important as well. To extrapolate to the Japanese case, challengers had greater reason to test the waters in the first elections under Japan's entirely new electoral *system*.

Moreover, the problem for the opposition was not merely that it could not find a *strong* candidate: In many districts between 1996 and 2003, the leading opposition party ran no one at all. In a number of districts, the party might have had available a local office incumbent or two, whom it could have run in the hopes of drumming up support for the party in the PR race or to start laying the seeds for success in future campaigns in the district. However, according to Japanese election law, when a sitting office holder submits his papers to run for a different office, he automatically loses his existing position, even if the local office holder's seat is not up for reelection for a number of years. Because such a move will immediately cost the party a seat at the local level, it is a major risk for a party with only a small number of office holders at the local level to run any of them in races for higher office (and therefore lose control over the lower office position). In contrast, parties with a larger number of seats at the local level – especially the LDP, which controlled so many subnational-level seats – can more safely afford to run some of their local incumbents in national-level races (even against entrenched incumbents).

OTHER EFFECTS OF SUBNATIONAL WEAKNESS
ON NATIONAL-LEVEL FORTUNES

The Japanese opposition's failure at the local level created three additional problems for opposition parties as they tried to compete at the national level.

Weak Bases in General

First, and most obvious, local-level failure made it dramatically more diffi-cult for the opposition to develop a foundation. The Clientelist/Financially

Centralized system already made top-down party formation especially likely, which harmed the opposition by making parties far more elite-based, with less of a grassroots base. As a result, at the nonelite level there was little energy and excitement generated for the parties (except perhaps by those who felt excitement about the opposition's leaders). Opposition failure in local elections simply exacerbated this problem.

Local Politicians as Campaigners

Second, with few local office holders, Japan's opposition parties lacked the local foot soldiers that all parties need. Ames (1994: 95) argues that local political organizations are key determinants of national-level electoral contests in many countries. In particular, he cites Columbia, Mexico, Venezuela, Italy, and Japan as countries where local politicians are able to use clientelist networks to generate support for national politicians and parties at election time. The problem is made particularly clear by Park in his comments on the advantages local politicians bestow upon parties in Japan:

Local politicians clearly serve as a primary force in national-level electoral campaigns. Securing the cooperation of local politicians is critical to the success of the electoral campaign. Local politicians are specialists in campaigning; they are not only knowledgeable but also willing to engage in campaigning. These politicians can identify the political loyalties of nearly every household in their home territories. And as they are engaged in politics as a career, they can volunteer their time for the campaign. Those in other occupations have to take time off from work to make a serious commitment to campaigning. In addition, as local politicians have their own personal supporters, Diet candidates can use their channels to secure easy access to ordinary voters. (1998b: 76)

In short, by lacking a base of local-level politicians, Japan's opposition was missing a group that is adept at creating citizen–party links and mobilizing voters. And local politicians' advantage in Japan is usually their well-organized, highly mobilizable bases of support, which their party and the party's candidates expect them to muster in national elections. Given the importance of the organized vote in Japan, parties without such a base of local politicians face much greater difficulty.

Concentration of the Vote

Third, the Japanese system provides incentives to develop concentrated bases of support, but opposition parties faced obstacles in their ability to develop them. Japanese campaign laws offer candidates and parties only limited access to television, radio, and print as a way to appeal to voters and, as a result, made it extremely difficult for candidates and parties to campaign on the grounds of broad-based, mass appeals. For years, the Japanese SNTV/MMD electoral system reinforced the effect of campaign laws, as politicians could win seats through the support of relatively concentrated geographical areas, which gave them an incentive to cultivate concentrated bases of support. Because each district in Japan's SNTV/MMD system contained multiple seats, a candidate garnering the bulk of the votes in a relatively small region within the district could win HR office with only a relatively small number of votes and without needing to engage in costly efforts to try to appeal to voters in different parts of the district.

Not surprising, under SNTV/MMD, LDP candidates on average maintained a more geographically concentrated base of support than opposition party candidates.[15] Opposition candidates' inability to develop similarly concentrated bases of support was no doubt due in part to their lack of access to geographically targetable clientelist benefits.

However, their lack of candidates with local political experience also caused problems for opposition parties' ability to develop concentrated bases of support. Very commonly, subnational politicians will represent relatively small geographic areas and presumably will maintain close ties with their constituents from those areas as their base of support in the future. Moreover, with Japan's restrictive campaign laws, local candidates who acquire local political experience are more likely to have built geographically concentrated or limited bases of support.[16] Data on other countries' levels of candidate vote concentration are difficult to come by, but Ames' (1995, 2002) analysis of Brazil provides insights into how such bases might continue to be maintained when local politicians run for national office. Ames finds that in Brazil – another system that, because of its open-list PR electoral system and emphasis on pork barrel, provides candidates an incentive to cultivate concentrated bases of support – large city mayors running for national legislative office maintain geographically concentrated bases of support. Detailed additional data would be needed to conduct a similarly systematic study of the vote bases of former local politicians running for national office in Japan, but my preliminary examination of the Japanese data on vote concentration suggests a similar trend.

Japanese opposition parties are therefore doubly disadvantaged. They cannot afford to waste campaign efforts by making broad appeals that will only appeal to unsubstantial constituencies thinly spread across a large geographical area, and because they have fewer local assembly members than the LDP, they are also less able to attract local, targetable, and concentrated bases of support. Thus the combination of limited campaign advertising

---

[15] This statement is based on my analysis of Miyazaki Appendix data set, which accompanied the JED-M data set (covering elections over the 1958–93 period).

[16] This is especially the case because there are even greater legal restrictions on local candidates' use of broadcast media (Akuto 1996: 317).

options and few local politicians (through whom opposition candidates can campaign) limits the effectiveness of opposition campaigning.

CONCLUSION

By preventing opposition parties from generating a deep pool of office holders at the local level, Clientelist/Financially Centralized systems create obstacles to opposition parties' ability to compete in national-level elections. This is especially the case in Japan, a system where strong candidacies are necessary in order to do well in national parliamentary races.

Even though I do not have detailed data on career backgrounds (such as whether a given new candidate for HR office was a former local office holder) for earlier elections, the Japanese opposition held very few local offices throughout the postwar (Chapter 5). It is therefore reasonable to assume that the Japanese opposition's difficulties in finding quality candidates were prevalent during the pre-1990s period, playing a central role in opposition failure throughout the postwar. Although individual candidacies were critical to success under the SMD portion of Japan's post-1994 mixed-member electoral system, quality candidates must have been even more important under the SNTV/MMD system, which Carey and Shugart (1995) argue encouraged personalistic/nonparty-based political behavior to a far greater degree than SMDs.[17]

These difficulties, though, became more obvious between 1996 and 2003 under the postreform mixed-member electoral system, as opposition failure continued despite many apparent opportunities for success. The opposition continued to fail despite the collapse of the economic bubble, the change in the electoral system, and the emergence of new parties, which consolidated the opposition and should have fostered a broader base of support than previous opposition parties enjoyed. There was a clear constant across the two periods: The Japanese opposition continued to suffer from problems growing out of the Clientelist/Financially Centralized system, the most tangible problem being a failure to develop a local base that could make strong national-level candidacies and national success attainable.

Strong, experienced candidates make the task of winning office markedly easier for any party. The DPJ won a large number of SMDs in cities, especially

---

[17] As noted in Chapter 2, the LDP did not win a majority of the vote after 1963, but LDP seat success appears to have been due very much to the quality of its candidates. Christensen's (2000) research on the SNTV/MMD period indicates that the opposition was often better than the LDP at nominating the "correct" number of candidates and evenly distributing the vote among these candidates, but that the LDP essentially won more votes per competitive candidate (or, as Cox [1996, 1997] puts it, per "winnable seat"). In short, the LDP won more seats because it had more votes for each of its main candidates – no doubt because of their higher "quality." A similar concentration of votes for quality candidates appears to also exist under the postreform system.

when it had quality candidates running. As of the early 2000s, it was still *somewhat* difficult for the opposition to acquire strong candidates in urban areas, but given the weaker organization of LDP-linked networks in urban areas, the lower levels of support for clientelism among urban voters, and the lower levels of dependence of urban local governments on the center, it was usually easier for the opposition to gain local-level strength in cities and therefore find more quality candidates to run for national office in urban regions.

But the opposition was stuck because substantial areas continued to support clientelism and were, naturally, largely impervious and often antagonistic to anti-clientelistic appeals. Nevertheless, when opposition parties had quality candidates, they were able to do well in national-level elections in such areas.[18] However, Japanese rural areas are particularly clientelistic and dependent upon the center, thereby representing the archetypal Clientelist/Financially Centralized case. As a result, these are the single most difficult areas for opposition parties to gain seats in at the local level and develop pools of strong candidacies.

Signs of Improvement

As of 2004, the DPJ was working hard to improve the quality of candidates. In the summer of 2004 – well before it faced another HR election – the party was already attempting to recruit "talented" candidates for all 300 SMDs (*Yomiuri Shinbun*, online, July 13, 2004). Among other things, it began offering new incentives (such as a substantial increase in the stipend it provided its candidates to support their living expenses during their time as DPJ standard bearers) to run for office as a DPJ candidate (*Asahi Shinbun*, online, January 15, 2004). And the party was beginning to close the gap on the LDP in terms of the number of bureaucrats running under its banner (*Asahi Shinbun*, online, November 6, 2003).[19]

Most impressive, the DPJ won the less important 2004 HC election, taking 50 seats to the LDP's 49. As in the 2003 HR election, the DPJ won the largest share of the national PR vote in 2004. Even more important, it won only three fewer (31 to 34) district seats than the LDP. The DPJ's success was due in large part to the party's ability to run a substantial number of quality candidates who defeated LDP incumbents and quality new candidates (Scheiner 2004).

Nevertheless, the DPJ's success in the 2004 HC election was unlikely to carry over to HR elections as much as opposition supporters would hope. HR districts are smaller than in the HC; therefore, the LDP can more easily

---

[18] Moreover, strong SMD candidacies are often thought to help parties win larger numbers of PR votes as well (Mizusaki and Mori 1998).

[19] The DPJ recruited eight former central government bureaucrats to run as new candidates for it in 2003, compared to 12 for the LDP.

provide targeted subsidies to them to maintain support. Also, unlike the HC, where a party need find only one or two strong candidates per prefecture, in the HR with its 300 districts the DPJ needs many more quality candidates, a tough task without a pool of local politicians.

Catch-22

Japan's opposition appears to face a Catch-22. The opposition needs strong local candidates to generate quality challengers for the national elections that determine who takes power. But without strength at the national level, opposition parties face great difficulty finding success at the local level.

As I discuss in greater detail in Chapter 10, the opposition appears to have three potential routes out of this vicious circle. As long as the Clientelist/ Financially Centralized system remains intact, the opposition must hope for further LDP defections at the national level. This situation is highlighted by the words of a staff member in the DPJ's local party organization bureau. When asked what needs to happen for the DPJ to truly succeed, he replied, "The LDP would have to split again."[20] That is, a large group of LDP politicians, compatible with those in the DPJ, would need to split off from the ruling party and link up with the Democrats.

That said, the system could change. In Japan in recent years, there has been widespread talk of a second potential route out of the vicious circle: decentralization or a devolution of financial independence to Japan's subnational units. In light of my analysis, this would dramatically alter voters' and politicians' relationships with the central government and the LDP and most likely would improve opposition parties' chances at the subnational level.

Moreover, as Japan's political economy has changed in recent decades, clientelism has grown increasingly unpalatable to many. Changes on this front, too, may offer a third route out of the vicious circle and have a substantial effect on opposition party fortunes in Japan. It is to this issue that I turn in Chapters 7 and 8.

[20] Interview, February 1, 1999.

7

Political Economy Changes and Their Impact on Party Systems

Comparative Analysis

The combination of clientelism and centralization of governmental finances is not sufficient to explain opposition failure at the national level. New parties in three other Clientelist/Financially Centralized systems – Italy, Austria, and Mexico – developed into solid competitors in their respective party systems.

Mexico is different from the other Clientelist/Financially Centralized cases. Presidential systems such as Mexico's offer an opportunity for success to any party with a popular individual candidate. Moreover, it is difficult to find adequate comparisons in the other cases to the high levels of politically motivated violence inflicted upon many who supported the opposition in Mexico. There is also an important difference between Austria and the other cases. Austria's PR electoral system removes the importance of having strong candidates. For this reason, despite the limits placed on opposition parties' success at the local level, even non-ruling parties have an opportunity to do well at the national level if they put forth a sufficiently popular message (although, without a base of local office holders, non-ruling parties are hindered in many other ways). Nevertheless, for my model, the problem of the success of new parties in Italy remains. In Italy (as well as Austria), a powerful backlash against clientelism fueled new party growth and a solid challenge to the ruling regime (Kitschelt 1995a).

Kitschelt argues that in the wealthier, more international global economy of recent decades, we ought to see a decline in support for patronage-oriented parties: "A highly educated, independently-minded electorate in the 1980s and 1990s perceives clientelist networks as a fount of corruption and lack of fairness. . . . [P]rivate enterprise associates clientelism and corruption with an increase in the cost of doing business and has been more opposed to it as international competition has increased" (1997: 141).

Indeed, Kitschelt's analysis describes recent events in Italy quite well and suggests that the changes to the Italian system look quite a bit like those occurring in other systems that had held little party competition. The *Uncommon Democracies* project (Pempel 1990) studied four cases of

146

longtime one-party democracy: Italy, Israel, Sweden, and Japan. To that group, it is reasonable to add a fifth case: Austria. Although, as I discussed in Chapter 1, Austria was not a case of *one*-party dominance, it was a clear case of opposition-party failure, as the two leading parties (in particular, the Social Democratic Party) jointly controlled the government for the bulk of the postwar period. In all these cases – *except Japan* – party competition emerged. Indeed, changes in each country's political economy appear to have played a major role in opposition party success. Italy, Austria, and Israel all maintained highly clientelist systems, and Kitschelt's prediction of the decline of parties maintaining such systems was borne out in those cases. In addition, the Swedish system's fusion of economic and political power was functionally equivalent to much of the governmental power exerted in clientelist systems so that, when faced with economic downturn, it generated a backlash against the ruling party similar to those faced in clientelist systems.

In this chapter, I discuss how changes in the political economies of these four countries – Italy, Austria, Israel, and Sweden – altered the party systems within them in recent decades. I place special emphasis on Italy and Austria, as both, like Japan, were dominated by clientelism for decades and, only in the 1980s and 1990s, saw a backlash against the clientelist system lead to the rise of serious alternatives to the existing regime. In Chapter 8, I consider why a similar backlash and political economic changes in Japan did not inject greater competition into its party system.

ITALY

Italy was dominated throughout the bulk of the pre-1990s postwar era by the Christian Democratic Party, which led a long series of coalition governments. Patronage, government favors, and clientelist exchange formed the cornerstone of Italy's political-economic system. The DC's base was an alliance of big business, small business, state employees, and the rural south. Although flare-ups within this unwieldy alliance did occur, the regime used the heavy distribution of pork and jobs to prevent serious conflicts between business and labor.

Italy found economic success in the early postwar period, in particular during the economic "miracle" of 1950–63. During that time, the country's growth rate doubled; in the 1960s, it was second only to West Germany's among European nations. A critical part of the economy's success was the large reserve of unemployed or underemployed workers, who were utilized flexibly. In particular, when industry required an infusion of large numbers of relatively "unskilled" hands, it absorbed much of the large agricultural workforce. Over 80 percent of industrial output came from the north of the country, which continually drew additional labor from the south (Hine 1993: 35–41). In 1951, 44 percent of labor was employed in agriculture; between 1951 and 1963, industry's share of the labor force grew from 29 to

40 percent and unemployment dropped from roughly 9 to less than 3 percent. Especially critical, the reserve labor force allowed investment and output to grow without major wage hikes.

Economic growth was export driven, and public investment – in particular, funding for the modernization of the steel and energy/petrochemicals industries – played a critical role in export success. Many of these industries were state-owned enterprises, each providing numerous patronage opportunities. And clear socioeconomic divisions emerged during this period as workers in the private sector resented the job protection and generous funding that public-sector companies received.

As labor grew stronger and more politically protected, wages rose, and investment became more likely to go abroad. Even though economic growth continued after a brief setback, Italy never again saw growth like that of the 1950s and early 1960s. In the 1970s, economic performance was poor, and wage costs continued as a major issue. During economic slowdowns, pork barrel spending was the primary tool used to attempt to kick-start the economy. In the 1980s, there was significant growth, but also constant concern over the inflation and high public debt that grew out of the massive pork spending (Hine 1993: 42–51).

Clientelist practices – not just patronage – were central to most political and economic relationships. Graziano points to survey data indicating that Italian partisanship was typically based on instrumental, clientelistic considerations, especially in southern Italy (1978: 321). Throughout the postwar period, the government was careful to provide protection through various forms of patronage to the DC's major clienteles. In exchange, the party was guaranteed a substantial set of votes. In the 1970s and 1980s, working in part through corrupt networks of power, the DC ran up huge government deficits to maintain its base in the rural south of the country, even as corporations in Italy's more urbanized north were highly successful in areas such as fashion and machine tools. Much of the patronage was simply public jobs, as over half of all Italian civil service positions required no competitive examinations (Pempel 1998) and the DC was able to use patronage of this kind to lock support into place.

Beginning in the late 1980s, a number of indicators demonstrated that Italy's economy was stronger. Particularly important was the increased productivity of numerous small private-sector manufacturers that had struck deals with labor (Pempel 1998: 130). Data compiled in 1981 shows that employment in large manufacturing firms fell by 13.5 percent over the previous decade; there was little change in employment in medium-sized firms; and employment in small firms (under 100 employees) grew by 11.5 percent (Hine 1993: 54). The success of small and medium-sized firms was in part the result of the DC's efforts, which served to maintain the firms in the DC's larger base for a while. As Woods writes, "In the north, the DC ... supported economic and administrative policies which benefited small and medium-sized businesses; even though it . . . meant maintaining a relatively large and economically inefficient service sector of shopkeepers" (1992: 63). As a result, although the economy grew, public debt was massive, rising to more than the total Italian GNP (Salvati 1995).

Although the north and its small and medium-sized businesses played a major part, the south was especially central to the success of Italy's economic system and the success of the DC. The Italian model of economic development was founded on low wages. As Allum explains: "The South's position in this system is clear. On the one hand, it acted as the privileged supplier of cheap labour; . . . on the other, it was a reservoir of votes for government parties, and in the first place the DC" (1981: 317). In the south, the DC controlled all "channels" through which grants and other financial sources flowed and used this to maintain its own power in the region. The south also held a position of advantage within the bureaucracy. People who had good options in the private sector were less likely to enter the civil service, but those from the poorer areas had fewer alternatives. Not surprising, therefore, 60 percent of senior civil servants were from the south. And "once having joined the civil service, recruits [were] rapidly socialized into a system conditioned by several decades of solidly southern domination" (Hine 1993: 239).

The south certainly benefited from the relationship. Northern regions paid roughly half of all Italian taxes, but for every 100 lire they paid into the central government, they got back only 25 lire in the form of governmental side-payments. In contrast, southern regions got back roughly 80 percent of every lire they paid the central government. The DC benefited hugely from the arrangement as well. Without its success in the south, the DC would have had difficulty gaining the type of dominance that it did. Perhaps more important, without the south, the DC would have had great difficulty maintaining its power later as the political economy of the rest of the country changed.

Over time, pressures for change exerted themselves in the Italian system. In addition to old dilemmas surrounding, among other things, high public debt, controversy over the following issues plagued the system beginning in the 1970s: the appropriate degree of government regulation of the labor market through wage-indexation, redundancy legislation, and social-security costs; the misallocation of resources from direct intervention in the manufacturing sector through state-holdings companies and from indirect intervention through extensive industrial subsidies and public procurements; and the very ad hoc (and clearly discretionary) redistributive mechanisms inherent in regional transfers, subsidies for low-productivity public-service employment, and fragmented welfare and pensions' networks (Hine 1993: 57).

International pressures for change also increased from the 1970s on, with many concerned about Italy's eligibility to be a full part of the European monetary union. Although it joined the European Exchange-Rate Mechanism in

1978, Italy restricted the degree to which it allowed its currency to float. However, the weakening of the competitive position of Italian industry (in part due to labor market policies) lowered foreign confidence in the lire, in turn discouraging foreign direct investment in Italy and encouraging capital flight out of the country. Over the same period, because of huge numbers of incompatible competing claims on the government and the immense spending on pork, budget deficits increased, forcing up interest rates and therefore penalizing domestic industry.

The European Community's Single Market Program added further problems for Italy because it required members to phase out much state assistance to industry that came in the form of subsidies, access to special credit, and tax concessions (Hine 1993: 58). As Hine explains:

All these pressures made many in Italy very aware of a variety of structural bottlenecks to future development. These lay in the labour market, in industrial structure, and, most importantly of all, in the nature of the state. The capacity of the Italian state to absorb resources that it used inefficiently – in the health service, education, transport, and public administration – was an increasingly acute problem. The divergent paths of productivity growth between the public and private sectors were difficult to ignore, but difficult to correct. (Hine 1993: 58)

Much of the problem was the way linkages between citizens and parties had been established. The parties benefited from the population shifts of the 1950s and 1960s because no other institutions were prepared to absorb and mobilize the new urban residents. However, after the relationships between parties and new urban voters were established, they reinforced the ad hoc and piecemeal nature of Italy's political economy, making more coherent, universalistic policy far more difficult. As Woods writes:

The network of particularistic interests and individualistic relations, a fundamental feature of clientele societies, undermines the aggregative capacity of political institutions. In Italy, clientelism contributed to the breakdown in the relationship in as much as it provided an incentive for fragments of larger groups to form and seek out their own particularistic contacts and "entitlements." Such an environment did not provide fertile ground for neo-corporatist relationships to develop, and instead a kind of "chaotic pluralism" emerged which the parties have had a hard time dealing with. (1992: 68)

Hine explains that even though the northeast, where much of growth had occurred, was traditionally the core of DC strength, economic and social change gradually pushed the DC away from urban centers and out to the rural periphery (1993: 82). Voters' continued need for clientelist benefits in the south maintained the DC's support there much longer.

All these problems laid the foundations for public outcry. Although revelations of massive corruption played a major part, divisions growing out of the changes in the political economy also played a critical role. Voters decried not just the corruption but the waste and inefficiency of the clientelist system in Italy. Parties such as the Northern League were able to tap into this frustration and gain significant ground at the polls.

Much has been made of cultural differences between Italy's regions, but socioeconomic differences were critical as well. Woods suggests that the regional leagues were an "epiphenomenal manifestation of the significant structural changes that have taken place in Italian society since the 1950s, which have shifted the locus of economic development, political identification and legitimation to regional units" (1992: 57).

The clientelist system came under fire as socioeconomic conditions changed when northern economic and social modernization created a middle class that was opposed to clientelism (even though many within it benefited from public-sector jobs and subsidies), while the more underdeveloped south remained dependent on the patronage system (Woods 1992: 440–1). As Kitschelt explains, much of the attractiveness of the Northern League in Italy was its attention to the corruption and inefficiency of the partocratic state and party machines (1995a: 175).

Bull explains that "the coalition between the Ministry of Finance and the Southern regions [maintained] numerical superiority over the Northern regions.... The new federalism advocated by the Northern League must be viewed in the context of this increasing frustration and sense of impotence on the part of the richest half of the country" (1994: 78). There were substantial differences between the bases of the old parties and those challenging the system. Residents of the northern areas, where much of the Italian opposition emerged, are on average wealthier, with higher levels of education and greater access to modern economic resources than those in the south (Woods 1992: 71–2). Not surprising, supporters of the Northern League tended to be better educated and younger than those of Italy's more "traditional" parties (Kitschelt 1995a: 193).

While the Northern League was gaining strength, the DC lost nearly all the support and seat strength it had maintained in the north, northeast, and center but for some time was able to hold on because the south controlled at least one third of all the seats in the country. Even as it weakened everywhere else, the DC clung to its base in the south, the area that most continued to benefit from clientelist arrangements in countless forms such as subsidies and public jobs (Gundle and Parker 1996: 5; Waters 1994). But with its base so weakened, when corruption scandals mounted in the early 1990s, the party imploded. By the 1994 election, the DC no longer existed and, after the election, a new government emerged, led in part by the Northern League that sought the demise of the clientelist system.

AUSTRIA

Austria was one of the top postwar economic performers in Europe. The system was founded first and foremost on a large public sector and close cooperation between its major interest groups. As Lauber explains, four elements were particularly central: (1) a commitment to hard-currency policy and trade liberalization; (2) promotion of investment and savings; (3) depoliticization of incomes policy; and (4) use of deficit spending to stabilize demand during recession (1996b: 127). This last feature – deficit spending – is particularly noteworthy, as one of Austria's more substantial problems, especially from the 1970s, was its large budget deficits.

The Social Democratic Party and the Austrian People's Party dominated Austrian politics throughout the postwar era. One or the other was in every cabinet throughout the period, and the two shared cabinet control for roughly three out of the first six decades after the end of the war. Most striking, the SPÖ either shared the government or held it by itself for all but four years between 1945 and 1999. The SPÖ core constituency was blue-collar workers, whereas that of the ÖVP's was the self-employed and farmers (Müller 1996a, 1996b.) At first, both were ideological and programmatic parties, but over time they increasingly reached out to voters through public-sector patronage, public housing, and industrial protection that were provided in exchange for support for the parties (Kitschelt 1994b).

Katzenstein explains that in Austria parties were active not merely during campaign periods but between elections as well, penetrating political interest groups and the state bureaucracy (1978: 124). Stirnemann depicts the parties' behavior as follows: "The quasi total organization of society by the parties has given rise to an almost consummate patronage system. The political parties enjoy the right to make proposals for very many not even indirectly political posts reaching far into the business world" (1989: 411). For years, the Austrian Freedom Party acted as a vehement critic of this patronage, but as long as the economy was good, the party found little success (Stirnemann 1989: 411).

The government's big budget deficits were of concern to Austrians for some time. The fear was that the government was overspending in maintaining its active and expensive public sector. As the 1980s moved on, the public sector faltered, and it was widely perceived that deficits were causing a drag on the more successful or productive private sector. In the late 1980s, concerns deepened, and many Austrians pushed for substantial privatization and tax reform, as well as a general restructuring of the public sector. In addition, roughly half of Austria's GDP was produced in sectors sheltered from competition (transportation, telecommunications, banking and insurance, and the marketing of agricultural commodities). In the late 1980s and early 1990s, public outcry fostered steps to increase competition in these areas, but government response was limited (Lauber 1996b: 138–41).

Concerns over the government's failure to act further on these issues and the FPÖ's willingness to raise them helped trigger a backlash against the state and its dominant parties, whereby voters increasingly turned their backs on the ruling parties (Kitschelt 1995a: 180–4). Diverse social strata became available for populist appeals challenging the established parties. As state-owned companies grew even less efficient and were perceived to strain the economy, those finding success in the private sector sought to end the clientelist state. In addition, despite state intervention, the declining state-run businesses forced restructuring (layoffs) on numerous blue-collar workers. By pushing greater market liberalization and attacking clientelism, the FPÖ could tap into the support of both the successful in the private sector and the unsuccessful blue-collar class that in the past had supported the SPÖ. Kitschelt finds that supporters of the FPÖ were particularly libertarian and highly educated and that blue-collar workers were especially likely to support the FPÖ (1995a: 193).

Even though the FPÖ also appeared to appeal to the more xenophobic and racist elements in Austrian society, the party was not merely a one-note right-wing party. It was undergirded by anti-clientelist principles. As Kitschelt writes, like the Northern League in Italy, the FPÖ expresses "the sentiments of a 'populist' antistatist segment of the electorate whose crucial common denominator is the alienation from the incumbent political elites in parties and public administration, and a generalized disaffection with the established channels of patronage-driven and clientelistic interest intermediation" (1995a: 160).

Beginning in 1986, FPÖ electoral success began to increase at the expense of the two dominant parties. In 1983, the party won just under 5 percent of the vote and 12 seats. In 1986, it won nearly 10 percent of the vote and 18 seats. In addition, it cut into the number of votes and seats taken by the SPÖ and ÖVP. By 1999, the FPÖ was on equal footing at around 28 percent of the vote and 52 seats (out of 183) with the ÖVP, and just behind the SPÖ's 33 percent of the vote and 65 seats.[1] Most striking, in 1999, the FPÖ/ÖVP coalition knocked the SPÖ out of power. Intraparty tensions got in the way of greater FPÖ victories, both within the government and in the 2002 election, but its mark had been made. After the 2002 election, the SPÖ was still out of power, and, for the first time since 1966, it ran second to the ÖVP in both seats and votes.

ISRAEL

In Israel from the 1930s until 1977, Labor (and its earlier iterations) was the dominant party, and its leader was consistently the head of the government.

In the 1950s, the party made a special effort to solidify its base of support to counter any advantages that the right wing might be able to gain in the economically distressed periphery. The party focused on the allocation of resources to communities loyal to it. By and large, until the 1960s, its

[1] For Austrian electoral results, see Müller (1996b) and *www-public.rz.uni-duesseldorf. de/~nordsiew/indexe.html.*

machines' primary task was channeling demands from Israeli citizens to the Labor government, and the government used the distribution of public jobs and housing to respond to these demands (Sheffer 1978: 66–81). As Shalev describes it, "[v]oters' personal indebtedness for distributional advantages like housing and employment was evidently integral to . . . success in instilling political loyalty" (1990: 107). Israel was founded on a strong central government. Along with the party's own bureaucracies, the public bureaucracies actively supported Labor politicians, "and the central government dominated every major interest group in society" (Sheffer 1978: 66).

Over time, however, the increased success and differentiation of the economy became Labor's undoing. At the same time that Labor had depended on asserting control through social and economic dependence on the party, economic growth helped big business grow in leaps and bounds. Similarly, previously dependent Arab groups grew more affluent and educated. The result was a "breakdown of clan-based patronage politics" (Shalev 1990: 119). Obviously, in a country like Israel with many serious religious and foreign policy divisions, it is difficult to pinpoint a single issue that by itself can bring about dominance or decline of a party. Nevertheless, it was clear by 1977 that numerous groups sought to eliminate what they saw as wasteful and somewhat unfair distributive practices, and Labor's undoing was in large part due to this effort. Labor lost the 1977 election and was replaced by a coalition government led by the Likud Party, which remained in power or competitive with Labor for the ensuing decades.

SWEDEN

The fourth case, Sweden, is a classic corporatist system, with a small number of vertically integrated interest associations (especially business and labor). The foundation of the Social Democratic Party regime was its Red-Green alliance between labor and agriculture. Farmers were well subsidized and protected against foreign competitors. Workers received public-sector jobs and unemployment protection (Esping-Andersen 1990). Later the SAP also focused on creating ties between blue- and white-collar labor. Although mostly domestically owned, very little business was nationalized, and corporate taxes were kept low. The SAP used this formula to maintain its dominance from 1933 until 1976, and then again from 1982 to 1991.

SAP success was premised on a positive sum formula, in which most groups benefited. As time passed, however, the beneficiaries of the system of public support and involvement became fewer in number. As Esping-Andersen explains:

By 1974–5, the economy was in acute imbalance; public expenditures grew tremendously as did wages and, of course, taxation. And with the onset of international economic crisis after 1973, the government's chief concern came to be focused on maintaining full employment. The means available for maintaining full employment were limited to the absorptive capacity of the active manpower programs, expansion of public sector employment (in welfare state services), and industrial subsidies. The government did succeed in retaining full employment but at enormous public budgetary costs. (1990: 53)

Government spending was already very high, indeed, the highest in the industrialized world. And public employment in Sweden more than doubled between 1960 and 1975 (Pempel 1998: 31).

As larger numbers of voters were forced to sacrifice more and more for these programs without gaining the same benefits as in previous years, unhappiness with the system grew. In 1976, the SAP lost power. In the aftermath, public policies and institutions actually changed relatively little, and in 1982 the party returned to power. However, over the 1980s, Sweden's exports lost competitiveness, and the policy of maintaining high wages in the public sector caused economic problems as well as resentment by more "productive" private-sector workers toward public-sector employees. Centralized wage bargaining began to break down in the early 1980s. Ultimately, large groups that had previously benefited from the SAP's policy profile lost confidence in the regime. A non-SAP coalition came into power in the early 1990s, reducing public spending and public-sector employment, and slashed corporatist arrangements and centralized wage negotiation institutions.

CONCLUSION

Changes in countries' political economies tend to be followed by changes in their party systems. These four cases are only a few examples of a general trend. In three of them, clientelism served to hold together parties' bases of support, but once political economic changes caused the economy to become more zero-sum, fissures developed and resistance to the clientelist-based system intensified. The result in many countries – in particular Italy and Austria – was party change.

8

Parallel Party Systems

*Political Economy Changes and the Limits
to Anti-Clientelist Appeals in Japan*

After seeing the rise of an anti-clientelist backlash in Italy and Austria, and the accompanying success of previously uncompetitive parties in those countries (Chapter 7), the question becomes why no such backlash penetrated and found success in Japan.

In reality, there *was* a similar backlash, which *did* help Japan's opposition, but it only occurred in particular parts of the country. In Japan, a divide emerged between groups that benefited from and groups that were harmed by the clientelist system and the pork barrel and protections that went with it. This division is most clearly evident in the differences between the urban and the rural areas of the country and led to the development in Japan of what might be called two parallel party systems: a one-party dominant system in rural areas and a competitive system in urban areas.

Although certain depressed urban regions may also support clientelism, the simplest rule of thumb is that rural areas support the clientelist structure, as a result of their lower education and skill levels – making people there less flexible in the face of threatened changes in the labor market – as well as the inefficient agricultural sector's general dependence on governmental subsidies and transfers of money for public works. By and large, voters in urban areas appeared to oppose clientelism and the features accompanying it. Indeed, in the 2000 and 2003 House of Representatives elections, the leading opposition party, the Democratic Party of Japan, actively campaigned on cutting public works and, in general, attacking the pork-driven LDP economic policy. The DPJ did extremely well in cities, especially in proportional representation races.[1]

---

[1] To remind the reader, beginning in 1996, Japan began utilizing in the HR a mixed-member system that combined proportional representation seats with single member districts.

For details on all of the statistical analysis discussed in this chapter, see the links at *www. ethanscheiner.com*. Tremendous thanks to Guillermo Rosas and Orit Kedar for their advice on portions of the statistical analysis and to Steven Reed, who provided much of the electoral data.

In 1996–2003 Japan, however, the regions most supportive of the clientelist state also had sufficient political clout – in particular, in the number of seats they held and the way these seats were allocated – to prevent greater success by parties that campaigned against the clientelist system and the pork, protections, and regulations accompanying it. Rural areas held approximately one third of all seats in Japan (with each SMD allocated to the plurality vote winner), effectively allowing party competition to occur for, at most, roughly two thirds of all seats to the country's Lower House of parliament.[2]

This chapter offers detailed empirical analysis of Japan's urban–rural split. Japan began the postwar era as a heavily rural society and economy, and, through clientelist exchange, the LDP was able to dominate the politics of the era. Over time, Japan became increasingly urbanized, altering much of the country's political economy and hindering the effectiveness of clientelist practices in many areas.[3] Indeed, changes occurred in Japan's political economy that were similar to the changes felt in countries such as Italy and Austria, and, as I demonstrate in this chapter, just as in Italy and Austria, the changes in Japan greatly impacted the country's party system. In many ways, my discussion here is similar to Pempel (1998) and Rosenbluth (1996), who emphasize the role of political economic changes in shaping the new forms taken by Japan's party system in the last decade of the twentieth century. It is especially close to Rosenbluth's in its emphasis on the importance of domestic institutions in maintaining LDP control and holding off changes in clientelist and protectionist policies.

But my use of data is different. Even though Pempel and Rosenbluth both examine macro-level trends and introduce useful anecdotal evidence, neither offers systematic empirical analysis of politicians and voters to bolster fully their claims linking Japan's political economy to its party system. I add onto and test their analyses by including a more systematic empirical dimension: First, through an analysis of the policy positions and appeals of national-level Japanese legislators and candidates in the mid-1990s, I demonstrate the greater emphasis rural and LDP politicians placed on appeals linked to clientelism. Second, I use survey data to indicate how clientelist voters were more likely to support the LDP, whereas anti-clientelist voters tended to

---

[2] Party competition was also less likely in some depressed urban areas that supported and benefited from government favors and protections.

[3] Arguments that focus on the urban–rural divide may appear to tread on unsteady ground because they give the appearance of using modernization logic (e.g., Huntington 1968), which links clientelism to early stages of socioeconomic and political development. As Kitschelt correctly argues, the problem with the "developmentalist" account is that it cannot explain the persistence of clientelism in advanced democracies such as Italy and Austria (2000: 857). However, my argument is not that low levels of socioeconomic or political development are necessary for clientelism, but rather that under certain conditions voters will be particularly supportive of clientelism and resist efforts to give it up.

support Japan's new parties. Third, I present electoral data from the 1996–2003 Japanese HR elections that indicate how these policy appeals and voter responses manifested themselves in electoral outcomes that favored the LDP and disadvantaged the opposition.

I find that Japan's traditional parties – especially the LDP and SDP[4] – and their supporters held policy positions that supported the clientelist system and ran counter to views held by a large proportion of residents of urban areas. In contrast, Japan's new parties and their supporters tended to favor chipping away at or eliminating the clientelist system. This analysis indicates that urban areas were the prime battleground between the LDP and opposition parties, largely because of the presence of many urban voters who hold views antithetical to Japan's clientelist system. It also suggests that future prospects are bleak for opposition parties in areas, which make up a large proportion of HR seats, that are more supportive of clientelism.

BACKGROUND ON JAPAN'S POLITICAL ECONOMY

Throughout the first few decades of the postwar period, Japan's economy was founded on carefully crafted policies of insulation. The Japanese government especially sought to protect and incubate manufacturing firms that, with sufficient time, money, and guidance, could become internationally competitive. Most noteworthy, the Foreign Exchange and Control Law (FECL) and Japanese Foreign Investment Law (FIL) imposed very strict quotas on the use of foreign money for imports. With the exception of explicitly delineated cases allowed by the government, the FECL prohibited all foreign exchange. Capital restrictions constrained foreign takeovers and the capital market remained under Japanese government control (Pempel 1998: 49–52).

Japanese domestic markets were almost wholly protected from competitive imports in areas such as agriculture and basic materials, with small businesses also well taken care of. Despite their inefficiency, farmers and small businesses were protected by the insulated capital market, and numerous restrictions were placed on foreign direct investment and imports. Moreover, farmers' subsidies kept agricultural prices high, allowing even inefficient farms to profit. Japan's Large-Scale Store Law gave small shops and firms the ability to prevent large stores from competing against them in their local markets, and, through the Fiscal Investment and Loan Program (FILP), the government channeled generous low-interest loans to small and medium-sized businesses.

Emerging from a devastating war, it was important for Japan to develop and maintain its own sources of goods. But insulating policies were not

---

[4] For most of the postwar period, the Socialists were the Japan Socialist Party, but they renamed themselves the Social Democratic Party in 1996.

designed merely for economic security. The LDP sought electoral success through the support it gave to a variety of groups, especially large firms, professionals, small subcontractors and distributors, and farmers. As larger firms grew internationally competitive, Japan's tremendous growth created a positive-sum economy, in which it was possible for the LDP to continue to support all of its major constituents. Pempel writes: "as long as exports brought high growth, economics and politics reinforced each other: there was little political incentive for government to dismantle protectionist barricades or for economic sectors to view their political interests as dramatically at odds" (1998: 63). For example, large businesses benefited from Japan's economic growth and maintained close ties to small contractors and distributors, who depended on protectionist measures and insulation.

Naturally, not everyone favored such policies. Militant labor (in the late 1950s) and pollution victims (in the 1960s and 1970s) fought the LDP-led system. However, labor was pacified and even brought to see business success as in its interest, as many workers came to support the party that ruled during the miracle economy. Moreover, by spending money raised through deficit financing on favors to its clients but also on pork barrel more broadly, the LDP was able to quiet the alarm raised over poor environmental conditions and even expand its electoral base. In this way, the LDP sought to identify itself as a catchall party and found little opposition from key socioeconomic blocs.

The LDP's ability to maintain such disparate groups' support depended upon the insulation of Japan's market and high economic growth, but neither could be sustained. Perhaps most important, over the late 1980s and early 1990s, Japan's economic bubble burst. As time passed, pressures prompted changes in the economic superpower. Slowed economic growth and increased pressures from foreign countries and firms increased the need for trade-offs between the different groups supporting the LDP.

These trade-offs divided Japanese business. Even though many large firms were internationally competitive, others – in sectors such as construction, food services, pharmaceuticals, chemicals, and financial services – were less so in the more market-liberal and unprotected world. Supporting noncompetitive sectors took its toll on the Japanese economy, especially as the Japanese government injected large amounts of public money into propping up these groups. For a number of years, Japanese budgets had been well balanced, but by 1995 – even with substantial new consumption taxes – the government's continued support of noncompetitive industries led it to finance more than one quarter of the budget through borrowing. By 1995, debt service was 18.6 percent (Pempel 1998: 147).

Especially in the 1980s and 1990s, many large firms determined that they no longer benefited from Japan's system of regulations (especially cartel regulation) and no longer wished to contribute to the LDP's campaign

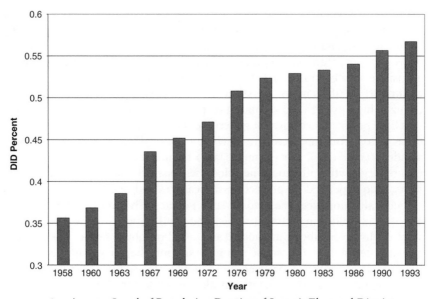

FIGURE 8.1 Average Level of Population Density of Japan's Electoral Districts
Source: Horiuchi and Kohno's Japanese Election District-level Census Data.

coffers.[5] Also, the movement of many Japanese to the cities over the years
meant that fewer benefited from protective agricultural policies, and many
individuals came to define their economic interests according to their position as consumers (Rosenbluth 1996). Figure 8.1 indicates the average level
of population density (DID), a common measure of urban-ness, in Japan's
electoral districts between 1958 and 1993. Over time, Japan had grown
substantially more urban,[6] and domestic big business and consumer groups
pressured the government to liberalize the economy, especially loosening restrictions on the distribution system – in which small businesses controlled
the distribution of goods in Japan, thereby maintaining high prices and keeping out large stores that might bring prices down – and agricultural imports.
Meanwhile, the business community split over (among other things) deregulation, exchange rate policies, taxation, fiscal stimulation through government procurement, and overall protection and oligopolization of utilities,
banks, the insurance industry, and holding companies (Pempel 1998: 166).

The Japanese government gradually enacted changes. As pressures from
abroad grew in the 1970s, Japan partly eased quotas on beef and citrus imports. Similarly, it liberalized its financial markets substantially, in particular
with the 1980 revision of the FECL and the deregulation of the corporate

---

[5] For example, when the LDP lost power in 1993, Keidanren, Japan's leading big business
organization, cut its donations to the party.

[6] Great thanks to Yusaku Horiuchi and Masaru Kohno for sharing their DID data.

bond market. Especially beginning in the late 1980s, the government began weakening the Large-Scale Store Law and reducing the tax breaks given to small-store owners. And, even before then, the government had begun devoting a smaller share of the budget to such businesses (Rosenbluth 1996). Then, especially in the 1990s, the government moved gradually toward liberalizing imports.

Many of Japan's biggest changes occurred in the financial sector. Consolidations occurred and newcomers – domestic and foreign – entered Japan's financial and capital markets. Foreign firms entered the telecommunications, semiconductor, autos and auto-parts, pharmaceuticals, and machinery markets. Foreign direct investment increased, and many Japanese firms moved production overseas.

While these changes occurred, there was little policy consensus within the LDP. Pempel (1998) explains that the LDP was split over how to respond to pressures for liberalization: Gradually it began to liberalize, shifting burdens from urban workers to those in agriculture and small business. The LDP had for years held on to many groups' support through protectionist policies, but as formerly loyal clients of the LDP lost government protection, they became less loyal to the party. Unwavering support for the party no longer made sense for now-unprotected groups. Linked to this trend, the number of unaffiliated or floating voters increased, and it became far more difficult to mobilize many previously loyal support groups. Already facing this negative trend, the LDP risked losing its entire base if it caved in fully to globalization and economic pressures. The rural (and, typically, agricultural) vote was a key to LDP success. Turning on its major constituency would cause electoral trouble for the LDP.

So, despite a number of changes, LDP policies continued to protect some of the country's least economically competitive electoral constituencies. In earlier years, government intervention focused on making larger firms internationally competitive. In the 1990s, more effort was spent on propping up declining industries. Between 1992 and 2000, the government passed eight fiscal packages, which together were worth over $1 trillion and were loaded with pork barrel construction projects and assistance for small and medium-sized firms (Pempel 2000). The government also sought to defray the costs of a massive bad loan crisis, extended the deadline for ending unlimited insurance on savings deposits, and was slow to implement planned deregulation.

Public works spending was as much a part of LDP policy as ever. In the 1960s, Japanese public works spending was roughly twice the average in other major industrial countries. In 1997, such spending was roughly three to four times the percentage of GDP that was spent in the major economies of Europe (Seaman 2003). The post-1993 makeup of the LDP's elite and support base continued to be rural. Probably most important, the organized vote system at the core of LDP electoral success was made possible through seemingly endless clientelist exchanges of governmental funding for party and candidate support.

URBAN–RURAL DIFFERENCES

Clearly, Japan's clientelist political economy remained in place, but pressures to alter the system had made their mark. As a result of the rift that developed between clientelist/protectionist and anti-clientelist/internationalist groups, divisions between parties and their supporters also emerged. A backlash within the Japanese party system emerged against clientelist business-as-usual.

These divisions are most neatly illustrated by the differences between rural areas, which tended to be dominated by clientelism-supporting organizations, politicians and voters, and anti-clientelist urban areas. Utilizing Kitschelt's (2000) procedural definition of clientelism (see my Chapters 1 and 3) makes measuring clientelist practices difficult. In part, I focus on the LDP's protection of certain industries and agriculture.[7] What is more useful from the perspective of Kitschelt's definition, I pay particular attention to public works and subsidies, which tend to be disbursed on a discretionary, case-by-case basis by the ruling party and the bureaucracy – often in exchange for votes and financial support – and are useful "tracers" of clientelism.

Overall, the Japanese opposition tended to do poorly in elections in the countryside but relatively well in cities (see Chapter 2). Why would such strong differences exist between urban and rural areas? One could point to culture, noting the traditional values held by many in the countryside, but from the perspective of my argument in this book, the socioeconomic/demographic differences between urban and rural Japanese are at least as important. Using public opinion survey data from the Japan Elections and Democracy Study (JEDS), which was conducted before and after the 1996 HR election, we can see that on nearly every measure urban voters had characteristics that suggest they were more likely to reject the clientelist system underpinning Japan's politics (Table 8.1.) In rural areas, average age was higher and education levels were lower, suggesting less labor flexibility. Such voters tend to be more dependent on traditional economic sectors and more reliant on the government during economic downturn. Urban businesses had more employees, suggesting greater international competitiveness and

---

[7] I categorize a wide array of policies as clientelistic, but admittedly many – in particular, regulatory and protectionist policies – do not fit Kitschelt's (2000) definition perfectly. The definition holds that a policy is not clientelist if it is applied universally, even to those who might not support the party. For example, because agricultural protection applies to all farmers of a particular type, irrespective of which party a given farmer supports, it is not necessarily clientelistic in Kitschelt's sense. However, regulatory and protectionist policies are clearly linked with the benefits used in the exchanges between the LDP government and organized bases of support that fit the definition of clientelism much more neatly.

TABLE 8.1 *Average Characteristics of Japanese Broken Down by Region and Party Affiliation*

Characteristic (scale in parenthesis)	Urban-ness of Residence			Party Supported in PR		
	Rural	Mixed	Urban	LDP	Old Left	New Parties
Age (20–87)	51.29	49.97	46.57	54.64	51.60	48.38
Education (1–7)	3.14	3.34	3.95	3.23	3.37	3.62
Pro-agricultural liberalization (1–4)	2.65	2.71	2.79	2.61	2.60	2.92
Non-clientelistic (1–4)	2.25	2.31	2.41	2.22	2.33	2.35
Anti-reform (0–10)	5.99	5.86	5.18	6.59	4.84	5.04
Ideologically conservative (0–10)	5.77	5.28	5.07	6.43	4.02	5.21
"Economy has worsened" (1–5)	3.83	3.70	3.92	3.75	3.90	3.88
"Worsened standard of living" (1–5)	2.99	2.84	2.99	2.80	3.05	3.03
Number of employees (1–5)	2.75	3.18	3.29	2.86	3.24	3.18
Proportion in each group who:						
Noted distribution of subsidies	0.23	0.17	0.09	0.22	0.24	0.18
Supports decentralization	0.11	0.16	0.12	0.09	0.13	0.21
Union membership	0.10	0.13	0.11	0.06	0.19	0.13

Summary data from JEDS96 data set.
For more information, see the Characteristics Key at the end of the chapter.

less need for government protection. And rural voters were more likely to indicate the central role of subsidy disbursements in the region's politics.

Rural voters were also more likely to hold issue positions consistent with support for clientelism. In particular, rural voters were on average more supportive of agricultural protection. In addition, JEDS includes questions that Japan elections researchers have used for years to measure clientelist tendencies,[8] and urban voters' responses indicated lower average clientelism scores than their rural counterparts.

---

[8] These questions involve the extent to which people see as proper the use of connections and assistance from others to achieve individual goals.

In sum, if there were to be an anti-clientelist movement in Japan, it ought to have occurred in the cities.

CANDIDATE POSITIONS AND APPEALS

As Table 8.1 indicates, support for parties broke down along similar lines, with voters who displayed more clientelistic characteristics and opinions supporting Japan's "traditional parties," the LDP and the old Left (the Social Democratic Party and the Japan Communist Party), and voters displaying anti-clientelist features supporting the leading new parties of the 1990s, the NFP and DPJ. In addition to differences in the characteristics already mentioned, new party supporters were on average more supportive of another position – decentralization. In the 1990s and early 2000s, many politicians pushed for greater financial decentralization. Many in the opposition – even some from rural districts – supported such moves out of a desire to force localities to raise more of their own funding[9] and reduce the heavy use of subsidies by the LDP-led central government for both (inefficient) economic policy and clientelist political gain.[10] However, to what extent were Japan's new parties of the 1993–2003 period truly anti-clientelist?

Interviews I conducted with both LDP and opposition (new party) politicians reveal differences between the two groups on public works. No LDP politician admitted to using public works as a tool to maintain political support. But, when referring to public works, one HR member from a rural district explained, "I don't want it, but that's the only economic policy we've got. As long as we create employment, digging a hole and filling the hole is not wasteful."[11] Hinting at the role of public works in maintaining LDP support, a rural LDP politician explained that he wanted to create a more decentralized system and reduce public works, but his constituents opposed the idea, and pushing the issue too hard would only lead to his own (and perhaps the party's) undoing.[12]

Opposition party members decried such policies. Each DPJ politician I interviewed – whether a former LDP member or former Socialist – described the LDP as interested in little more than distributing pork in exchange for the party's own political health. One DPJ leader described government construction spending as equivalent to 1980s military spending in the United States, much of which, in his mind, focused on local patronage given to supporters and not overall planning. Despite hailing from a rural district, he

---

[9] Interview with a leading DPJ politician, May 21, 1999.
[10] Interview with leading DPJ politicians, August 12, 1999.
[11] Interview August 1999.
[12] Interview August 1999.

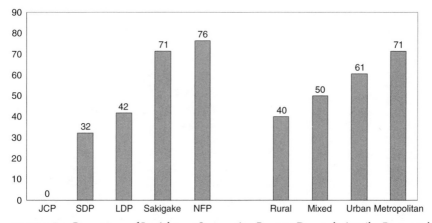

FIGURE 8.2 Percentage of Legislators Supporting Prompt Deregulation (by Party and Type of District)
Respondents were given two options: (1) "Economic restrictions should be promptly relaxed or completely abolished based on the free and individual responsibility in principle while giving considerations to the weak." (2) "Deregulatory efforts should be gradually promoted in consideration of the weak." The small number of respondents who provided a different answer were eliminated from the analysis.
Data come from the results reported in Bungei Shunju (1996).

railed against the LDP's use of pork and saw its downfall as critical because of its role in the decline of Japan's economy.[13]

The government's regulatory power was an important tool in the LDP's clientelist/anti-market-liberalization policy kit. The party was able to use a variety of regulations to protect its leading constituents in finance, agriculture, and small business in exchange for votes and monetary contributions. Not surprising, many LDP members were averse to eliminating such controls quickly. In 1996, *Bungei Shunju* published a survey conducted with a large group of Diet politicians from all parties (see Figure 8.2), in which legislators were asked about their position on deregulation. Politicians from the old Left (the SDP and JCP) overwhelmingly opposed significant, immediate deregulation; LDP politicians were mixed but on average leaned toward making only slow moves to deregulate; and NFP politicians strongly favored prompt deregulation.[14] In addition, support for prompt deregulation corresponded with urban-ness: Legislators from urban areas were more likely to support prompt deregulation.[15] In addition, even controlling for different

[13] Interview May 1999.
[14] The DPJ did not exist until after the survey.
[15] I use a four-point scale (rural, mixed, urban, and metropolitan based on population density) from a data set developed by Steven R. Reed.

factors,[16] (a) urban legislators were more likely than more rural ones and (b) NFP legislators were more likely than those from the LDP and SDP to support prompt deregulation.[17]

Additional information can be gleaned by examining the pitches politicians make during campaigns. Prior to every election in Japan, each prefecture publishes "Election Information" (*Senkyo Kōhō*), in which each candidate is given space equivalent to roughly one third of a newspaper page to present his or her campaign message. In most cases, candidates advertise their policy goals (even independent of their party's plans) and what they have achieved in the past. Using these platform messages, I analyzed the campaign appeals made by 145 politicians in the 1996 HR election.[18]

What issues did politicians raise in their campaigns? Many focused on valence issues, such as the importance of ending bullying in schools and the need to promote citizen welfare, which politicians of all parties and all areas emphasized. Candidates rarely took opposing views on a given issue and, aside from Socialist and Communist cries to protect the peace clause of the Constitution, few raised major national issues. This serves to underscore what I have argued throughout this book: Electoral competition in Japan is typically founded less on debating the central "big" issues of the day than it is on clientelist and personal politics.

There were important differences, though, between regions and parties in the issues that were emphasized. The clearest difference between urban and rural areas was in appeals based on public works. Rural candidates mentioned, on average, 1.6 projects, while urban candidates mentioned only 0.7, and even controlling for other variables, as districts grew more urban, the number of public works mentioned declined. Also, candidates from non-LDP parties were less likely than those from the LDP to mention public works projects. Reform – vaguely writ – was a major theme in 1996. There was no discernible difference between the LDP and new opposition's support for "reform," but urban candidates were more likely than rural candidates to mention reform.

There was little difference between urban and rural areas on most of the other issues I coded, but (even controlling for level of urban-ness), substantial differences existed between the different parties. Like the *Bungei Shunju* data, the platform data indicate that NFP candidates were more likely than LDP candidates to support deregulation and, similar to the *Bungei Shunju*

---

[16] See the links to the supplementary Web site at *www.ethanscheiner.com* for details on statistical analysis that controls for party, urban-ness of district, and number of terms in office.

[17] Japan's traditional parties – the SDP even more than the LDP – were less likely than the new ones to support prompt deregulation.

[18] I coded the platforms of candidates from Akita, Fukui, Iwate, Kagoshima, Kanagawa, Niigata, Osaka, and Tokyo, ensuring a wide array from both urban and rural districts. See the links to the supplementary Web site at *www.ethanscheiner.com* for detailed discussion of the coding and statistical analysis.

data, the old Left was even *less* likely than the LDP to support deregulation. This is in line with the old Left's general stance against a liberal market economy. No LDP, NFP, or DPJ politicians outside rural areas even mentioned the primary sector (agriculture, etc.), but many *urban* Socialist and Communist candidates emphasized the protection of agriculture, fisheries, and lumber industries. DPJ candidates were more likely than LDP candidates to initiate appeals for making information more public about government activities and for eliminating the "sticky" relationship binding together politicians, bureaucrats, and business. Candidates from both the NFP and DPJ were more likely than LDP candidates to seek a reduction in power held by bureaucrats (and an increase in politician activism) and less likely than the LDP to make appeals to protect small and medium-sized business.

Patterns of Parties' Issue Stances and Locations in Issue Space

Are there particular issues that tended to go together in politicians' appeals? Using principal components factor analysis, we can see the extent to which there were patterns to politicians' sets of appeals.[19] I find that candidates made their appeals along two main dimensions. First, on a public works dimension, many candidates put together campaign appeals that promised to provide public works and protect agriculture (and then also many candidates who promised neither). Second, on a "Liberalization" dimension, candidates put together platforms that pushed for deregulation and decentralization while ignoring (typically noncompetitive) small and medium-sized business and platforms that did the opposite.

What does this mean in terms of what each party offered the electorate? Figure 8.3 plots where the average (mean) candidate from each of the major parties fell on these dimensions. It shows that LDP candidates strongly emphasized public works in their appeals. So did NFP candidates, an action most likely explained by the fact that a number of the NFP's leading politicians defected from the LDP and no doubt continued to campaign for cheap votes through public works types of appeals. As expected, both DPJ and the old Left candidates offered little in the way of public works appeals. Most interesting, we can see the divide between the new parties and the old on the liberalization dimension. Both the LDP and the old Left fell to the bottom half of the liberalization dimension, largely as a result of their support for small and medium-sized business. In contrast, the DPJ's and NFP's support for action such as deregulation left them as the clear proliberalizing parties.

[19] In the analysis, I include all major (nonvalence) appeals made by politicians in the platforms and the output of the model indicates the existing patterns. See the links to the supplementary Web site at *www.ethanscheiner.com* for more information.

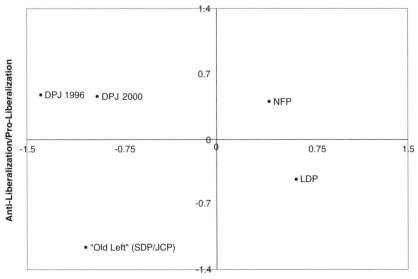

Anti-Public Works/Pro-Public Works

FIGURE 8.3 Types of Campaign Appeals Made by Candidates of Different Parties
Mappings are based on the average scores for candidates of each party (determined
through principal components factor analysis).
Source: Author's coding of 145 candidate's campaign platforms from the 1996 HR
election.

I also extrapolated from the data to determine what issues underpinned
the party system after 1996. In 1998, a "new" DPJ was formed out of a
marriage of the "old" DPJ (born in 1996), the bulk of the former Democratic
Socialists (DSP) who were part of the NFP in 1996, and a portion of the
"conservatives" (former LDP and Japan New Party members) who were
also part of the NFP (see Chapter 2). While losing a few key (former LDP)
members to defection, the new DPJ provided the leading challenge to the LDP
from 1996 on. Drawing from the 1996 candidate platform data, I determine
the average issue positions for candidates who joined the new DPJ between
the 1996 and 2000 elections. In Figure 8.3, I denote these candidates with the
label "DPJ 2000." Candidates from DPJ 2000 were different on the public
works dimension from the 1996 NFP, but similar to DPJ 1996: The new DPJ
(DPJ 2000) appeared to be opposed to heavy use of public works projects
and in favor of an increase in deregulation and liberalization. Because there
is no reason to believe that the issue positions of LDP candidates changed
markedly between 1996 and 2000, it appears that the party system in the
late 1990s and early 2000s divided over these issues.

This mapping – based on actual candidate platforms – is similar to the
analysis of Schoppa (2001), who intuits that the most salient cleavage in

post-1993 party politics divided two sets of groups: those favoring protection of declining and uncompetitive sectors and those seeking to make the economy more efficient and productive.

It is interesting that the old Left fell into the bottom, left-hand quadrant in Figure 8.3, indicating its opposition both to public works and to liberalization and deregulation: Despite their longtime opposition to the LDP, old Left parties shared a key similarity with the LDP. The old Left and LDP diverged on public works. Indeed, it would have been odd for the old Left to push issues on the positive end of the public works dimension because they were parties that had long been out of power and cut off from the core of national public works spending. However, they shared the negative half of the Liberalization dimension with the LDP. The support given by old Left parties to the clientelist system in the form of appeals to protecting small and medium-sized businesses and maintaining substantial regulations should not be surprising. For years, the Socialists were less successful in urban districts and Japan's centrist parties took over much of the city opposition vote (in part through their control of the city union vote). Both the Socialists' and Communists' bases long rested on public-sector union members and rural agricultural cooperatives, making it nearly impossible for them to push a deregulatory, anti-agricultural subsidy set of appeals.

Because the Socialists, the LDP's primary challenger for years, were unable to tap into the potentially potent yet latent liberalization dimension, it is little wonder that the LDP faced so little competition. Despite internationally competitive big business's apparent desire to liberalize, the ruling party was the only realistic outlet for big business votes.

In the 1990s, the Socialist Party was also fundamentally a conservative party in the sense that it did not seek serious change in the Japanese system. Curtis suggests that much of the reason that the Socialists and LDP could form a coalition government together was that both "were unable to articulate any new goals or vision," so that the coalition "was built on the basis of a cautious and incremental approach to dealing with pressing domestic economic and social issues and with a changed international system" (1999: 199). Otake puts it even more strongly:

The LDP represented the interests of local constituencies, self-employed sectors (including agriculture), and specific industries (especially the construction industry).... [The Socialists] represented the interests of public servants in railroads, the postal service, telecommunications, education, and local government. The two major parties came to compete less on the basis of policies or principles than on who would win a greater share of the pie. (2000: 295)

In this way, the anti-clientelist and free market appeals of the NFP and DPJ represented not merely a difference between them and the LDP, but in fact a challenge to Japan's traditional party structure that maintained the clientelist system.

Candidates from Japan's new parties pushed greater liberalization of the economy, in contrast to the traditional parties' efforts to maintain the clientelist Japanese economic system. Speaking after the formation of the new DPJ version of the party in 1998, party leader, Kan Naoto, explained that "[s]ince the LDP had failed to undertake Thatcherite liberalizing reforms, the Democrats would have to do so when they came to power" (Curtis 1999: 194).[20] This effort by Japan's new challengers grew more intense in the 2000 election, in which the DPJ – as a party – campaigned almost exclusively on the issue of drastically reducing public works, as such spending threatened the survival of Japan's economy (e.g., *Yomiuri Shinbun*, June 14, 2000).[21] Trying to bring greater attention to the issue, the DPJ introduced a bill to control public works projects (*Asahi Shinbun*, May 22, 2000) and promoted other, similar measures, arguing that they were absolutely necessary even if they caused short-term economic pain. While public works were the focus of the DPJ's attack, the party also sought to distinguish itself from the LDP by claiming that only the DPJ was truly committed to economic deregulation (*Yomiuri Shinbun* interview with DPJ leader Hatoyama Yukio, June 4, 2000). In the 2003 HR election, the DPJ pushed this even further, offering a manifesto that promised to cut public works spending by 30 percent (*Asahi Shinbun*, September 19, 2003).[22]

VOTER PREFERENCES

Typically, the issues discussed by politicians frame the political debate. However, to what extent did voters respond to appeals made by Japan's parties?

Patterns of Voters' Issue Stances and Locations in Issue Space

Utilizing responses from the 1996 JEDS survey of Japanese voters, I sought to map voters' issue positions (by support for political parties) as I did for candidates. Unfortunately, this is not a straightforward task. In the case of campaign platforms, politicians mentioning an issue in the first place indicates the salience (to them) of the issue. In contrast, we cannot tell the relative salience of an issue for voters simply by using their responses to questions about where they stand. That is, surveys may reveal voters' positions on issues raised by the questioner, but they provide less sense of whether voters consider these issues important. Mapping issues for voters as I did for

---

[20] However, Kan was not a pure Thatcherite. He also argued that "[t]hey would also simultaneously have to adopt new social-welfare policies – thus the Blair moderation of Thatcherism – to cushion the adverse impact on society's weakest members that would result from increased competition and less government management of the economy" (Curtis 1999: 194).

[21] Unless otherwise noted, all newspaper citations in this chapter refer to online editions.

[22] However, as noted in footnote 20 of this chapter, the DPJ was not purely free market. It also promised to increase spending on small businesses.

candidates could provide misleading results by grouping together issues that hold salience for voters and those that do not. As a result, the analyst might overemphasize the presence of particular issue positions that are not salient to the voter.

All that said as a caution, for illustration's sake, I did unscientifically experiment with different combinations of voter survey responses to issues related to the previously mentioned candidate platform model to see what patterns appeared. The clearest patterns emerged from a principal components factor analysis where the main variables were voters' self-placements of their level of ideological conservatism, voters' self-placement of their general support for reform, voters' support for agricultural liberalization, a measure of their clientelist tendencies, and their support for noninterference with individuals' choices. This simple view suggests that voters were distributed on two main dimensions. First, we can see a progressive/conservative dimension, where voters fall into groupings of general conservativeness and unwillingness to engage in reform (with the opposite of each also grouped together). Second, we can see a liberalization dimension, which grouped together clientelist tendencies and opposition to liberalization of agriculture (with the opposite of each also grouped together). Mapping the results in Figure 8.4's issue space is illustrative. Each plot in the figure represents the average position for supporters of a given party in PR balloting in 1996. The figure suggests that LDP voters were more conservative than new party (NFP or DPJ) or old Left voters. Most important, the figure indicates differences between voters supporting the LDP and the new parties on issues relating to liberalization: New party voters were more market liberal than voters supporting the other parties.

Determinants of the Vote

In short, we see a liberalization dimension in both the candidate and the voter models. LDP candidates and voters both appeared to be less market liberal, while new party candidates and voters appeared to support moves to liberalize. There are reasons to treat the voter mapping as only tentative, but using a model that includes other variables allows us be to more certain of these findings. Specifically, I conducted statistical analysis (multinomial probit and multinomial logit models) to analyze the JEDS public opinion survey data and to draw out what determined vote choices in SMD and PR races in 1996. In particular, I looked at what distinguished the vote for the LDP, the new parties (NFP and DPJ), and the old Left (Socialists and Communists) from one another.[23]

---

[23] For details of the statistical analysis and the different results, see the links to the supplementary Web site at *www.ethanscheiner.com*.

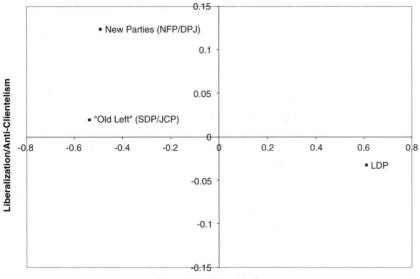

FIGURE 8.4 Voters' Issue Positions
Mappings are based on the average scores for PR supporters of each party in the 1996 HR election (determined through principal components factor analysis). Data are from JEDS 1996 public opinion survey.

Multinomial probit analysis reveals that roughly identical factors shaped voters decisions in both SMD and PR races, the main exception being incumbency:[24] Controlling for other factors, voters in SMDs were more likely to support incumbent candidates, irrespective of their party, but by and large the presence of an incumbent (no matter from what party) did not appear to affect voters' likelihood of casting a ballot for one party over another in PR.

Factors other than incumbency were also important. Ideology played a role in shaping voters' decisions. Self-described conservative voters were more likely to cast ballots for the LDP in both SMD and PR, whereas self-described progressive voters turned to the old Left. Those ideologically in between were more likely than those on the left and the right to support new parties. And voters were more likely to support new parties over the LDP when their satisfaction with their standard of living was low.

What is more interesting, factors relating to clientelism and market liberalization shaped voters' support for different parties in both SMDs and PR. Older voters were more likely to support the old Left and LDP. Voters who were more supportive of liberalizing agricultural markets were more

---

[24] Unfortunately, data of the kind I used in Chapter 6 to examine quality new candidates were not readily available for 1996.

TABLE 8.2 *Probability of Supporting Specific Parties*

	Type of Voter			Region of Voter		
	Clientelist Voter	Average (Mean) Voter	Anti-Clientelist Voter	Rural	Mixed	Urban
SMD vote						
LDP	0.623	0.493	0.329	0.522	0.470	0.432
New parties	0.204	0.411	0.614	0.327	0.352	0.380
Old Left	0.173	0.096	0.057	0.151	0.178	0.187
PR vote						
LDP	0.471	0.382	0.208	0.400	0.354	0.316
New parties	0.288	0.475	0.721	0.449	0.478	0.516
Old Left	0.241	0.143	0.071	0.151	0.168	0.168

Figures represent predicted probabilities of support for each of Japan's major parties in 1996. (Results are based on multinomial logit analysis of JEDS96 public opinion survey.)

likely to cast votes for new parties, whereas those who emphasized the role of candidates in delivering subsidies to their district were more likely to cast ballots for the old Left and LDP. And voters who supported decentralization were more likely to vote for new parties.

To sum up: The results here indicate the centrality of individual candidacies in shaping success in SMD races, further highlighting the importance of strong candidates discussed in Chapter 6. Perhaps more important, the analysis also confirms the results of the tentative patterns found in the voter mapping in Figure 8.4. On a simple progressive–conservative scale, old Left voters were the most "progressive," LDP voters were the most "conservative," and new party voters were somewhere in between. More striking, voters for new parties were quite different from old Left and LDP voters on issues related to clientelism and liberalization. Those emphasizing subsidies and agricultural protection (as well as opponents of decentralization) – the hallmarks of Japan's clientelist state – were far more likely to support their traditional options of the old Left or LDP.

To demonstrate the impact of the clientelist system in maintaining LDP support, in Table 8.2 I use the results of multinomial logit analysis (where I use variables identical to those in the multinomial probit analyses) to predict the likelihood of different types of voters casting ballots for each party. In the top left-hand grouping, I list the different probabilities for average Japanese voters, clientelism-supporting voters, and clientelism-opposing voters supporting each party in SMD balloting in 1996.[25] The table indicates how

[25] A clientelism-supporting voter is one who (a) emphasizes (and presumably supports) the disbursement of subsidies by a candidate in his or her district, (b) opposes liberalizing Japan's agricultural market, and (c) opposes decentralization. A clientelism opponent is the opposite. All other variables are kept at their means. See the links to the supplementary Web site at *www.ethanscheiner.com* for information on computing the likelihoods.

voters' likelihood of supporting any given party's candidate varies with their support for clientelism. Most striking, LDP candidates were extremely likely (with a 62.3 percent chance) to get the support of pro-clientelism voters, but new party candidates had relatively little chance of receiving support from them (20.4 percent chance). In contrast, the LDP (32.9 percent chance) and old Left (5.7 percent chance) were likely to do markedly worse among anti-clientelist voters in SMD races, while the new party candidates did much better, with a 61.4 percent chance of receiving their vote.

URBAN-RURAL DIFFERENCES REDUX

In short, an anti-clientelist backlash appears to have developed in Japan, with new parties the primary beneficiaries and, to some extent, the leaders of the campaign. But what prevented the new opposition parties from converting this backlash into greater success? Earlier in the chapter I discussed the differences between urban and rural voters. The root of the *new* opposition's problems lies in these differences.

The right-hand side of Table 8.2 also lists the likelihood of an average voter supporting Japan's leading parties at each level of urban-ness in 1996.[26] That is, based on my statistical analysis, what was the likelihood of the mean rural voter casting a ballot for a given party? What of the mean urban voter? The mean voter in districts that are mixed? As Table 8.2 shows, because of the presence of older voters, lower levels of education, and more pro-clientelist issue positions, the gap in likely success between the LDP and new parties was wide in rural districts. However, urban voters – because they are younger, more educated, and more likely to hold anti-clientelist issue positions – were roughly as likely to cast ballots for either an LDP or a new party SMD candidate. As the bottom half of Table 8.2 – which shows the likelihood of voting for each *party* based on the voter's issue positions and the characteristics of the mean voter in each type of district – indicates, these trends grow stronger in PR races, where voters, no longer relying on personal candidacy cues, were more likely to cast ballots for new parties, especially when maintaining anti-clientelist positions.

Electoral Results

These findings are all based on an analysis of individual-level voting decisions. What was the effect of these individual vote choices on overall electoral outcomes?

[26] This division, based on the population density of each district, was designed by Kabashima Ikuo and his Tokyo University seminar for the districts in 2000. Their measure placed 100 districts in each category (with the densest districts categorized as urban and the least dense categorized as rural). I extrapolated for the minor redistricting that occurred prior to 2003 and divided the 300 SMDs into 100 urban, 99 rural and 101 mixed districts.

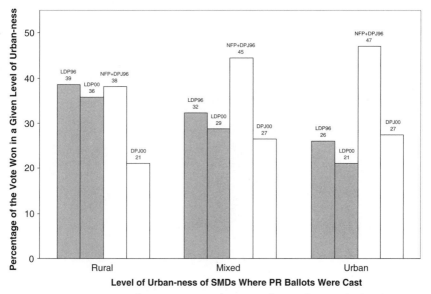

FIGURE 8.5 Percentage of Votes Won in the PR Balloting by Level of Urban-ness: 1996 and 2000
1996–2000: 100 seats in each type of district. 2003: 99 rural, 101 mixed, and 100 urban.
Note that two parties are summed and listed for the opposition in 1996.

According to an index based on population density, we can divide roughly evenly Japan's 300 SMDs into categories that we can term "urban," "rural," and "mixed."[27] Table 8.2 indicates that in 1996 the probability of voting for a new party in the PR balloting was always higher than that of voting for the LDP in any type of district, even in rural areas. Figure 8.5 plots the percentage of PR votes that each party actually received in each area in 1996 and 2000.[28] The results are similar to those found in the predictions in Table 8.2. In rural areas in 1996, the new parties' (NFP and DPJ) combined PR vote was roughly equal to the LDP's, and in 1996 new parties actually received markedly more votes in mixed and urban districts. In 2000, the splintering of the opposition left the focus of efforts to challenge the LDP in the hands of the DPJ.[29] As Figure 8.5 demonstrates, the DPJ by itself did not

[27] See footnote 26.

[28] As of the writing of this book, I did not yet have available PR results broken down to the SMD level. However, it should be noted that the DPJ did especially well in PR races in 2003 and was often even on roughly equal footing with the LDP in PR races in the countryside.

[29] In both elections, other parties ran as opposition challenges to the LDP. However, I am primarily concerned here with the development of the leading challengers to the LDP because they will (a) tend to be the center of any coalition around which a group of opposition parties might form and (b) most likely to win the more important district races. In 1996, the NFP

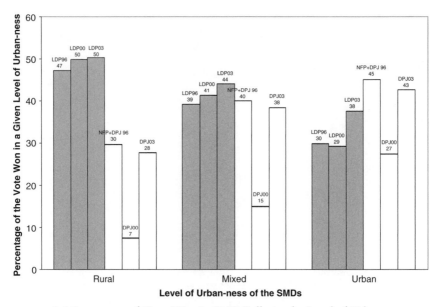

FIGURE 8.6 Percentage of Votes Won in SMD Balloting by Level of Urban-ness 1996–2000: 100 seats in each type of district. 2003: 99 rural, 101 mixed, and 100 urban.

Note that two parties are summed and listed for the opposition in 1996.

match up to the LDP in rural areas but ran roughly even with it in mixed districts and was stronger than the LDP in urban areas.

Such figures indicate substantial opposition strength, but PR balloting determined only 200 of Japan's 500 HR seats in 1996 and only 180 out of the country's 480 seats in 2000 and 2003. The heart of the system is in the SMDs. Here the difference between parties and between regions is much starker. As I noted previously, statistical analysis shows that the LDP was particularly advantaged when it had an incumbent and when it faced voters who were interested in subsidies. The LDP maintained a large advantage over the other parties in the number of incumbents it *ran* in SMDs in the rural areas in the 1996 election, with 70 rural incumbents compared to only 28 for new parties.[30] In addition, attention to subsidies was markedly

was clearly the leading new and opposition party, but the DPJ was also seen as much more than just a minor splinter party. In 2000, I focus solely on the DPJ. The NFP no longer existed. The relatively new Liberal Party also sought to challenge the LDP, but few saw the Liberals as having much chance to develop into a larger organization. Moreover, until only a few months before the election, the Liberal Party had been in a coalition government with the LDP.

[30] However, the new parties had roughly as many incumbents as the LDP in mixed SMDs and far more than the ruling party in urban districts in 1996.

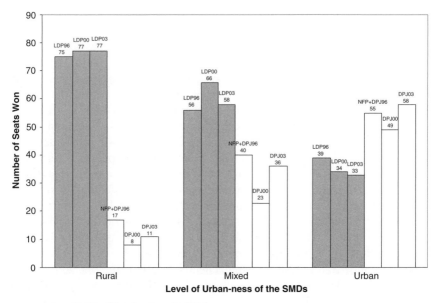

FIGURE 8.7 SMDs Won by Level of Urban-ness
1996–2000: 100 seats in each type of district. 2003: 99 rural, 101 mixed, and 100 urban.
Note that two parties are summed and listed for the opposition in 1996.

higher in rural areas than in urban. For example, in rural areas, 23 percent of respondents in the JEDS survey mentioned that the first candidate they thought of in the district had an ability to deliver subsidies, as opposed to 17 percent in mixed districts, and only 9 percent in urban districts (see Table 8.1). The combination of many incumbents and an electorate looking to their incumbent politician for subsidies gave the LDP an especially large boost in SMD races over PR ones in rural areas. As Figure 8.6 demonstrates, the LDP won a much larger share of the SMD vote than the major opposition parties in rural areas. The major new parties took a much greater share of the SMD vote in urban districts than they did in rural.[31]

The pattern is even clearer when we turn to the number of *seats* each party won in SMDs. As Figure 8.7 shows, the LDP won a massive number of seats in rural SMDs. Despite the fact that there was rough parity (and, indeed, great urban strength on the opposition side) in the remainder of the districts, the LDP's advantage in rural districts left the ruling party with a significantly greater sum total.

[31] The drop in the success of the new parties between 1996 and 2000 is primarily due to the fact that many within the NFP joined non-DPJ alternatives when the NFP split. New party success went back up with the additional consolidation of the opposition around the DPJ in 2003.

TWO PARALLEL PARTY SYSTEMS: IMPLICATIONS
FOR OPPOSITION FAILURE

Japan's new parties of the 1990s were founded in very large part on a
backlash against Japan's clientelist system. Otake (2000) articulates this
neoconservative basis to the new parties' appeals but argues that voters
sharing the political economy ideals of these new parties failed to shift their
allegiances to these new parties. My analysis suggests that voters with such
ideals *did* in fact support the new parties. Urban voters in particular were
antagonistic to Japan's clientelist system, and the new parties found great
success in urban areas with the backing of these voters. In rural areas, however, voters were not only more supportive of Japan's clientelist system but
often even dependent upon it. Support for clientelism led to support for the
LDP and its candidates. In large measure as a result of this support, the
LDP dominated SMD races in rural areas, winning three quarters of all rural
seats. In short, Japan maintains not one party system, but two parallel party
systems – one rural, LDP-dominated, clientelist system and one competitive,
urban system. And the opposition is greatly hindered by this fact. Despite
the fact that rural SMDs constitute only about 20 percent of all seats, rural
SMD victories provide the LDP with nearly one third of all the seats it needs
to win a majority. To win a majority, the LDP needs to take only around
40 percent of the remaining seats.

While preferences favoring the clientelist system are strong in rural areas,
preferences in the rest of the country are mixed. In urban areas, there are
more voters with anti-clientelist views, but there are also those – for example,
countless small and medium-sized businesses owners – who benefit from the
clientelist system (see Chapters 3 and 5) and therefore continue to support
the LDP. As a result, even though the opposition found considerable success
in urban areas, this success did not sufficiently counteract its poor prospects
in rural areas. Indeed, even if an opposition party won 30 percent of the
rural SMDs and one third of all PR seats – an overall result greater than the
DPJ was able to achieve in 1996–2003 – it would still need to win 75 percent
of the remaining seats (mixed and urban SMDs) to win a majority. As long
as the LDP exists and preferences in nonrural districts remain as mixed as
they are, this is difficult to imagine.

In part the opposition's problem is malapportionment. Under SNTV/
MMD, the system was malapportioned to favor the countryside. At times
there were more than five times as many eligible voters per seat in the most
underrepresented urban district as there were eligible voters in the most
overrepresented rural district. There have been many analyses of malapportionment's effects in Japan (e.g., Lijphart, Pintor, and Sone 1986), and many
of the most systematic analyses (Baker and Scheiner ND; Christensen and
Johnson 1995) estimate that malapportionment may have manufactured parliamentary majorities for the LDP in a small number of elections. With the

introduction of the new electoral system in 1994, malapportionment was not eliminated, but it was substantially reduced. As of the 2003 election, the most underrepresented urban district had just over two times the number of eligible voters of the most overrepresented rural one (*Japan Times*, September 3, 2002). Under a perfectly proportional system, there would be a shift of about 10 seats from rural to urban areas, probably leading to a small swing in the number of seats held, respectively, by the LDP and the opposition. In this way, malapportionment continued to provide a bit of protection for the LDP and rural interests that benefit from clientelism.

However, in post-1993 Japan, the opposition's problem was due much more to the existence of a candidate-centered, winner-take-all, small-district electoral system. Even in rural districts, the LDP as a party received less than 40 percent of the PR vote. The opposition would unquestionably have profited from a more proportional electoral system. By allowing the LDP to win 75 percent of rural SMDs with only 50 percent of the SMD vote, the small-district system gave clientelism- (and, hence, LDP-)supporting groups a very large bang for their voting buck (or yield for the yen). In these ways, Japan's clientelistic, rural areas received a form of institutional protection – they received a very large and pivotal set of seats – that, in turn, aided greatly in the success of the LDP and the failure of the opposition.

This offers an important contrast to the Italian system. In Italy, the beginning of the DC's rapid decline occurred under the country's now-defunct PR system, which included a "preference vote."[32] The candidate-centered, preference-voting rule advantaged the DC, but the heavy proportionality of the system ultimately helped bring down the longtime dominant party.

Under the system, southern Italy, the bastion of Italian clientelism and DC support, received a substantial number of seats that helped maintain the dominant party. The preference-voting component of Italy's electoral system, whereby (on top of casting a ballot for a party) voters had the option to cast ballots that expressed a preference for particular candidates within their chosen party, aided the DC in the south by attracting greater support for the party of the preferred candidates. In the Italian PR electoral system, total numbers of seats were allocated according to the number of votes won by each party. The ballots cast expressing a preference for particular candidates were used to help rank the candidates on the party PR list and thereby determine which individuals won seats for a given party (Golden 2000). Voters in Italy's south were twice as likely to use the preference vote as those in the north, and government parties such as the DC received more preference votes than other parties.

Hine writes that "the preference vote has had its effect on the struggle for public resources: jobs in the public sector, grants, licensing and regulatory

---

[32] Italy used this PR system until 1994, when it introduced a new mixed-member electoral system (using PR and SMDs).

authority, etc. Control of such resources is vital in mobilizing preference votes because party members have to be rewarded for their services, whether those services involve merely voting or campaigning more directly" (1993: 131). Even when the DC grew increasingly unpopular, its more clientelistic politicians were able to continue to win office because of the preference vote that rewarded them for being good clientelistic patrons.

However, the fact that it was a proportional system made it far easier for other parties to cut into the DC's base of support, even where the DC was at its regional strongest.[33] The very large number of SMDs as a proportion of the total number of seats in Japan made it far more difficult for smaller, less-popular parties to chip away at the LDP's foundation in rural areas.

CONCLUSION

My main argument in this chapter is largely an institutional one. Even within Clientelist/Financially Centralized systems, a variety of voters and regions oppose the clientelist system, particularly as the economy grows increasingly zero-sum. At the same time, certain areas – those that benefit from the clientelist system – remain very supportive of it. As more regions and voters oppose the system, electoral institutions play a major part in determining the extent to which clientelist-supporting areas are sufficient to protect the regime that maintains it.

Nevertheless, as I noted in Chapter 3, we should be careful not to overstate the impact of institutions. Anti-clientelist positions and characteristics consistent with them grew stronger with each level of urban-ness in Japan (see Table 8.1). My analysis of Italy and Austria in Chapter 7 suggests that increasing urbanization in those two countries helped increase antagonism toward the clientelist system, which in turn exacted political costs from their ruling regimes.[34] Continued urbanization in Japan may well continue to do much to undercut the clientelist system there as well.

Japanese wealth may actually hinder the Japanese government's maintenance of the clientelist system. As I note in Chapter 3, increased wealth injects a greater sense that the marginal benefits brought about by additional public works projects are not worth the negative side effects. Moreover, economic decline in the 1990s and early 2000s reduced the perceived acceptability of continued "infrastructural" spending. Opposition to such spending is

---

[33] Johnson (2003) correctly notes also the importance of the independent Italian judiciary in helping to bring down the DC through arrests precipitated by the corruption of many party members. Nevertheless, support for the DC had declined even before the Tangentopoli scandal broke in 1992.

[34] However, urbanization largely affects party competition only through its impact on the level of support for clientelism. That is, urbanization does not directly affect competition.

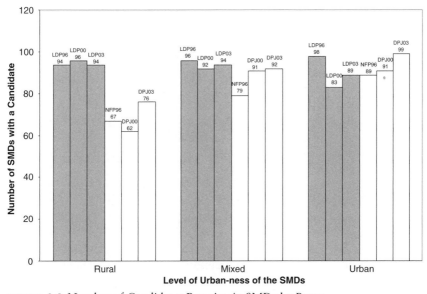

FIGURE 8.8 Number of Candidates Running in SMDs by Party
1996–2000: 100 seats in each type of district. 2003: 99 rural, 101 mixed, and 100
urban.

particularly prevalent in (urban) areas that do not especially benefit from
clientelist spending. It is therefore conceivable, as I also noted in Chapter 3,
that popular opinion against the clientelist system may ultimately outweigh
the power of institutions in upholding it.

My discussion in this chapter has focused on issues related to clientelism
and institutional protections as an explanation of opposition failure, but it
is important to highlight also the conclusion of Chapter 6, the tremendous
importance of quality candidates in shaping a challenge to a ruling regime.
Quite simply, the presence of quality candidates makes the task of winning
office markedly easier for any party. In the late 1990s and early 2000s, the
DPJ won a substantial number of SMDs in cities. In part its relative success
was due to the more anti-clientelist views of urban voters, but it was also due
to the larger presence of quality candidates running under the DPJ banner.
On the other hand, the opposition faced a more strongly pro-clientelism
population in rural areas, but it also had great difficulty generating any sort
of candidacies there. In contrast, as Figure 8.8 illustrates, the LDP was able
to run candidates in most districts throughout the country. The NFP in 1996
and the DPJ in 2000 ran candidates in most urban districts, but they were
able to find candidates to run in, respectively, only 67 and 62 out of the total
100 rural districts. The DPJ was able to run more in 2003, but still had no
candidate in 23 rural districts.

Given urban areas' lower levels of clientelism and dependence on the center, it was usually easier for the opposition to gain local-level strength in cities and therefore find quality candidates there to run for national office. But the opposition was stuck because many rural districts continued to support clientelism and were, naturally, largely impervious to anti-clientelist appeals. In such areas, opposition parties were able to do quite well in national-level elections *when they had strong candidates*. However, rural areas in Japan are particularly clientelistic and dependent upon the center, thereby representing the archetypal Clientelist/Financially Centralized case. As a result, they made it difficult for opposition parties to gain seats at the local level and develop pools of strong candidacies.

In short, a combination of two factors constrained opposition parties' capacity to take advantage of what appeared to be a substantial anti-clientelist backlash in Japan. First, opposition parties faced great difficulty developing a strong candidate base, especially in rural areas, which are dominated by quintessentially clientelistic and centralized politics. This created a tremendous disadvantage for the opposition under Japan's candidate-centered electoral system. Second, the use of a small-district, first-past-the-post electoral system that overrepresents the rural areas provided a massive advantage to clientelist interests and the LDP with whom they are intertwined. Malapportionment offered rural, clientelist-dominant districts roughly 10 extra seats that could be added to their national total. Moreover, the winner-take-all system allowed the clientelist bare majority to take more than 70 percent of all the seats in the rural regions.

These problems were sufficient to hold off greater opposition strength in the face of apparent opportunities for success. In Chapter 10, I consider what possibilities exist that might allow Japan's opposition to overcome these problems.

CHARACTERISTICS KEY FOR TABLE 8.1

Age: age of respondent.

Education: seven categories from completion of primary school (1) to graduate school (7).

Pro-agricultural liberalization: runs from "To protect Japan's agriculture, liberalizing imports for agricultural products should not be allowed" (1) to "Liberalizing imports in agricultural products should be allowed for the sake of manufactured products exports from Japan" (4).

Non-clientelistic: runs from "It is better to depend on an influential person at your place of work or in your neighborhood to get things done the way you wish" (1) to "It is better not to depend on somebody but to do it by myself to get things done where you work or live" (4). This wording has been used for many years as an indication of clientelistic tendencies.

Anti-reform: "There are people who think that it is better to reform politics, while other people think that politics should remain the same as much as possible. Which opinion best fits you?" Options run from "Reform" (0) to "Stability" (10).

Ideologically conservative: "The words conservative and progressive are used to express some positions in politics. If progressive is a "0" and conservative is a "10" what number do you think you might best indicate your own position on these matters?" Options run from "Progressive" (0) to "Conservative" (10).

"Economy has worsened": What is your estimation of the economy? Runs from "Very Good" (1) to "Very Bad" (5).

"Worsened standard of living": respondents' satisfaction with their own standard of living running from "Very satisfied" (1) to "Very dissatisfied" (5).

Number of employees: number of employees in the respondent's workplace. Runs from one to four (1) to 1,000 or more (5).

Proportion: The last three characteristics refer to the proportion of respondents who (1) noted the ability of their first-named HR candidate to provide subsidies, (2) supported decentralization, and (3) were union members.

9

The Problem of Organization and Coherence in Top-Down Party Formation

New parties face special problems, beyond those of opposition parties in general. This has been important in Japan, where the leading opposition between 1993 and 2003 was made up of new parties.

As they develop, new parties often encounter many problems, even beyond their very newness. For example, in systems where new parties have little incentive to consolidate into larger wholes, they often have a hard time presenting a unified front against large existing parties. New parties in Clientelist/Financially Centralized systems face problems growing out of the way they were born. In such systems, new parties are likely to form from the top down. That is, after the party system is established, new parties have incentives to form not from the grassroots, but rather out of splits from and/or mergers between preexisting parties.

Aldrich's (1995) description of the early American Democratic Party suggests how new parties can benefit from such conditions. The presence of preexisting party organizations that new parties can borrow from can make creating new local organizations easier. However, in 1990s' Japan, new parties' top-down formation created difficulties for the opposition. In earlier chapters, I noted a number of ways in which top-down party formation patterns hurt the opposition in Japan, not the least of which being that it made the opposition more of an elite-level party with less of a grassroots base. In this chapter, I discuss a different problem growing out of the top-down party formation pattern: For the new parties of the 1990s, bonding together preexisting parties made party unification and party organization difficult and hindered their ability to present clear, coherent messages. The new parties' electoral chances were harmed as a result.

For details on the statistics and the politician survey discussed in this chapter, see *www.ethanscheiner.com* and its links to Chapter 9 of this book.

BACKGROUND

New party formation can occur according to two types of patterns: grass-roots or top down.[1] Even in the face of an existing party system (in contrast to brand-new party systems emerging in new democracies), party formation from the ground up makes sense because it allows parties to tap into issues that are not being handled by the system. Bottom-up formation can be seen in many different systems. In Britain's (programmatically oriented) party system in the first decades of the twentieth century, the Labour Party was able to become a force on the strength of workers' support.[2] And among the decentralized cases considered in Chapter 4, both Brazilian (especially the Workers Party or PT) and German (the Greens) new-party development was clearly from the ground up.[3]

However, Clientelist/Financially Centralized systems create incentives for parties, faced with an existing party system, to form from the top down: that is, through the actions of national-level elites. We can see this in new-party formation in a number of Clientelist/Financially Centralized countries. The electoral rules that permit alliances between multiple small parties help to block the necessity of such top-down formation in Italy, but even still, it is striking that a number of parties there emerged out of splits within preexisting parties. In Austria, despite the presence of a proportional representation electoral system that should have promoted greater new-party entry from various societal interests, there has been little new-party formation. The only major challenge to years of SPÖ and ÖVP supremacy has been by the FPÖ, which itself has long been a part of the system. A Green party did emerge in Austria, but it found almost no success. The best comparison to Japan may be Mexico, where the two leading opposition parties were the PAN and PRD. The PAN was a longstanding (very weak) opposition party, so the PRD was the only really new party of the two. Greene (2002) emphasizes bottom-up elements to PRD formation. But, Bruhn (1997) explains that, in many ways quite a bit like the new parties formed in Japan in the 1990s, central to the party's formation was the fact that the PRD was born out of the split of Cuauhtemoc Cardenas and other national-level politicians from the national ruling PRI.

---

[1] Similarly, Duverger distinguishes between "extra-parliamentary" party formation and those instigated by groups in the national legislature.

[2] Grassroots (especially workers-founded) new-party formation is more likely in any type of system at the time of the introduction of universal (male) suffrage. That said, the workers' parties grew far less in the clientelistic Japanese system where the workers' parties rarely had access to state resources.

[3] In the United States, all new-party formation is difficult because of the majority-determining (Electoral College) presidential system, single member districts, and campaign laws that privilege the two leading parties.

In Japan, with the exception of *Kōmeitō*, created in the 1960s to represent a lay Buddhist sect, every major new party formed from the top down. This was the case with both the LDP and Socialist Party in the 1950s; each formed out of a joining of preexisting rival parties. After the 1950s, the most important new-party formations occurred in the 1990s. First, small parties emerged out of defections from the LDP. Then in 1994, the NFP formed out of a merger of conservative former LDP members, JNP members, union-based Democratic Socialist members, and *Kōmeitō*. In short, the NFP was hodge-podge of very different preexisting parties.

The next major new-party formation involved the DPJ, which organized just prior to the 1996 election out of the merger of Socialist Party moderates and junior members of *Sakigake*, a splinter from the LDP. The emergence of both the NFP and DPJ pleased voters who had long been frustrated by the lack of pragmatic challengers to the LDP. But the wide range of groups that came together to form the new parties confused many because it was not clear what each stood for as a group – aside from opposition to the LDP.

After its defeat in 1996, the NFP gradually unraveled, as individuals and groups splintered off, until the party officially disbanded at the end of 1997. In its place, in April 1998, a "new" DPJ was born, combining former Socialists, former Democratic Socialists, former *Sakigake* members, and former *Shinsei* members (the more "conservative" group of LDP defectors).[4] Consolidation continued in 2003 when the Liberal Party (an Ozawa Ichirō-led splinter from the NFP) merged with the DPJ. Minus the Communists (on the left) and *Kōmeitō* (in the center), the DPJ had former members of nearly every party in the Japanese system. With such a wide assortment of characters in a single party, commentators and voters expressed concern regarding the party's ability to maintain principles of its own.

INCENTIVES FOR AND AGAINST CONSOLIDATION

In short, after the 1993 split of the LDP, there was much party splintering and merging in Japan. To what extent does the Japanese political system provide incentives for longer-term fragmentation and consolidation?

Japan's electoral institutions offer mixed incentives for new and opposition party consolidation. The new mixed-member (part single member district/part proportional representation) Japanese electoral system increased incentives for coordination among opposition parties. It is widely believed that an opposition bloc of the type that arose under the new system would have been difficult to achieve without single member districts.

---

[4] I will refer to more "progressive" and "conservative" groups within the DPJ. By "progressive," I mean former members of (or those with links to) the Socialist and Democratic Socialist Parties. By "conservative," I mean former members of the LDP, *Sakigake*, or *Shinsei*.

As a number of opposition party staff and Diet members explained, without the consolidating influence of SMDs, most small parties that formed the NFP and DPJ would have been unwilling to give up their autonomy.[5] They merged because small parties can rarely survive in SMDs. However, the proportional representation component hindered consolidation by allowing smaller parties to remain separate and made it easier for the NFP to split into smaller splinter parties. In addition, Japan's parliamentary (rather than presidential) structure reduces the pressure for consolidation toward a two-party structure.

On the other hand, Japan's public financing of political parties created incentives for party consolidation. Parties that have won a specified number of votes and seats in the previous election are eligible to receive substantial amounts of public funding.

PARTY CONSOLIDATION AND ORGANIZATIONAL DEVELOPMENT: TOP-DOWN PARTY FORMATION

As discussed in Chapters 4 and 5, Japan's Clientelist/Financially Centralized system makes top-down formation likely because local politicians and groups have little incentive to join a party that has limited ties to the central government. This led to new party formation that was focused on merging existing parties into a single one, even when lacking unifying backgrounds or ideologies. As I discuss in this chapter, new parties therefore had difficulty organizing themselves and providing a clear picture of what they stood for.

LOCAL PARTY ORGANIZATION

Aldrich (1995) explains that new parties ought to more easily develop local organizations when they are able to build on existing groups. In the case of nineteenth-century America, the Jacksonian Democrats "organized first where state and local politics were already more organized, making them less costly to develop and where the benefits would be highest, which meant organizing in states expected to be the most competitive" (1995: 112). The Jacksonian Democrats were a party composed of politicians from many preexisting party-like structures. The Democrats therefore decided to create local organizations first in areas where they had the greatest preexisting electoral strength and established organization. However, most of these organizations were fairly new; as a result, there were relatively few intraparty battles over turf within each state and locality. In contrast, in 1990's Japan, the histories of the parties coming together to form new parties created a number of difficulties.

---

[5] Interviews, December 1998–August 1999.

The NFP made little effort to build local organizations, leading it to have few local party foundations to help it compete.[6] The DPJ actively sought to avoid the NFP's bad judgment in this area.[7] Beginning soon after its formation in 1998, the new DPJ made one of the most serious efforts of any party in Japan in recent years to create local party organizations. The party set out to create well-structured, unified party organizations in each of the country's 47 prefectures. A unified party organization was one in which all the groups within the party in the prefecture formally accepted the merger of the party into a single headquarters and expressed a willingness to work together to elect DPJ candidates in the prefecture, irrespective of the candidates' party past and support groups.[8]

Sitting Diet members were important in creating local organizations because they were the center of most local party activity. The DPJ's central office in Tokyo and Diet members from the prefecture provided the main organizational push. Originally, the Tokyo headquarters was mostly concerned with Diet-related issues and left the localities to deal with their own affairs. At first DPJ prefectural assembly members and affiliated unions exerted great influence within prefectures in choosing DPJ Diet candidates, but by 2002 the central headquarters, through a panel of judges within the party, took over the job (*Asahi Shinbun*, May 30, 2002).[9] Although not to the same extent as *Kōmeitō* or the Japan Communist Party, which had strong organizations by Japanese standards (Foster 1982), the DPJ put together a substantial set of local party organizations. The focus was on building organizations to serve the party as a whole, unlike the LDP's far more candidate/incumbent-oriented ones that made little effort to help build a *party* base.[10]

At the time of its birth, the DPJ did not have a clear underlying policy or sense of solidarity. A large proportion of the party had come from the Socialist Party, frequently not for policy reasons but to create a more potentially competitive party. Oftentimes, when Socialists joined the DPJ, their old local-party organization continued to exist, simply removing the "Socialist" nameplate and putting up the "DPJ" label instead. Yet many remained uncomfortable because they were not yet used to the new party and its culture. Much of the key to organization came down to the party's relationship with the unions. Most former Socialists and Democratic Socialists within the party had unions as their base of support, so the key to building a successful organization was developing the relationship between the unions and the party.[11]

---

[6] Interview with staff member of former NFP Diet member, November 17, 1998.

[7] Interview with DPJ election bureau staff member, December 16, 1998.

[8] Interview with member of DPJ's local organization bureau, February 1, 1999.

[9] Unless otherwise noted, all references to newspaper articles in this chapter are from online editions.

[10] Interview with member of DPJ's local organization bureau, February 1, 1999.

[11] Interview with a leading member of the DPJ's local organization bureau, August 11, 1999.

Much of the problem in creating the organization was what one DPJ member described as "cultural."[12] Discord arose, for example, in the DPJ's January 2001 convention over the proper discussion format for the meeting. Former Socialist and Democratic Socialist members expected that all DPJ members would be welcome to participate in the meetings' discussions freely and therefore felt affronted when the party leadership cut off their speaking time. In contrast, the leadership had insisted on holding its principal discussions before the beginning of the convention, a practice more common in the LDP. As mentioned in a column in the *Daily Yomiuri* on the convention,

Those [DPJ] members who were familiar with [the JSP's and DSP's more open, participatory] tradition naturally felt irritated at a convention being run in such a way that all the items on the agenda were passed by applause expressing unanimous approval. No doubt they wondered whether a convention that was no different from LDP conventions, which are merely formalities, deserved to be called a convention at all. . . . It is no wonder that [DPJ] members have different views about what a party convention should be like, depending on the parties they once belonged to and other aspects of their political backgrounds. (*Daily Yomiuri*, January, 31, 2001)

Japanese politics analyst and erstwhile candidate for the DPJ in Saitama Prefecture, Matsuzaki Tetsuhisa, explained that the different parties that came together to make up the DPJ had very different cultures. Matsuzaki gave the following example. Disagreement emerged in the party over the choice of words used to describe less serious supporters of the party. Most of the party was able to agree on the word *tōin* to describe serious supporters, but one group sought to call less serious supporters *sapōtā* [supporter, a loan word from English], while other groups sought to call them *tōyū* [party friend, a compound of Japanese terms]. It was widely felt that disagreements of this kind could not interfere with the ultimate goals of the party, but they did somewhat undermine the individual relationships that underpinned general party activities at both the national and local organizational levels.[13]

Formation of Local Organization

Although all DPJ prefectural organizations unified, the ease of the process varied. In some cases, unification occurred almost immediately: Oita and Hokkaido each unified within a month of the new party's birth. In others such as Aomori, however, unification did not even occur within the first year and a half of the 1998 DPJ merger. The main trends were that unification was (1) quickest and easiest in prefectures where there were few sitting Diet members, which, as a result, also provided the party less overall electoral

[12] Interview with Matsuzaki Tetsuhisa, February 10, 1999.
[13] Interview with Matsuzaki Tetsuhisa, February 10, 1999.

benefit and (2) less cohesive in prefectures where the party had a larger potential base, possibly harming the party's ability to take full advantage of opportunities available to it.

In the United States, the Jacksonian Democrats organized first where, as Aldrich (1995) explains, costs were the lowest and benefits were potentially the highest (i.e., in those states where party organizations already in place could be used for the purposes of the new party and where the party could expect its greatest support). As Aldrich points out, working to the American Democrats' advantage was the fact that the Democratic Party, as the only group attempting to generate a mass-based party at the state level, could pick and choose in which states to build.

In the case of the Democratic Party of Japan in 1998, the party had no such luxury. Other parties had established mass bases throughout the country, and the DPJ, therefore, needed to organize quickly everywhere in order to compete at the national level. Like the Jacksonian Democrats, the DPJ organized fastest where the costs of organization were lowest. However, the nature of the costs was different in Japan, and, perhaps even more important, the greatest potential benefits tended to be in areas where the difficulty of organizing was the greatest.

Unlike the American Democrats who organized quickly in states where the party expected success, in the case of the Japanese DPJ, it does not appear that order of unification had much to do with anticipated electoral success. I have ranked each of Japan's 47 prefectures according to how quickly the DPJ unified its prefectural organization.[14] By and large, the DPJ unified late in prefectures where it was weakest. The average unification rank was 34 in the 10 prefectures in which the DPJ was least successful relative to the LDP in PR balloting in the 2000 HR election, the first after the 1998 party merger. However, the DPJ also did not unify quickly in places where the likely benefits were the highest. In the 10 prefectures where the DPJ found its greatest electoral success, the average order of unification was twentieth.

Instead, unification occurred most quickly in places where little coordination was necessary. The earliest unifications usually occurred in prefectures with few preexisting parties – usually just one party – providing a Diet member to the DPJ.[15] When few parties needed to unite to create the local DPJ organization, the effort to build the organization was less difficult because time-consuming and contentious negotiations over power and

---

[14] The party unified first in Oita and last in Aomori. See the links to the supplementary Web site at *www.ethanscheiner.com* for the specifics on each prefecture.

[15] The presence of only a small number of preexisting parties was a useful precondition for very quick unification because it dramatically reduced the costs of coordination. But it was no guarantee that the DPJ would unify rapidly. The DPJ was also quite slow to unify in a number of prefectures where the party was built from only one preexisting party.

administrative logistics were unnecessary. Iwate prefecture, the sixth prefectural party branch to unify, provides an extreme example. In Iwate, despite the fact that the DPJ had no Diet representative and no prefectural assembly member in the prefecture, unification occurred quickly. The reason was that there was a single city assembly member in the prefecture representing the DPJ and the party's organization simply was founded on him and his support organization.[16]

The first two cases of DPJ unification, Oita and Hokkaido prefectures, demonstrate the importance of low costs. Oita prefecture's DPJ unified first. Oita has substantial pockets of leftist union strength, as evidenced by the longtime success of Murayama Tomiichi, a Socialist who served as prime minister in a coalition government with the LDP in 1994–5. As a result, Oita Socialists were more loath to join the DPJ than were Socialists elsewhere. The lone DPJ HR member in Oita was longtime LDP member Hata Eijirō, who had defected from the ruling party in 1993. For this reason, Oita unification was easy; the party was primarily founded on Hata's *kōenkai*, or personal support organization.[17] But the Oita DPJ was quite weak because it did not acquire the strong Socialist core affiliated with Murayama.

Hokkaido unified second. Unlike most other quick unifiers, Hokkaido's DPJ was composed of two preexisting party groups – the Socialists and former LDP members who had joined *Sakigake*. But Hokkaido was unique in that the entire Socialist Party switched over to the DPJ. As a result, forming the organization was nearly as smooth as simply changing the name on the party headquarters' door. Moreover, the leader of the *Sakigake* group in Hokkaido was Hatoyama Yukio, one of the founders of the DPJ and its top leader for a number of years. As a national party leader, Hatoyama made special efforts to work out quickly any measures necessary to unify the organization.[18] Hokkaido was a rare case where rapid unification at low cost went along with electoral strength. However, except for Hokkaido and Fukuoka, the party was not electorally strong in prefectures where unification occurred quickly (e.g., Akita, Iwate, Oita, Tochigi, and Yamagata). And unification was slower in prefectures where the potential benefits – in particular, the number of potential supporters of the party – were greater (e.g., Aichi, Hyogo, Osaka, and Saitama).

According to a staff member heading the DPJ's local organization bureau, unification of the party at the national and local levels was not a clear-cut process. Many politicians joined the DPJ for no reason other than they had left another party with which they had grown disaffected. They joined the DPJ merely because they needed party affiliation. Some politicians even delayed joining the DPJ until campaign rules kicked in that encouraged joining

---

[16] Interview with DPJ local organization bureau, February 1, 1999.
[17] Telephone interview with the DPJ Oita prefectural organization, August 1999.
[18] Telephone interview with the DPJ Hokkaido organization, July 1999.

a party rather than running as an independent – for instance, the right to keep one's campaign posters up longer (Scheiner 2003). In this way, local organization was primarily just a matter of compromises at the local level.

Perhaps the hardest part of creating a unified local party organization was getting local support groups to work together. The local organization bureau staff member explained, "For local party unification, getting DPJ politicians to work together is not too tough, but supporting organizations and groups matter a lot! For example, doctors' associations strongly support the DPJ, but some can also support the LDP. Also, there are some private-sector labor unions that have very close relationships with the LDP. The relationship with labor unions can be difficult – it all depends on the groups."[19]

Nagano prefecture in 1998 provides an example of support-group unification problems. One of Nagano's leading political stars was Kosaka Kenji, a former LDP member, who ran and won under the NFP banner in 1996. With the collapse of the NFP, Kosaka considered switching over to the DPJ but was met with fierce resistance by his *kōenkai*, who did not want to join together with a group of former Socialists. As a result, Kosaka returned to the LDP, under whose banner he easily won office in the 2000 HR election (Scheiner 2003; *Yomiuri Shinbun*, paper version, June 19, 1998).

Although anyone joining the DPJ was expressing a greater willingness than Kosaka and his supporters to work with former enemies, similar problems existed within a number of DPJ prefectural organizations. Such problems were more likely in prefectures where the party was potentially strong – and therefore the benefits of unification were greater – because part of the reason for the party's strength in such areas was the many groups that came together in the DPJ.[20] That is, in prefectures where a large number of pre-existing parties united to form the DPJ, the party would attract the support of many different types of voters, but at the same time the presence of multiple groups made creating a unified front more difficult.

Relative to the LDP in the PR balloting, the DPJ's second and fourth most successful prefectures (in terms of PR votes relative to the LDP) in 2000 were, respectively, Tokyo and Kanagawa. In each, the party unified moderately quickly (Tokyo was sixteenth and Kanagawa eleventh), but in neither case was unification a total success. In each, the organization was officially unified, but they were actually divided into fiefdoms, each controlled by a different influential politician. Serious party building was largely eschewed for at least the first year-plus of the "unified" organization.[21] The lack of

---

[19] Interview, August 11, 1999.
[20] In the nine prefectures in which the DPJ outpaced the LDP in PR voting in 2000, the average number of parties holding national Diet members who united to form the organization was 3.22. In the prefectures where the LDP did better, it was 0.76.
[21] Interviews with DPJ Kanagawa prefectural organization (February 8, 1999) and DPJ Tokyo organization (February 9, 1999).

unity of the party in areas like these was so great that the local organization staff bureau member compared them to the European Union, a set of
sovereign units with loose ties to a larger organizing body.

Other prefectural organizations were even worse off. The local organization bureau staff member described these as similar to Yugoslavia, where the
different parts of the party were not only kept separate, but each part saw
an enemy in the other. Aichi, Hyogo, Osaka, and Saitama, among the DPJ's
most successful prefectures in terms of PR votes relative to the LDP, fit the
"Yugoslavia category."[22] The most problematic was Aichi, where moderate, private-sector unions associated with the old Democratic Socialist Party
were strong, and public-sector ones associated with the former JSP were
leftist, a combination that, owing to years of competition and differing ideologies, typically led to serious battles between the two. These battles made
any sort of organizational unification impossible for a year and a half after
the creation of the DPJ in April 1998.[23] In the words of the local organization bureau staff member, without a clear "Tito-like" leader, truly unifying
the warring factions would never be complete.[24] Similar problems existed in
Hyogo, Osaka, and Saitama, although not to the same extent. In Saitama,
for example, old conservative forces and the progressives frequently clashed,
typically over issues such as which group would get to put up its candidate
in the next election. In addition, unions were slow to back conservative candidates, and conservative (former LDP) candidates' support groups were not
easily mobilized to provide support for labor union candidates.[25]

Finally, prefectures like Nagano provided a different sort of problem. The
DPJ's organization in Nagano unified moderately quickly and was the DPJ's
most successful prefecture in the 2000 HR election in terms of PR votes
relative to those won by the LDP. However, it would be a stretch to call
the DPJ Nagano's local administrative body a *party* organization. The most
powerful politician in Nagano was Hata Tsutomu, one of the leaders of the
reform movement of the early mid-1990s, who defected from the LDP and
was an important founder of the new DPJ. Similar to Oita's organization, the
DPJ's party organization in Nagano was founded foremost on Hata's *kōenkai*
and was less involved in DPJ party affairs, as the party itself scarcely existed
in the prefecture except in national-level elections.[26] DPJ success in national

---

[22] Chiba, another prefecture where the DPJ found substantial PR vote success, was also put in
the Yugoslavia category.

[23] Telephone interview with the DPJ Aichi organization made up of former members of the
Democratic Socialist Party, August 1999. At the time of the interview, the DPJ had two Aichi
prefectural organizations: one made up of former Democratic Socialists and one made up of
former Socialists.

[24] Interview, February 1, 1999.

[25] Interview with DPJ Saitama prefectural organization, February 10, 1999.

[26] Telephone interview with DPJ Nagano organization, July 1999, and written correspondence
with Nagano prefectural reporter, May 23, 1999.

races in Nagano was due far more to Hata's power within the prefecture than to popularity held by the party itself there (Scheiner 2003).

Effects

Usually, where unification occurred swiftly and costlessly, the party was not able to benefit because its electoral support was so thin. In contrast, in most prefectures where the DPJ had substantial electoral support, it was not able to get the entire party working together in tandem.

I determined for each prefecture the number of additional SMDs the non-Communist opposition could have taken from the LDP had the opposition pooled its votes in each district in the 2000 HR election. Out of 57 SMDs that the LDP won in the nine prefectures where the DPJ was especially popular (outpolled the LDP in PR voting), greater opposition coordination could have netted the DPJ and its mates as many as 17 additional seats (roughly 30 percent of all seats the LDP won in those areas). In contrast, out of 120 SMDs won by the LDP in the remaining prefectures, better coordination would have yielded only an additional 12 DPJ seats (just 10 percent of the total). Moreover, 7 of those 12 were in prefectures where the DPJ was made up of multiple preexisting parties.

In part, this finding merely reflects the fact that the opposition could only make errors in prefectures where it was already strong enough to have an opportunity to win. Where the opposition did not have enough votes to win seats – where it was unpopular relative to the LDP – errors were essentially impossible for the DPJ. Nevertheless, the finding is significant: It was in the prefectures where the DPJ could have won extra seats that the party was fraught with internal organizational and coordination problems. These problems afflicted DPJ candidates in districts where other opposition candidates also ran, and they also hindered individual DPJ candidates' ability to draw support from various groups within their own party. If such problems were an obstacle to intraparty cooperation, they certainly also made interparty coordination even more difficult. In sum, a lack of truly unified organizations no doubt prevented greater opposition success in areas where it potentially had the most to gain.

OVERALL PARTY COHERENCE

In the early years of a party system's development, internal mobilization – that is, party formation by elites within the state – may not create too many obstacles. An example from U.S. history is illustrative. As Aldrich explains, when the American Democratic Party was formed in the nineteenth century, the founders focused on bringing together key figures such as office seekers and office holders (1995: 104). The leadership was drawn from sitting members of the national legislature (who were supportive of Jackson). A key factor was that the party formed without any commitment to policy, particularly important because many of the existing state and local groups that formed the Democrats had already developed platforms that contradicted those of others likely to join the new party. Before the Jacksonian Democrats, no real "party in the electorate" or "party in the organization" had existed in the United States: Voters generally did not see themselves as supporters of a particular party, and there were no real party organizations. As described by Aldrich, the main purpose in forming the party was to create an organization through which the Democrats could mobilize voters to support their candidates. The major national news about the party related to Jackson, who was notably ambiguous in his policy appeals.

In short, the American Democratic Party was aided by the fact that little was known about it. It could sell itself however it wanted and the media could not instantly recognize and demonstrate inconsistencies within the party across the country. Although many American Democratic Party candidates were relatively new to politics, they faced media that were less than fully capable of pointing out their differences. The primary aim in forming the Jacksonian Democrats was voter mobilization, and given that this occurred separately in each locality, consistency of program and method across the various states was not critical.

In contrast, in more established party systems with active media, such as Japan's, consistency is important in establishing a party's reputation. Consistency was especially important for Japan's new parties of the 1990s because voters were suspicious of parties in general after years of being disappointed by them.

Perceived Divisions

The new DPJ sought to present a united front, but it had the appearance of being divided on key issues that had long received substantial press in Japan.

The most obvious division was over the use of the military and revision of the Constitution's "peace" clause. In the fall of 2000, DPJ leaders Hatoyama Yukio and Kan Naoto made a series of remarks suggesting that the party should discuss the advisability of Japan's participation in United Nations peacekeeping activities ("peace-enforcement") and potential revisions of the Constitution. The proposal shook a number of senior members within the party, who suggested that such remarks could compromise Hatoyama's party leadership, as a number of DPJ Diet members were set against expanding Japan's peacekeeping role. There were reports that, within the party, members' views about national security were far apart on such sensitive issues as Japan–U.S. security arrangements and revision of the Constitution (e.g., *Yomiuri Shinbun*, September 29, October 2, and December 1, 2000). Some observers, such as DPJ Vice President Yokomichi Takahiro, a former longtime member of the Socialist Party, threatened to push for

Hatoyama's resignation from the leadership of the party if he did not stop speaking in favor of Constitutional revision (*Yomiuri Shinbun*, December 18, 2000).

In addition, the party faced divisions in other areas. Party executives did not actively cooperate in handling Diet affairs and party conventions, where many junior members, especially from the factions of the former Socialist parties, were left out of the debate. Moreover, as the LDP pushed reform of the Upper House electoral system, a divide emerged between leading DPJ members in the House of Representatives and the House of Councillors. Distrust grew to where DPJ HR leaders began to fear a secret deal between HC members and the LDP on the issue (*Yomiuri Shinbun*, October 2, 2000).

As such divisions emerged, I sought to understand what principles truly underlay the new DPJ (and its predecessor, the NFP). In the summer of 1999, I conducted a survey of HR Diet members, in which I asked members and their staff from a variety of different parties what the primary differences between the leading parties were. My survey also included questions about differences between a number of different parties, but the following are the most important: the differences between the LDP and the conservative (former LDP) members of the DPJ, the differences between the LDP and the DPJ as a whole, and the differences between the LDP and the prior leader of the opposition, the NFP.

The survey was conducted from mid-May to mid-August 1999 and targeted roughly 300 (out of a total of 500 members in the entire chamber) HR members, primarily from the LDP and new DPJ, with responses from 116. The surveys were not open-ended, but rather included as possible differences all the responses listed in Table 9.1 except for the last five, which respondents wrote in the "Other" category. However, respondents were given room at the end of each question to explain their answers in greater detail. The respondents were first asked: "What do you think is the biggest difference between LDP and DPJ Diet members?" Then, respondents were asked the same question, but this time inserting first "conservative DPJ" and then "the now-defunct NFP" in place of "DPJ."[27]

Table 9.1 summarizes the results. The most common description of the difference between the LDP and the *conservative* members of the DPJ was "No difference between them." Many politicians saw no difference between the LDP and conservative DPJ members. Among those who did see a difference, the most common distinction was bureaucrat versus politician power: They perceived conservative DPJ politicians as eager, relative to the LDP, to shrink the power of the bureaucracy and increase the role of politicians.

Respondents perceived four main differences between the DPJ *as a whole* and the LDP. They saw the DPJ as more interested in shrinking bureaucratic

---

[27] For additional details of the survey, see the links to the supplementary Web site at *www. ethanscheiner.com*.

TABLE 9.1 *Total Number of HR Members Perceiving a Difference Between Politicians from the LDP and Those from Other Parties*

Issue on Which Respondent Is Comparing New Party to the LDP	New Party with Which Respondent Is Comparing LDP		
	DPJ (Conservative Wing)	DPJ (Whole)	NFP (Whole)
Economic policy	10	13	13
Military policy	16	32	9
Foreign policy	9	14	7
The Constitution	9	29	9
Electoral system	5	6	8
Liberalization vs. protectionism	2	1	2
Centralization vs. decentralization	17	27	9
Bureaucrat vs. politician power	30	35	11
Political reform	16	17	26
Social welfare	7	13	2
No difference between them	31	3	29
Other	6	5	13
All	1	2	2
I don't know	0	1	2
Depending on the person, it differs	0	0	0
Big vs. small government	0	1	0
Religion	0	0	1
Things having to do with the presence of the JSP in the DPJ	0	3	0
DPJ is not a real party: it is made up of too many different groups	0	16	0
Raw totals	159	218	143

Each figure indicates the number of respondents citing a difference between the LDP and the new party on the issue cited in left column. Note that the number of answers exceeds the number of respondents because multiple answers were possible.

Source: Author's survey of Japanese HR members (summer 1999).

TABLE 9.2 *Answered That There Was No Difference Between Politicians from the LDP and the Conservative Wing of the DPJ*

Party of the Respondent	Total No. of Respondents	Number Citing "No Difference"	Percent Within That Party Citing "No Difference"
LDP	46	21	45.65
DPJ	49	4	8.16
Liberal Party	7	3	42.86
Kōmeitō	13	3	23.08
Independent	1	0	0.00
Raw totals	116	31	

The final column represents the percentage of a party's respondents who cited "No Difference" between politicians from the LDP and those from the conservative wing of the DPJ (i.e., column 4 is equal to the percentage derived from dividing column 3 by column 2).
Source: Author's survey of Japanese HR members (summer 1999).

power, more dovish on the use of Japanese troops and other military questions, more anxious to hold off Constitutional revision, and more interested in decentralization. Most striking, however, was the frequently articulated view that the DPJ had little coherence – 16 respondents offered an answer that was not even available in the survey questionnaire: namely, "the DPJ is not a real party: it is made up of too many different groups."

As for perceived differences between the LDP and the NFP, 26 respondents cited political reform, explaining that the NFP was more reform-oriented. But even more respondents (29) saw no difference between members of the NFP and the LDP.

In short, a very large number of respondents saw little difference between LDP politicians and those who had earlier left the LDP and joined the NFP and then the DPJ. At the same time, a large number of respondents found a substantial difference between the DPJ as a whole and the LDP. One of the respondents, a fairly experienced LDP politician from Ehime Prefecture, explained: "Differences between the conservatives really just come down to electoral need. Basically, everyone wants to stay in the LDP, but those who can't [run under the LDP banner], then run for conservative opposition parties. As for the DPJ, there is no such thing as an overall party. Within it there are conservatives and there are Socialists."[28] That said, how could the DPJ remain intact if composed of such different groups?

In reality, the responses were much more nuanced than these results suggest. The results change when we break down the responses by party. Of the 16 who said that the DPJ was not a "real" party, 15 were LDP members (and one was from Kōmeitō). No DPJ member made such a claim. Table 9.2,

[28] Telephone interview, July 23, 1999.

TABLE 9.3 *Number of Respondents Perceiving a Difference Between the LDP and DPJ (Whole Party) on Four Key Issues*

Party of the Respondent	Total No. of Respondents	Number of Respondents Perceiving a Difference on:			
		Military	Constitution	Centralization Vs. Decentralization	Bureaucrat Vs. Politician Power
LDP	46	17 (.37)	17 (.37)	2 (.04)	4 (.09)
DPJ	49	7 (.14)	5 (.10)	23 (.47)	26 (.53)
Liberal Party	7	4 (.57)	2 (.29)	0 (.00)	2 (.29)
Kōmeitō	13	4 (.31)	5 (.38)	2 (.15)	3 (.23)
Independent	1	0 (.00)	0 (.00)	0 (.00)	0 (.00)
Raw totals	116	32	29	27	35

Figures indicate the number of respondents citing a difference between the LDP and DPJ on the issue listed at the top of the column. (Listed in parentheses is the proportion of respondents from the party listed in column 1 who cited a difference on the issue.)
Source: Author's survey of Japanese HR members (summer 1999).

which breaks down the responses by the respondents' party affiliation, shows that most politicians claiming no difference between LDP and conservative DPJ politicians were from non-DPJ parties. Only four (out of 49 total) respondents from the DPJ made a similar suggestion. Similarly, as Table 9.3 shows, politicians stating that there was a major difference between the DPJ (as a whole party) and the LDP on issues of Constitutional revision (peace clause) and military policy were generally members of the LDP, Liberals, or *Kōmeitō*. Few DPJ members found major differences between themselves and the LDP on these issues.

The pattern reverses if we ask about differences between the parties on centralization versus decentralization and on the power of politicians versus bureaucrats (Table 9.3). Many DPJ Diet members saw significant differences – notably, they favored increased local governmental power and limiting the power of bureaucrats – but politicians from other parties claimed to see little difference between the LDP and the DPJ.

Why did non-DPJ members see a contrast between the parties on one set of issues and DPJ politicians see distinctions on a completely different set? A partial answer is no doubt wishful thinking, denial, and/or obfuscation: DPJ members did not want what is potentially a major difference between its members to become a point of contention that truly does divide its members and/or gives the public the idea that it does.

But this does not appear to be the whole story. Many non-DPJ politicians' perceptions of the DPJ were undoubtedly shaped by the fact that former Socialists tended to express stronger feelings about military issues. Nevertheless, with the end of the Cold War, military and peace Constitution issues were no longer a central focus of interparty politics. Moreover,

Constitutional revision and military questions divided not only the DPJ but the LDP as well.[29]

It is also possible that, on average, LDP and DPJ members did hold different positions on military and Constitutional issues, but DPJ members simply did not locate such issues at the core of the debate driving Japanese politics. Moreover, such issues did not appear to play a central part in the split of the LDP in 1993 and did not determine who joined the DPJ in 1998. As Reed and Scheiner (2003) indicate, urban–rural issues were important in those moves and it was around these issues that divisions within the parties appeared to grow. Even though most LDP politicians I interviewed did not think the issue of decentralization or a concern with reducing bureaucratic power were significant in dividing the parties, every DPJ politician I interviewed concurred with the view expressed in the results of the last two columns in Table 9.3: The DPJ sought to differentiate itself from the LDP by promoting issue positions and policies that could undercut the clientelist tradition of the LDP.

In the words of Kano Michihiko, one of the leading former LDP members in the DPJ, the difference between the parties can be summed up in a simple Japanese phrase, *shūken kanji, bunken jiji* or "Centralized/Bureaucratic Power versus Decentralized/Politician-based Power."[30] That is, to Kano and many in the DPJ, the LDP's pork-based clientelist system was founded on power that was derived from Japan's *central* government, in particular the *bureaucracy*. The DPJ pushed for a more *decentralized* government system, which also gave greater power to *politicians*. To some extent, an opinion like this ought to be expected from any party that is out of power and lacks access to the centralized bureaucracy: The DPJ could not benefit from the centralized system and the powerful bureaucracy within it. In contrast, these two features of the system were at the heart of much of the LDP's power. Therefore the DPJ had great incentive to push for an end to the particular features that were critical to LDP dominance, even if the DPJ could not bring an immediate end to LDP dominance itself. LDP leaders I spoke to argued that DPJ efforts to push decentralization and weaken bureaucratic power were simply ploys to enhance DPJ political position and reflected no real difference between the two parties.

Nevertheless, an important policy difference, and not just a means to power, seems to underlie the DPJ's position here. To DPJ leaders, the clientelist system needed to be phased out to fix the ills of Japan's sagging economy. Here, the DPJ saw a clear difference between itself and the LDP,

---

[29] It also appears that former Socialists within the DPJ over time grew less vehement in their stances on military issues as the Cold War became an increasingly distant memory. In 2003, the DPJ joined the LDP in passing emergency military legislation, with former Socialist Party members within the party grudgingly assenting to the bill (*Asahi Shinbun*, May 15, 2003).

[30] Interview, May 21, 1999.

which sought to maintain the existing clientelist system. Referring to the system established with the birth of the LDP in 1955 (along with the consolidation of the ruling party's socioeconomic base under the system), one staff member in the DPJ national headquarters explained that, compared to urban areas, rural areas maintained a different sort of socioeconomic structure, which had been developed through the "1955 system." This structure, he argued, was founded on massive subsidies paid out by the central government. Every DPJ politician and staff member I spoke to argued that this structure contributed to Japan's economic ills. For this reason, the DPJ staff member explained, "the DPJ is looking to change the social structure. The main objective of creating the DPJ was to truly change the 1955 system."[31]

There were certainly LDP members, especially from urban areas, who did not match the preceding description of the LDP, but overall this discussion suggests – similar to Chapter 8 – a sharp distinction between overall LDP and DPJ visions of the correct direction of the Japanese economy. In contrast to the overall image of the LDP, the DPJ emphasized greater market liberalization and a government more concerned with producing public goods, rather than distributing favors and private goods to stay afloat in a more controlled economy. Indeed, unless there was a genuine difference between the two parties over issues like these, it is hard to make sense of the new parties' expression of anti-clientelist views and the voters' response to this effort, described in Chapter 8.

In addition, in highlighting the *shūken kanji, bunken jiji* division between itself and the LDP, the DPJ was almost certainly attempting to attract a specific set of LDP politicians who were most likely to defect from the LDP and link up with the DPJ. Those in the LDP who said the LDP and the DPJ differed on the *shūken kanji, bunken jiji* dimension were also among those who were perceived as unhappy with the LDP over its position on the issue and had therefore given thought to leaving the LDP to link up with the DPJ. In public statements, Katō Kōichi, long a leading member of the LDP (until scandal in 2002), agreed with the DPJ on a number of issues related to the *shūken kanji, bunken jiji* issue, particularly on the need for structural fiscal and economic reform and deregulating information technology. This position placed Katō (and Prime Minister Koizumi) squarely at odds with the recent LDP leadership, which sought to stimulate the economy through continued tax cuts and public works (*Yomiuri Shinbun*, November 16, 2000). And indeed, Katō and Koizumi were typically seen as the most likely LDP leaders to link up with the DPJ. As prime minister, Koizumi focused his reform efforts not on the banking system as many had expected, but on the foundations of LDP clientelist mechanisms: the postal system, construction, and roads. The opposition held out hope that a failure of Koizumi to achieve his agenda would lead the prime minister to break up the ruling party. Katō

---

[31] Interview with national DPJ headquarters' staff, August 11, 1999.

was even likelier to leave the LDP and join the opposition. In 2000, he nearly left the LDP in an effort to bring to an end both the Mori administration and the party's massive pork barrel spending (*Reuters*, November 18, 2000). Given the conclusion of Chapter 5, that it is critical to the success of the opposition in Clientelist/Financially Centralized systems such as Japan's to bring in defectors from the ruling party, it made sense for the DPJ to play up issues that might attract defectors from the LDP.

Nonetheless, even if the DPJ had been able to present these principles (anti-clientelism, decentralization, curtailing bureaucratic power) clearly to the public, other problems made it hard for voters to recognize what the party stood for. There were still many divisions within the DPJ. Many DPJ junior members formed within the party separate study groups, the bodies that drove much of both policymaking and group dynamics within the party. The media sometimes characterized these groups as precursors to a new round of party defection and realignment, in particular as the divisions appeared to be along old party lines.

At the same time, people inside the DPJ explained that the apparent splits within the party, such as those between Hatoyama and Yokomichi regarding Japan's participation in United Nations peacekeeping and the revision of the Constitution, had more to do with jockeying for internal power and leadership of the party than with actual policy. Moves by Yokomichi's group seemed more founded on pushing his own candidacy for party president than on policy issues (*Yomiuri Shinbun*, July 8, 2002). Other key disputes within the party appear to have been based more on a desire for new blood to lead the party than on a desire for new policies to drive it (*Asahi Shinbun*, July 4, 2002; *Yomiuri Shinbun*, July 10, 2002). In addition, one DPJ party staff member argued that the party was unlikely to split unless the LDP also had a massive split, an event that would probably lead the conservatives in the DPJ to join an anti-clientelist/pro-market liberalizing group from the LDP in forming a new party.[32]

A second part of the DPJ's problem in advertising its principles involved political coverage by the media in Japan. Members of the DPJ whom I interviewed argued strenuously that they were truly attempting – through speeches and reports – to demonstrate differences between themselves and the LDP on nonmilitary/Constitution-related issues, but the media did not cover such efforts. Indeed, attending a number of speeches made by party leaders where such principles were laid out, I found substantial truth to the DPJ's argument about media coverage.

Finally, perhaps the most serious problem for the DPJ was its own history. As Kumagai Hiroshi, one of the leaders of the DPJ (until he split from the party to become head of the New Conservative Party in December 2002)

---

[32] That said, there was a small split in the DPJ in December 2002, when four members of the party left to join the New Conservative Party (*Asahi Shinbun*, December 25, 2002).

said, "With all the people coming in and out of the opposition, it seems that all conservatives are the same and that the DPJ does not have any party principle. The next issue for us will be how we can gain the trust of the public."[33]

These results may suggest confusion on the part of politicians over what the DPJ stood for, as well as a lack of clarity in the way the DPJ was presented to the public. To what extent does this confusion get passed on to voters? Unfortunately, I do not have public opinion data covering the new DPJ, but I am able to examine data from 1996. These data indicate that voters were more uncertain about Japan's new parties than about the LDP. Analyses of U.S. elections by Alvarez (1997) and Bartels (1988) and Mexican elections by Magaloni (1997) indicate that voters tend to be leery of casting ballots for parties they are uncertain about. I find that Japanese voters are similar, suggesting additional problems for new parties that cannot advertise their principles clearly.

Voter Knowledge of New Parties

To what extent did voters have a clear sense of Japan's new parties? I answer this question using results from the 1996 JEDS data set. Among the many ways the data set offers to measure such uncertainty, the most obvious is self-placement, asking voters how well they knew each party. Voters felt that they knew the NFP and DPJ quite a bit less than they did the LDP. Although 30 percent claimed to not know the LDP or know it only by name, 41 percent were similarly uncertain about the NFP and 62 percent, about the DPJ.

JEDS also asked respondents to place parties on a scale from 0 to 10 on three different issues: the extent to which parties are progressive or conservative, the extent to which they support political reform, and the extent to which they support administrative reform. By and large, the overall responses regarding each party appear accurate. For example, the Progressive–Conservative measure runs from 0 as the most progressive to 10 as the most conservative, and the average Progressive–Conservative score for each party correctly places the LDP (7.6) as the most conservative party, followed in order by the NFP (5.9), DPJ (5.2), SDP (4.7), and JCP (2.4).[34]

---

[33] Interview, May 27, 1999.
[34] Among political analysts of Japan, there are likely to be disagreements over exactly where each party stands on a particular issue. For example, many would argue that the NFP was to the right of the LDP on certain market liberalization or military issues. However, overall, the Progressive–Conservative ordering by the JEDS respondents appears quite accurate.

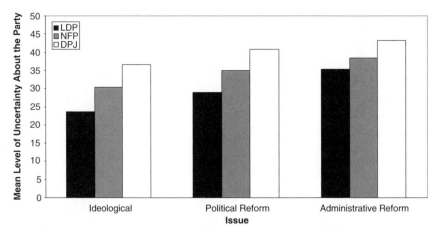

FIGURE 9.1 Voters' Levels of Uncertainty about Each Party by Issue
Uncertainty refers to the degree of dispersion of voters' impressions of parties' positions. Higher uncertainty scores indicate greater variance from the mean position attributed to a given party.
Source: JEDS96 public opinion survey.

However, to what extent was there confusion surrounding what each party stood for? Borrowing from Alvarez (1997) and Magaloni (1997), I define voter uncertainty regarding a given party as the degree to which there is disagreement among voters over the party's "true" position. Like the earlier studies, I define voter uncertainty as the extent of dispersion (variance) of respondents' placement of the party around the "true" position of the party (the mean position of all scores for that party).[35] As Figure 9.1 demonstrates, voters were more uncertain (there was less consistency) about the positions of the NFP and DPJ on all three of the issues mentioned earlier.

Part of the confusion was probably caused by the very newness of the new parties, but one important part of the confusion over Japan's new parties had little to do with their newness: the fact that the new parties were formed out of the merger of a number of (seemingly incompatible) extant parties. Many sitting Diet members in 1999 saw the DPJ as not a "real" party but rather as a collection of very different groups.[36] To what extent did voters have similar perceptions about the new parties in 1996?

The JEDS96 survey includes a question in which respondents were given a list of all of Japan's parties and for each were asked if it was "A party which has no programmatic center (which is a coalition of policy-wise different

---

[35] See the links to the supplementary Web site at *www.ethanscheiner.com* for all details of my analysis of uncertainty (including statistics).

[36] Politicians were clearly not saying this merely because the DPJ was a fairly new party. The Liberal Party, too, was quite new, but in my survey, no politician made any such statement about the Liberals.

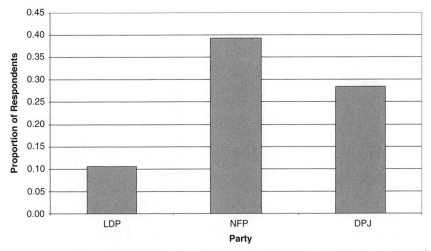

FIGURE 9.2 "Party Which Has No Programmatic Center (Which is a Coalition of Policy-wise Different Groups)"
Source: JEDS96 public opinion survey.

groups)." As Figure 9.2 shows, many more respondents felt that the NFP and DPJ (as opposed to the LDP) were not programmatically "centered." Most striking, more respondents cited the NFP than the DPJ. If responses to this question were merely a result of the short amount of time the parties had existed, more would have cited the DPJ, which formed just prior to the election, than the NFP, which was born more than two years earlier. Instead, voters correctly recognized that the NFP was in fact made up of a larger number of preexisting parties than the DPJ in 1996 was.[37] In short, it appears that, even though uncertainty about Japan's new parties was probably partly due to their newness, uncertainty about what they stood for was also due to the confusing mish-mash of different preexisting party incumbents they placed in their political lineups. As Otake writes, "the NFP failed to project a fresh image among voters, who viewed it as nothing more than a coalition of existing political parties (which it was)" (2000: 305).

Effect of Uncertainty

Did such perceptions actually hurt Japan's new parties?

Uncertainty and Support for Parties. The correlation between certainty about a party and support for that party tended to be high. Figure 9.3 graphs the average level of uncertainty for the three issues combined into

---

[37] Presumably, then, voters recognized that the post 1998 DPJ was a considerably less coherent party.

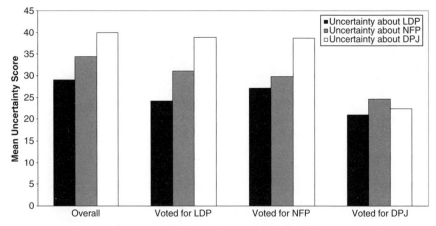

FIGURE 9.3 Support for Parties in PR and Voters' Levels of Uncertainty about Each Party

Uncertainty refers to the degree of dispersion of voters' impressions of parties' positions (on all three issues listed in Figure 9.1). Higher uncertainty scores indicate greater variance around the mean position attributed to a given party.
Source: JEDS96 public opinion survey.

a single score for each party's policy positions. As noted previously and shown in a different form in the left set of bars in Figure 9.3, voters overall felt greater uncertainty about the NFP and DPJ than about the LDP. What is more striking, the relative levels of uncertainty vary depending on the party respondents voted for in PR balloting in 1996. LDP voters demonstrated less uncertainty than the overall population regarding their own party but felt greater uncertainty about the two new parties than they did about the LDP. NFP voters' level of certainty regarding their own party was roughly the same as their sense of certainty about the LDP. Interestingly, DPJ voters felt markedly more certain about all three parties, with little difference in the level of certainty. This is most likely due to the fact that DPJ voters had *markedly* higher education levels than other party voters.

I also examine levels of uncertainty about the policy positions of the LDP, NFP, and DPJ, while controlling for sociodemographic features. A number of findings emerge.[38] As a group, women were markedly less certain about parties' issue positions, whereas more educated and urban voters were more certain. Most important for my purposes here, even controlling for other variables, there was a high correlation between voters' support for a given party and their level of certainty about it. Japanese appear less likely to vote for parties that they are uncertain about.

---

[38] For details of the statistics, see the links to the supplementary Web site at *www.ethanscheiner.com*.

The Impact of Perceptions of Incoherence. To deal further with the argument that uncertainty was simply an outgrowth of the newness of the parties, I also conducted more systematic statistical analysis of PR vote choice in 1996 in which I included voters' perceptions of whether a given party was "a coalition of policy-wise different groups." Even controlling for a number of other factors, the results indicate that voters were less likely to cast ballots for the LDP or NFP when they perceived that the party was such an incoherent collection of politicians. A voter maintaining such perceptions about the NFP was often more than 10 percentage points less likely to cast a ballot for the party than an identical voter who lacked this view of the party. My statistics suggest that votes for the DPJ in 1996 were unaffected by perceptions of incoherence, but voters who knew the party less well and were more uncertain about it, according to my definitions, were less likely to vote for it. Again, however, it is important to emphasize that the partisan makeup of the DPJ in 1996 was not terribly complicated – the largest proportion of members were moderate former Socialists. But when the party re-formed in 1998, it became difficult for many politicians (outside the DPJ) to reconcile the unification of so many politicians from different party backgrounds. Given the difficulties faced on this front by the NFP in 1996, it is likely that for this reason DPJ popularity in later years was harmed as well.

Counterarguments. Counterexamples might be raised against my analysis in this chapter. For example, when the LDP was born out of the merger of the Liberal and Democratic Parties in 1955, many doubted that two parties made up of so many seemingly incompatible personalities and policy positions could stay together for long (Calder 1988). In part, power (control of the government) helped maintain the merger. And, despite the seeming lack of coherence within the party, voters had no difficulty voting for the LDP. This might suggest a problem with my analysis of the importance of party coherence and voter certainty for party success.

However, even beyond government control, there is an important difference between the 1955 LDP and the 1990s new parties: the electoral institutions being used. In the 1950s, Japan used the single nontransferable vote in multimember districts system that gave voters ballots to be cast for individual candidates. In 1958, the first election after the LDP merged, voters did not have to worry about what *party* to support but could continue to cast ballots for their preferred *candidates*. In contrast, in post-1993 Japan, new parties in PR balloting had to attract *party* support, which was difficult given the lack of coherence within them and the voter uncertainty and perceptions of incoherence that arose in turn. This was one more problem for the opposition, which already had a massive disadvantage relative to the LDP in district-level, candidate-oriented balloting.

The 2001 Japanese Upper House election raises a related question. Not long before the election, Koizumi Junichirō rose to the presidency of the

LDP (which also made him prime minister). Based in large measure on his pro-reform stance, Koizumi's popularity skyrocketed and led to a sharp increase in support for the LDP. As a result, the LDP had its most successful election in years in the 2001 Upper House race. At the same time, Koizumi's ascendance raised uncertainty about the LDP. Here was a highly clientelistic party led by a reformer who sought to undercut the clientelist system. Given likely confusion about what the LDP stood for, then, why was the party so seemingly successful in 2001?

First, many simply supported the LDP in the hopes that Koizumi would indeed achieve his reform aims. In a survey conducted by the *Yomiuri Shinbun*, 27 percent of respondents who said that they supported Koizumi but not the LDP voted for the ruling party in PR balloting (*Yomiuri Shinbun*, August 11, 2001). Second, even though the LDP won many seats, the election hardly indicated a groundswell of support for the ruling party. Leading up to the election, Koizumi and his cabinet received support ratings of 70–80 percent, yet the LDP won only 38.6 percent of the PR votes. The LDP's greatest success, again, was in district-level races where voters could cast ballots for individual candidates only.

Ultimately, these two examples serve to highlight the additional importance of electoral institutions and LDP's advantages in races contested by individual candidates.

CONCLUSION: ADDING INSULT TO INJURY

Confusion over what they stood for was especially damaging for Japan's new parties of the 1990s because their base of support was in urban areas. If the NFP and DPJ had been established in rural areas, where individual candidacies, pork barrel, and clientelist practices carry greater weight than "issues," confusion about their policy positions might not have been as harmful. However, in cities, voters place greater emphasis on party- and issue-based voting. The JEDS survey includes questions asking respondents (a) if they based their voting decisions more on the individual candidate or the party and (b) if they preferred candidates who make "serious efforts on behalf of the local area" or ones who are mainly active in national problems. Urban voters were markedly more likely than rural ones to emphasize party and national issues. As a result, uncertainty surrounding new-party issue positions was likely to harm new parties particularly among urbanites, who also provided the electoral base in which these new parties were most anxious to find support.

The analysis here works with the findings in Chapter 8 to offer a more complete picture of Japanese voting behavior. As shown in Chapter 8, new parties sought to campaign against clientelism. The differences the DPJ saw between itself and the LDP lay largely in its sense of being an anti-clientelist party, and the LDP as clientelist. Such issues appear to have been at the heart of the DPJ's policy proposals. On the other hand, because the DPJ was a new party, relatively little was known about it, except – as painted by both the media and LDP leaders – that it was a confusing mixture of former LDP members and former Socialists. As a result, there was uncertainty surrounding it.

At the same time, among groups that systematically supported the new parties, there was less uncertainty. Analysis of the JEDS data set indicates that young voters were more certain about the new parties than older voters were. Those who supported the liberalization of the agricultural market were more certain about the new parties than those who were more protectionist. Those who supported decentralization were more certain than "anti-decentralizers." And those who were less supportive of subsidies were more certain than pro-subsidy voters. In short, even though the correlation between the variables is not at a level that is likely to cause problems for statistical analysis, voters with specific characteristics that ought to have made them more supportive of the new opposition parties also were less likely to be uncertain about them.

10

Conclusion

Democracy Without Competition

Democracy is unthinkable save in terms of parties.

E. E. Schattschneider (1942: 1)

Above everything, the people are powerless if the political enterprise is not competitive. It is the competition of political organizations that provides the people with the opportunity to make a choice. Without this opportunity popular sovereignty amounts to nothing.

E. E. Schattschneider (1960: 137)

Japanese democracy is a puzzle. We typically conceive of democracy as based on competition. One-party democracy is not supposed to happen. This study sought to understand the puzzle of party competition failure and explain how, even when facing a cynical and alienated public, a single party could remain so dominant and an opposition could be so ineffective.

Competition is critical to democracy. Fundamental to democracy is the principle that all rule is ultimately accountable to the people. Within modern democracy, this process works through representatives who, themselves, are accountable to citizens through regular elections. To overcome collective action and social choice problems, representatives organize in political parties (Aldrich 1995), which makes parties also accountable to the public. When parties enter the government, as Manin, Przeworski, and Stokes note, they "are 'accountable' if voters can discern whether governments are acting in their interest and sanction them appropriately, so that those incumbents who act in the best interest of citizens win reelection and those who do not lose them" (1999: 40). One would assume that incumbents who get reelected are those deemed by voters to be working in their best interest. The presence of a governing party that continues to get reelected when it is *unpopular* indicates a failure of accountability. In a country where the ruling party is unpopular, a lack of party competition is not merely a puzzle. It is also a problem of accountability and, therefore, very much a problem for democracy – one that we would do well to understand.

AN EXPLANATION FOR OPPOSITION FAILURE IN JAPAN

Observers of Japanese politics in the 1990s and early 2000s often asked questions about Japan's opposition that implied that the unsuccessful challengers to the ruling regime were not merely failures, but untalented, unintelligent failures: Why didn't an opposition party simply campaign against the terrible state of Japan's economy and the corruption scandals that involved the ruling LDP? Why couldn't the opposition work creatively to find an issue that could capture the attention of the Japanese public? But in the decade after the LDP's 1993 split, opposition parties in Japan *did* campaign in such a fashion; they did raise new issues and garnered substantial support as a result. In proportional representation races, non-LDP parties channeled such campaigns into more than 60 percent of the vote, even topping 70 percent in some elections.

Many observers of Japanese politics blame opposition failure on a public sense of opposition party incompetence and irresponsible behavior in the legislature. The suggestion that opposition parties were not taking advantage of the poor Japanese economy and LDP corruption in their campaigns is part of this notion of opposition incompetence. Historically, such observations were not incorrect. In particular, the pre-1993 opposition was not wholly "pragmatic." But such behavior was in part a *result* of the systemic and structural foundations that made it difficult for the opposition to succeed. Because these foundations gave them little hope of gaining power, opposition parties were placed in an awkward position within the parliament (Diet): They could work quietly behind the scenes – with only marginal policy influence for which they would receive little public credit – or they could obstruct ruling party policy, thereby bringing themselves greater attention, but also harming their image as viable (and possibly respected) parties. Given the options, it should not be surprising that they often chose the latter (Pempel 1975). In the end, opposition party behavior was less a root cause of their failure than a result of it, which in turn further reinforced the failure. And from this behavior, the opposition developed a reputation that it was slow to shake even as it grew more pragmatic in the 1990s.

My explanation for opposition failure (which applies to both pre- and post-1993 Japan) is quite different from those that have come before in that it does not focus on Japan's now-defunct single nontransferable vote in a multimember district electoral system, public perceptions of opposition incompetence, longtime economic success, or cultural predisposition to support a particular party. I focus on Japan's clientelist system. Clientelism, combined with financial centralization and substantial institutional protections for clientelistic regions, was critical to Japanese opposition failure. Opposition parties face a disadvantage in any clientelist system because it is usually government benefits that political parties use in clientelist exchange.

But party competition in other clientelist systems shows that opposition parties are not bound to fail in such systems.

In Japan throughout the bulk of the postwar period, however, the combination of clientelism and government financial centralization made it difficult for opposition parties to succeed in local elections, except in regions that did not rely financially on the central government. As a result, the opposition developed weak local foundations and had few politicians who could credibly run for national office in areas that depended on the central government for funding. In turn, weak local foundations and the lack of a candidate pool harmed the opposition's capacity to win national office, especially in candidate-centered district races.[1] My discussion in Chapter 6 of the weakness of opposition party Diet candidates focuses on the single member districts of the post-1993 HR electoral system, but the opposition had been weak at the local level throughout the postwar. Given that the SNTV/MMD system utilized in the HR through 1993 was even more candidate-centered than the post-1993 SMDs, local weakness and a lack of experienced (quality) candidates for national office was no doubt even more of a problem for the opposition in the years prior to electoral reform.

Alternative arguments might posit that the lack of opposition success was not due to LDP candidate strength but rather to the LDP's long-term reputation for policy effectiveness (compared to untried opposition parties) and the unwillingness of Japanese voters to support the painful reforms suggested by the opposition. One argument of this type involves *non*voters. Prior to the 1990s, nearly three quarters of eligible Japanese voters participated in HR elections, but in 1996–2003 turnout dropped to roughly 60 percent. It might be argued that the drop in turnout and the inability of the opposition to gain power in the 1990s were both due to an increase in nonvoters who had no great love for the LDP but did not wish to cast a ballot for the opposition out of fear that a non-LDP government would enact painful economic reform. However, this argument does not hold water. Nonvoters in Japan tend to be young and urban. Such voters have little reason to support Japan's clientelist elements and are, if anything, more likely to support reform. Moreover, turnout is lower in cities where Japan's opposition is most successful.

Also, it is unconvincing to suggest that votes *for* the LDP were due to fear of untried opposition parties and painful reform. If voters cast ballots based on such fear, the LDP as a party would have done markedly better in PR races, and non-LDP parties would not have won 60–70 percent of the PR vote. If voters' support for LDP politicians was due to positive (or less negative) feelings about the Liberal Democratic *Party*, this predilection would have appeared in Chapter 6's analysis of candidate success. Instead,

---

[1] Cox (1997) indicates coordination problems the opposition faced under SNTV/MMD, but my analysis in Chapter 6 demonstrates that this has been less of an issue in Japan's SMDs that make up the core of the new system.

I found that after controlling for candidate quality, LDP candidates were no more likely to win than opposition candidates.

The opposition's inability to develop a strong candidate pool in financially dependent areas was important because the post-1993 opposition's anti-clientelist message ran against the basic rural political economy and could not win many SMD races in such areas. Because their residents had less education, were older, and maintained fewer employment options, rural areas had less reason to buck a clientelist system that provided them benefits in exchange for political support. Rural areas relied on the central government for public financing, and the central government provided protection and subsidies to rural areas' farmers.

Agricultural protection does not fit neatly into Kitschelt's (2000) definition of clientelism, which rules out universalistic doling out of benefits (e.g., protection for all rice farmers, irrespective of where they live or whom they support). However, the LDP's relationship with rural businesses, such as construction companies, part-time farmers who also were employed by construction companies, and specific financially dependent prefectures and localities fits the definition more cleanly. The LDP central government's subsidization of such groups is well known. Moreover, the benefits the government provided regularly appeared to be tied to the extent that such groups/regions provided the LDP with monetary contributions, mobilized political support, or simply voted for the LDP and the ruling party often threatened to withdraw funding from areas that did not support it.

As a result, such areas and groups had good reason to support the clientelist system and the LDP that maintained it. Japan's opposition made anti-clientelist appeals, but these were unlikely to build support in rural areas, which relied on the clientelist system. The average rural voter displayed attributes and attitudes that made support for clientelism likely and support for Japan's new opposition parties unlikely. Moreover, voters cast ballots for candidates and parties in Japan – especially in rural areas – based not only on their ability to provide patronage but also on candidates' personal qualities, reputations, and especially organized bases. Therefore, the failure of opposition parties to develop strong local bases and find experienced candidates in rural areas was devastating because finding strong candidates was most likely the opposition's only chance in the countryside under the existing system. As a staff member of the DPJ's election bureau explained, "Especially because of our image and policies, we have higher support in cities than in the countryside. In [much of] the countryside ... we have the image of being outsiders or strangers. But where we have a history of maintaining candidates (from our precursor parties), we are relatively strong. ... In [most rural areas] we have no sitting national politicians, so the party cannot breed an image [in such areas]."[2] This would be less of a problem for the opposition in

[2] Interview, December 16, 1998.

(1) systems that emphasize party characteristics, rather than attributes of the individual candidates, and (2) PR electoral systems that do not overrepresent district winners.

Ironically, just as the opposition was less able to find strong, experienced candidates in areas where it needed them most (i.e., rural areas where its policy appeals were less popular), it had a better chance of finding experienced candidates in areas where it needed them less. In large measure because of such areas' greater financial autonomy, the opposition was able to develop greater subnational-level strength in urban areas. The opposition therefore had a larger pool in urban areas from which to draw experienced and potentially strong national candidates. At the same time, new, inexperienced candidates were more likely to win in urban areas than in rural ones, and new opposition parties' anti-clientelist issue appeals were more likely to resonate with urban voters. As a result, while the opposition's deeper pool of candidates in such areas also helped it find greater success there, the opposition had better chances in urban areas in general even without quality candidates.

However, because Japan's Clientelist/Financially Centralized system generated incentives for party formation to occur from the top down, there was a different impediment to greater opposition success in urban areas. Top-down formation meant that the country's more successful new parties had to form from mergers of existing parties, which created two problems for new parties. First, in prefectures where politicians from multiple parties joined together to form the Democratic Party of Japan, unification tended to be slow and typically was unification in name only. In such prefectures, the different groups within the party tended not to work together well and sometimes were even antagonistic to one another (Chapter 9).

Such problems existed even though mergers of this kind tended to occur in prefectures where the DPJ was most popular. Despite efforts to build a real *party* organization – something usually missing from Japan's parties (Foster 1982) – the party apparatus was not working on all cylinders in regions where the party had the largest potential base of support. Such problems were particularly burdensome in urban areas, where anti-LDP and anti-clientelist feelings ran strongest. In these prefectures, the opposition was also more likely to have coordination problems that allowed LDP candidates to win office even though the combined opposition vote was greater.

Second, because the two new leading opposition parties – the NFP and DPJ – were composed of multiple preexisting parties, voters questioned their ideological coherence. In the DPJ, for example, it was often difficult to justify on ideological grounds the union of former members of two longtime enemies, the LDP and the Socialist Party. Despite the fact that the parties sought to focus policy appeals on issues that the different groups within them agreed on, many voters remained confused about what such parties stood for. Given that voters who viewed a given party as incoherent were less likely to vote for it, this hurt the new parties' ability to attract additional support. The damage was most likely in urban areas, where, compared to rural regions, voters emphasized party and national issues rather than candidates and local issues in their voting decisions. In short, the apparent policy incoherence of Japan's new parties, which was in large part due to mergers of seemingly incompatible preexisting parties, harmed the parties most in areas where they seemed to have the most to gain.

THE MODEL: CLIENTELISM, FINANCIAL CENTRALIZATION, AND "INSTITUTIONAL PROTECTION"

This book seeks to go beyond mere description of Japanese campaign behavior and instead consider what components of democratic systems can impede party success. The main finding is that opposition parties face substantially greater obstacles in clientelist systems. More specifically, clientelism in conjunction with a centralized governmental structure (where localities depend on the central government) and institutional protections for regions supportive of clientelism is sufficient to explain opposition failure.

None of these factors by itself explains failure. There are many examples of opposition party success in clientelist systems, ranging – geographically as well as alphabetically – from Austria and Belgium to Venezuela. As Austria and Italy illustrate, even the problems that grow out of Clientelist/Financially Centralized systems are insufficient to explain opposition party failure. Moreover, the combination of clientelism and institutional protections for regional beneficiaries of clientelism is not sufficient to explain opposition failure: Where Japanese opposition parties were able to generate strong candidacies, they were successful even in areas that favored clientelist practices.

It is the *combination* of clientelism, financial centralization, and institutional protections for those areas that support clientelism that leads to opposition party failure because it leads to (1) difficulty developing strong local foundations and deep pools of strong candidates, (2) limited zones of competition, and (3) problems of organization and coherence for new parties. The problems of organization and coherence are not sufficient to lead to party failure, but they intensify the difficulties created by the problems of weak local foundations, poor candidate recruitment, and limited zones of competition.

To be more specific: The most important variable is clientelism.[3] By controlling the goods used to attract voters in clientelist systems, ruling parties have a substantial advantage over the opposition. Note that I am not arguing

---

[3] Once established in Japan, one-party dominance and clientelism also reinforced one another. With little party competition, the LDP worried less about forging programmatic appeals to distinguish itself.

that one-party dominance is impossible where parties compete with each other on programmatic grounds. The Social Democratic Party's longtime rule in Sweden disproves that notion. Rather, I am arguing that when conditions appear ripe for opposition success (e.g., because of economic decline or a backlash against corruption), opposition failure is unlikely in programmatic systems. It should not be surprising that SAP dominance dissipated during a period of economic decline. Similarly, competitive party politics are the norm in other programmatic systems, such as Germany and the United Kingdom.

In Clientelist systems, the degree of financial centralization has a marked effect on party success. In Financially Decentralized systems such as Brazil's, opposition parties have many opportunities to develop strength at the local level, but Financially Centralized systems create problems for opposition parties because they impede the capacity of parties that are not in the national government to develop local-level strength. As a result, these parties are left with weak local foundations and a shallow pool of potentially strong candidates for national-level offices.

However, two types of institutions may counteract the difficulties such systems impose. (1) Presidential systems, such as Mexico and Taiwan, offer an opportunity for success to any party with a single attractive presidential candidate, irrespective of the number of strong candidates the party runs in legislative races. (2) It is less important to develop a strong pool of candidates in systems, such as in Austria and Israel, where party characteristics play a greater role than candidate characteristics in elections (e.g., because of the presence of a party-controlled, PR, closed-list electoral system). In these systems, the presence of strong candidates atop PR lists is helpful for any party, but it ought to be outweighed by party image when the party's appeals are popular. In short, the full negative impact that a Clientelist/Financially Centralized system has on opposition parties' ability to generate strong candidacies, and hence on overall party fortunes, will be felt in Parliamentary systems that use candidate-centered electoral systems.

Even in more candidate-centered systems, opposition parties can succeed, as illustrated in Italy. However, when such systems provide institutional protections – in particular, when they allocate a substantial number of seats through a nonproportional formula – to regions that benefit from the clientelist system and provide the primary base of support for the ruling party, opposition parties are unlikely to succeed (unless they are able to dominate the remainder of the seats being contested). The serious decline of the longtime ruling Christian Democrats in Italy began under the (preference voting-permitted) PR system that governed the country until 1994.[4] As a result, voters who opposed the DC and Italy's clientelist system – even voters residing in the DC's bailiwick, the heavily clientelist south – were able

---

[4] For a brief description of this system, see Chapter 8.

to have their votes count toward a substantial number of seats for non-DC parties. As clientelism grew increasingly unpopular, even though the DC continued to maintain a relatively large number of seats there, other parties were able to develop a foothold in the south.

In contrast, the core of Japan's post-1993 Lower House electoral system was the single member district tier, whereby in any given district the plurality winner takes all. This allowed the LDP to win roughly 75 percent of the seats in Japan's clientelist rural areas – which were allotted one third of all seats – merely by winning a plurality in most rural districts. It meant that, unlike the Italian opposition, the Japanese opposition was unable to use to its advantage the small pockets of disenchantment that existed in LDP-held rural districts.

The combination of these forces is sufficient to generate opposition party failure. Moreover, where the leading opposition party is a new party, additional problems exacerbate the situation. The evidence from Japan suggests that in Clientelist/Financially Centralized systems, the top-down development of large new parties makes it hard for these parties to organize and present a coherent, united front.

IMPLICATIONS

Japanese Bureaucrats, Politicians, and Inability to Reform

Some might argue that opposition failure is not a very serious problem in Japan. According to the bureaucratic-dominance school of Japanese politics analysis (e.g., Johnson 1982), the best-known English-language interpretation of Japanese politics, politicians hold relatively little power in Japan, because the bureaucracy makes the bulk of the important decisions.[5] By extension, opposition failure is of little importance because politicians are merely an outlet for voters to express themselves, and not central to policy making.

In this book, I am not primarily concerned with how much influence the LDP has been able to exert in the policymaking process. However, irrespective of how much control the LDP actually had over postwar policy, it is difficult to imagine that the entry of other parties into the government would not have had an impact on policymaking. Indeed, where non-LDP parties exerted substantial legislative influence in recent years, major policy

---

[5] There are other interpretations. In the 1980s, more pluralistic approaches – for example, Muramatsu and Krauss's (1987) model of "patterned pluralism" – gained greater favor. In the 1990s, Ramseyer and Rosenbluth's (1993) arguments about *politician* dominance attracted attention. Recent efforts attempt to identify the conditions under which different groups in Japan's government gain greater power and discretion (see Scheiner, Muramatsu, and Krauss 2004). However, the notion of Japan as bureaucracy-dominated has always been the most well known.

changes followed. The most obvious case is the electoral and campaign reform measures enacted by the non-LDP government in 1994. Previously, no
LDP government had ever passed such legislation, but the non-LDP government completely overhauled Japan's electoral system and instituted new
structures governing Japanese campaign behavior.[6] Some might argue that
the new system did not live up to expectations and maintained continuities
from the old system (see McKean and Scheiner 2000), but its impact was
substantial. No doubt partly because of the elimination of SNTV/MMD,
factions within the LDP lost influence (Cox, Rosenbluth, and Thies 1999),
altering the power balance within the ruling party. And opposition consolidation into a single, more pragmatic, larger opposition force probably would
not have been possible without SMDs.

If the bureaucracy dominated policymaking, then these changes were relatively meaningless in the policy arena because they simply altered the rules
of the game played by a group of powerless individuals (politicians). Yet even
if the bureaucratic dominance characterization is correct, the reforms were
also important in the spending restrictions and reporting requirements on
contributions that they imposed. The reforms somewhat reduced the "money
politics" that played a major role in Japanese corruption.

What is probably more important is the observation that when opposition
parties have had power, they have played a central and defining role in other
types of policymaking, indicating that politicians can play a significant part
in the Japanese legislative process. The clearest example is the set of financial
reform laws the Diet passed in October 1998. At the time, the LDP controlled
the government but held a minority of the seats in the House of Councillors.
Led by the DPJ, the opposition pushed its own proposal, which the LDP,
lacking a majority in the HC, was forced to accept. The reforms are notable
because they altered the rules governing Japan's financial system *and* were
passed despite fierce opposition by the Ministry of Finance (Amyx 2000).

Policy Immobility

As this example suggests, the lack of party competition has been significant
as it appears to have promoted policy immobility, even in the face of serious
economic and political problems. Clearly, politicians can have an enormous
impact on policy. And when the opposition briefly held enough seats, it
played an important part in altering policy. After Japan's economic bubble
burst, many believed that LDP and bureaucrat policy paralysis was harming the country's chances for economic reform and recovery. When Prime
Minister Koizumi Junichirō came into office in 2001 promising to enact reforms to deal explicitly with Japanese economic inefficiencies, he was hailed
as a savior for both the LDP and the country as a whole. However, many

---

[6] To be fair, the LDP was involved in the legislation.

of Koizumi's efforts were blocked by members of his own party because his reforms were aimed at the clientelist system that undergirded the support of much of the LDP.[7]

The fact that the LDP could maintain power despite – and possibly even because of – its immobility (which aided the very clientelism-benefiting groups that were protected by Japan's SMD system) on major economic reform no doubt gave party leaders the sense that there was no *electoral* need for reform, even when there was a clearly perceived *economic* need. Similarly, voters, pundits, and politicians regularly decried the frequently reported cases of politician corruption – often a direct result of the clientelist system – but LDP legislators rarely paid more than lip service to the issue. Although it is by no means clear that reforms by non-LDP alternatives would have aided economic recovery and helped eliminate corruption, greater party competition almost certainly would have made genuine attempts more likely.

At the same time, it is not clear how far a non-LDP government could go in seeking to reform the Japanese system. Much of Japan's economy is founded on inefficient business sectors that receive government protection and are often funded through clientelist forms of exchange. There is therefore a structural bias against policies that would alter the system too dramatically. Politicians have many reasons not to pull the rug out from underneath such firms, including a fear of the economic consequences. Presumably, the *way* a non-LDP government came to power would influence its willingness to challenge such constraints. A party founded on backlash against the system would be likely to seek reform. But one founded on defectors merely seeking to run away from an electorally sinking LDP might be less capable of change, as genuine reforms might undercut their basis of support.

Conditions of Party Competition Failure and Maintenance of Clientelism

More broadly, my analysis suggests conditions under which party competition can be impeded. Political structures – such as presidentialism or parliamentarism, type of electoral system, and the degree of financial centralization – play a major role in shaping party competition and opposition failure. Constitutional designers and institutional engineers seeking to create systems that avoid opposition failure of the sort seen in Japan ought to consider these factors as they develop or alter rules that govern their systems.

The predominance of clientelism has a major effect on opposition parties' abilities to compete. And the institutions in which clientelism is embedded clearly structure the impact clientelism has on party competition. However,

---

[7] Indeed, it is striking that Koizumi appeared to make greater effort on issues at the core of the LDP's clientelist system, such as the postal system, construction, and transportation funding, than he did to reform the most talked about problem in the foreign press: the Japanese banking system.

it is important to note that political structures alone do not determine the degree to which clientelism remains a powerful force in a democratic political system. If clientelism becomes less central to Japan's political economy, its decline will be first and foremost due to social and economic changes that lead Japanese voters and politicians to seek its elimination.

Clientelism in any country depends on some kind of popular support. As the Italian, Austrian, and Japanese cases indicate, it can maintain popular acceptance only as long as sectors and groups that rely on it are not perceived to act as a drain on sectors and groups that do not rely upon it. Without popular acceptance, political structures can help maintain the clientelist system by channeling votes in favor of the system into electoral success for clientelism-supporting parties. But, in doing so, they generate tension between those for and those against the system's maintenance. In turn, this tension is likely to manifest itself in battles within the political system.

A Caution for the Reader

None of this is to say that clientelism is automatically a "bad" thing for democracy. It is not uncommon for people to see clientelism as undercutting democratic accountability, but the impact can be quite the opposite: By creating a relationship based on a direct exchange, clientelism offers tight accountability and responsiveness (Kitschelt 2000: 851–2). Indeed, in Japan, the LDP was highly responsive to its clients. Moreover, as Piattoni (2001) writes, clientelism has clear advantages. Through clientelist modes of exchange, voters generally know what they will get from elected representatives, and clientelist practices can be used to buy off groups that may otherwise destabilize the system. As Piattoni notes the advantages of clientelism, "it is simple, it is open, and it defuses conflict" (2001: 202).

THE IMPORTANCE OF NATIONAL ELITES: LITTLE CHANCE FOR "VOTER REVOLT"

As Japan entered the twenty-first century, clientelism remained central to its political economy, and Japanese parties existed in a context in which the combination of clientelism, financial centralization, electoral rules, and seat apportionment all impeded opposition party success. Nevertheless, even though I am arguing that structures create incentives for particular types of behavior, I am not positing that they are deterministic: There is nothing inevitable about party competition failure in systems like Japan's. However, the structures I discuss here do greatly constrain the ability of opposition parties to succeed. These constraints affect both voters and elites, but the impact is most striking with regard to the latter: Japan's structures, especially the combination of clientelism and centralization, make it hard for *voters* to bring about party competition. And because of these structures, *national-level politicians* – rather than voters – are the key to parties' electoral outcomes in Japan.

National Politicians

As long as Japan remains heavily clientelistic and financially centralized, the key to party success is the behavior of national politicians. Clearly important everywhere, national elites are especially critical in Clientelistic/Financially Centralized systems. In such systems, parties' abilities to develop local-level strength depends upon their strength at the national level. Without substantial national-level power, it is very difficult for parties to develop at the local level, so that top-down, elite-level party formation becomes the key to party development and success in Clientelist/Financially Centralized systems.

Therefore, without a change to the fundamental structure of Japanese politics, elite defection from the ruling party is the opposition's greatest hope for success. But defection from the ruling party is fraught with difficulties: Politicians need exceedingly good reasons to leave the party in power and sufficient confidence in their ability to survive outside. Reed and Scheiner (2003) find that those who left the LDP in 1993–4 Japan typically were pursuing particular electoral and reform-oriented objectives. However, lacking strong incentives, politicians should not defect. There are great rewards, especially prestige and access to government resources, associated with staying with the ruling party and tremendous risks, especially loss of both power and access to resources, associated with leaving.

Even after defection, elites do not easily develop a challenge to the ruling party. Because of the difficulty in Clientelist/Financially Centralized systems of generating grassroots-based new parties, it is usually necessary to create fairly large new parties out of the merger of preexisting ones. Defectors often find it difficult to get the different groups to align. For example, in 1998, former LDP politicians had a hard time getting their support organizations to join former Socialists in the DPJ (Scheiner 2003). Moreover, even once the party is formed, intraparty coordination is difficult.

Also, in Japan, a legacy of defection failure has emerged that might serve as a cautionary tale for those considering such a step in the future: The history of defections from the LDP offers little reason for future renegades to think that they could succeed. There have been three particularly important cases of defection (or near-defection): the New Liberal Club in 1976, the 1990s' new parties, and Katō Kōichi in 2000. The NLC emerged when a small group of politicians, angry over LDP corruption scandals, left the ruling party. The NLC was extremely popular, but it never grew much or created any serious challenge to the LDP. A larger number of politicians defected from the LDP in the early 1990s and offered the greatest hope to those who sought to overcome the LDP. By 1994, though, the LDP was back in power. The case of Katō was actually a near-defection. Seeking to topple the inept Mori prime ministership in November 2000, Katō, a top LDP member, planned to lead his faction in joining an opposition vote of no-confidence in the government. He realized that supporters of the move were likely to be expelled from the party (*Reuters*, November 18, 2000)[8] and, upon learning that he had insufficient numbers to make the motion work, he backed down from his plan. In the aftermath, Katō's position within the party was vastly weakened. As a result of these three failures, LDP politicians were given reason to believe that defection from the ruling party had little to offer them.

This legacy does not eliminate the possibility of defection; it simply creates stronger incentives not to defect. In reality, politicians in Japan have defected from the LDP and the opposition's greatest opportunity for success was a direct result of defections in 1993–4.

The inability of the 1993–4 anti-LDP coalition government to hold onto power and take full advantage of its opportunity suggests that perhaps opposition failure in Japan was due to factors other than those I have outlined, but actually the example also bolsters my argument further: I have focused on structural factors as an explanation for opposition failure, but, as with anything else, other, more contingent and contextual features can play an important part in eventual outcomes. The direct cause of the anti-LDP government losing power after only 10 months and 20 days in 1994 was a strategic error. When the anti-LDP group held power in 1993–4, LDP defector Ozawa Ichirō, one of the leaders of the group, did not work hard to maintain overall coalition unity. Believing that the left would never link up with the LDP and that more defectors from the LDP were soon to come, Ozawa antagonized the Socialist Party, which made up a significant proportion of the coalition. When the Socialists left the coalition, the government lost its majority, and when they aligned with the LDP, the longtime ruling party was back in power. In short, tactical errors in coalition arrangements by opposition leaders allowed the LDP to regain power and led to renewed opposition failure (Curtis 1999: Chapter 5).

But the preceding example reinforces my argument that the combination of clientelism and fiscal centralization weights politics to the elite side. Only through party defection – national elite realignment – was the opposition in Japan presented an *opportunity* to take power. And the failure of the anti-LDP group to coordinate with national politicians was what led the group to lose power.

In Clientelist/Financially Centralized countries, politicians need to be close to national governmental power because access to government resources maintains the pipelines that fuel the clientelist relations, thereby making possible many of the linkages between national politicians, local politicians, and the groups organized at the bottom. Simply holding power is not enough. Under these conditions, national politicians must hold power long enough

---

[8] Unless otherwise noted, all news references in this chapter are to online editions.

to tilt the distributive bias of politics toward their clients at the other end of the pipeline and ensure that they will continue to deliver needed votes, money, and organization to those at the top. This kind of power generates "virtuous cycles of dominance" (Pempel 1990), founded on a belief by those at the local level that national politicians reward their followers and punish their enemies.

The combination of clientelism and centralization cements these virtuous cycles strongly into place because of the central government's discretionary capacity to take away funding from groups throughout much of the country. Once clientelist relations between local actors and the central government becomes established, the virtuous cycles begin spinning and are difficult to stop.

Voters

In such systems, voters play a weaker role than national-level politicians in party competition. It is much easier to bring about a voter "revolt" against an unpopular regime in other types of systems. It is easiest to imagine a national groundswell of support for the opposition against the ruling regime in a presidential system, where a personally popular candidate can mobilize the support of a plurality of voters in the single national executive race. Such a revolt against an unpopular regime is also more likely in a programmatic system, where voters who are unhappy with ruling party policies will usually cast their ballots against the party.

In systems like Japan's, however, such a revolt will be far more limited. As long as clientelism resonates with substantial groupings, it is difficult for parties to develop programmatic appeals to counter the ruling party's advantage. This is especially problematic where there are institutional protections for clientelist-supporting groups such as those I discuss in this book. These factors make it extremely difficult for a full-scale voter revolt to occur in clientelist systems, *unless clientelist practices lose their popular support* and/or institutions are altered to eliminate the electoral advantage offered to such groups. Moreover, the combination of clientelism with fiscal centralization makes it difficult for opposition parties to develop a pool of viable candidates. For this reason, even if voters want to use the ballot box to revolt against the ruling party, they will be much less likely to if faced with the choice between a neophyte opposition candidate and an experienced incumbent with a history of district service. In addition, coordinated action would be needed: Revolts would have to occur separately in hundreds of districts where voters, though unhappy with the national ruling party, had long been perfectly content with the behavior of their individual representative.[9]

---

[9] This is similar to Fenno's (1975) discussion of American voters who "love" their member of Congress but hate the institution.

In Japan in 1993, voters sincerely sought to replace the LDP government (Kabashima 1994; Reed 1997). However, LDP incumbents did well in the election, and the principal opposition party candidates who benefited from the "revolt" were incumbents who had defected from the ruling party.

In Japan, these factors are exacerbated by substantial restrictions on the use of "mass" forms of campaigning, such as Japanese legal limits on the use of print, radio, and television advertising in political campaigns (Christensen 1998: 990–1). As a result, there are few permissible ways to create a national campaign against the ruling party, and, to find success, campaigns need to focus on developing organized, mobilizable bases of support at the local levels.

In short, given a level of support for clientelist practices and the structures I have described, it is very unlikely that voters can drive the engine of party competition in such systems. The behavior of "elites" – national politicians – is far more critical.

This situation raises one more important question about the quality of the democracy in such a system. Not only is competition – the cornerstone of democracy – kept at a minimum, but the electorate, the group typically held up as the ultimate sovereign in a democracy, is limited in its capacity to bring about greater competition. None of this is to suggest that Japan is somehow nondemocratic: Japan maintains free elections and the requisite liberties that place it squarely in the company of early twenty-first-century democracies. I also plainly reject the possibility that Japanese are predisposed to follow their leaders blindly or that there is an undemocratic cultural ethos. My argument regarding the state of party politics in Japan rests on the country's combination of clientelism and particular government structures. However, the lack of party competition and the obstacles to "voter revolts" of the kind often seen in other democracies suggests that under this system it may be harder for Japan's voters to assert their "sovereignty" in a meaningful way.

Those concerned with the workings of democracy would do well to consider the different components of the Japanese system that have prevented greater competition within it. Opposition failure and a failure of party competition suggest a failure of democracy. In a system where voters are content with the status quo, opposition failure is not troubling. If there is contentment with the existing arrangements, no change need occur. However, this is not the sort of failure I have been discussing. Rather, I have examined the failure of opposition parties in a context in which voters are deeply unhappy with the existing system and, in particular, the ruling party. Recall the public opinion survey to which I alluded in Chapter 2: The LDP was the most hated party in Japan, disliked by 44.4 percent of the public (*Asahi Shinbun*, March 13, 2001); cabinet approval ratings of even the most popular prime ministers typically rested under 50 percent; and the LDP as a party rarely received more than 30 percent support ratings.

It is a system where the vast majority of voters were unrepresented. In such a system, there is clearly something askew with the mechanism that links voter preferences to political outcomes. From a normative perspective, we should be troubled any time this mechanism appears to break down in a system that is founded on democratic principles. As one veteran member of the LDP, even, explained, "It is dangerous that there is no real opposition in Japan. Unchecked power is very dangerous."[10]

POTENTIAL PATHS TO OPPOSITION SUCCESS IN JAPAN

As long as the foundations I discuss here remain in place in Japan, the LDP's advantage will remain, and the opposition will have great difficulty challenging the ruling party. However, this does not mean that there is no hope for party competition in Japan. As of the early 2000s, potential paths to power exist for the Japanese opposition.

From the late 1990s, although the LDP typically had a majority in the House of Representatives, its submajority status in the HC led it to form coalition governments with *Kōmeitō*. In this way, *Kōmeitō* became an important pivot or "casting vote."[11] *Kōmeitō* showed great willingness to act strategically and use its pivot position to great advantage. If the DPJ gained enough seats, it could, with the right set of promises, entice *Kōmeitō* to join it in a coalition government *against* the LDP. The shift to regular coalition governments in the post-1993 era lowers the bar for opposition success. However, the DPJ's capacity to enter into a government coalition is conditional upon it gaining substantially more seats than it had in 2004.

Given the continued maintenance of the Clientelist/Financially Centralized structure, new defections of politicians from the LDP offer the opposition the greatest and most likely hope of success. That said, a strategy of encouraging or waiting for such defections would hardly be reliable.

Components of Japan's postreform electoral system offer some assistance to the opposition. The emphasis on SMDs, where only the top voter getter wins the district seat, created incentives for politicians and voters to converge strategically on a single concentrated opposition force, which played a huge role in the DPJ's relative success and almost total decline of the Socialist and Communist Parties in the 2003 HR election (Scheiner 2003/2004). Concentration of opposition forces into one party no doubt eliminated a psychological disadvantage faced by the fragmented opposition of the past, which left candidates and voters with little sense that there was one clear opposition force on which to focus their efforts. However, as of 2004 the opposition as a whole had not benefited as much as might be expected (Chapter 2). The

---

[10] Interview, July 23, 1999.

[11] *Kōmeitō* also played a substantial role in mobilizing votes for the LDP in district races (*Asahi Shinbun*, July 13, 2004).

DPJ's fortunes improved in 2003 and the party had the most successful election of any single opposition party in the postwar era. However, the DPJ's improvement in 2003 seemed to be less a result of attracting new voters or LDP supporters and more due to the greater concentration of opposition forces in one party. In 2003, the opposition as a whole did not especially improve, and the LDP had its most successful election in terms of votes and seats under the postreform system.

One subtle element of Japan's postreform electoral system may ultimately help the opposition entice defections of politicians who are not yet national-level incumbents for the LDP. As discussed in Chapter 6, much of the opposition's problem has been its inability to attract potentially strong *new* candidates, such as former local office holders, for national HR races (especially in rural areas). The irony is that, while unwilling to defect to the opposition out of fear of LDP and/or voter reprisal, many of these candidates are left dissatisfied because the LDP puts up other candidates (often incumbents) instead of them in HR races. This suggests a type of coordination failure between the opposition, which needs HR candidates, and the LDP nonincumbents, who want a party to nominate them for HR office.

Typically, the opposition's greatest difficulty attracting candidates has been in rural areas, but in a small number of rural cases, the DPJ has begun to lure such candidates away from the LDP.[12] Japan's postreform electoral rules help explain the opposition's ability to attract them (Reed and Thies 2001). Postreform Japan offers voters two ballots, one for a candidate in an SMD and one for the party in PR. Many run as dual candidates, competing in both an SMD and on the party's PR list. Because party-affiliated Japanese SMD candidates can gain office through the PR route even if they lose their district races, opposition parties can offer not only an SMD nomination to HR wannabes who are turned down by the LDP, but also the possibility of gaining office through the PR list, which then buys them time and exposure to challenge the LDP incumbent in the future. In fact, in 2004 the DPJ defeated the LDP in the less important Upper House election, in large part because of the presence of many quality DPJ district-level candidates (Scheiner 2004). The DPJ's success in the election could create a psychological advantage, generating among voters and candidates a sense of momentum and increased likelihood of gaining control of state resources, thereby encouraging greater affiliation with the party.

However, there is reason to be cautious in predicting continued opposition gains. Those most likely to switch over to the DPJ because they share the opposition party's political philosophy tend to come from urban areas, where the DPJ is already fairly strong and has incumbents of its own blocking the entry of new candidates. Defections by voters and candidates to the

---

[12] Personal communication with Steven Reed.

DPJ are less likely in rural areas, which are not inclined to share the DPJ's stated vision of cutting back the clientelist state. In addition, even though the DPJ ran a number of quality candidates in the 2004 HC race, it is far more difficult to find enough strong candidates for the 300 SMDs in the Lower House (Chapter 6), especially in rural areas. It is possible that the DPJ will be able to attract more LDP politicians in the future, but for it to do so, it will need to overcome incentives created by the Clientelist/Financially Centralized system for elites (especially in areas dependent upon the central government) to affiliate with the ruling party.

Nevertheless, the Clientelist/Financially Centralized structure need not be permanent, and changes to the system are possible. If such changes did occur, competition would be likely to emerge.

Decentralization

Especially beginning in the mid-1990s, the Japanese government and media increasingly discussed decentralization of power, including plans to create greater local financial autonomy.[13] And transfers from the center to the periphery declined over time (*Japan Statistical Yearbook*, various years). A continuation of such moves would dramatically alter voters' and politicians' relationships with the central government and the LDP, and most likely improve opposition parties' chances at the subnational level.

In part, decentralization was pushed as part of the Koizumi reform efforts by the central government, which had less money to spend because of economic decline. However, further measures were also pushed by the subnational governments themselves. Because of a growing decline in financial support from the central government, a number of prefectural governors in the early 2000s sought to increase their governments' autonomy and began to implement new programs that relied more on local programmatic innovation than support from the center.[14] Such moves by subnational governments offered perhaps the greatest opportunity for a genuine shift in the centralized system.

Nevertheless, there are reasons to believe the central government will not give up control over localities, a power that helps the LDP-led central government command great strength. As of the early 2000s, most serious proposals to decentralize only reduced the amount of funding to subnational governments and offered only partial autonomy over how to spend. Moreover, decentralization efforts were often blocked by central governmental ministries. A number of ministries pressured localities to oppose decentralization

---

[13] See, for example, *Asahi Shinbun*, July 17, 2001, and October 13, 2004; *Yomiuri Shinbun* December 19, 2003.
[14] Personal communication with Kay Shimizu, Stanford University Political Science Ph.D. candidate doing research on Japan's regional bank policies.

moves (*Asahi Shinbun* and *Yomiuri Shinbun*, October 6, 2004) and even planned to refuse to give up control over transfers and how localities were to spend them (*Asahi Shinbun*, October 19, 2004).

Moves Against Clientelism?

Changes in the clientelist system are the most likely route to competitive party politics and opposition success in Japan. These changes could take either of two forms. First, voters' socioeconomic/demographic conditions could change sufficiently to eliminate the base of clientelism-dependent supporters of the system. Second, economic necessity could force the LDP itself to alter the system.

Open antipathy toward Japan's clientelist practices has increased in recent years (see Chapter 8) and is likely to grow in the future. The public appears increasingly frustrated as Japan's economy stagnates and the population grows more affluent, educated, consumer-based, and urban – all characteristics of groups who do not benefit from clientelism. In this way, urbanization has a potential effect on opposition success, but only an *indirect* one: Urbanization reduces voters' tolerance for clientelist practices, which in turn undercuts the political viability of these practices, thereby potentially weakening the ruling party's grip on power. The LDP's greatest success occurred in the early postwar when Japan was more rural. As it grew more urban, Japan developed two parallel party systems – one rural and LDP dominant, one urban and competitive. As Japan urbanizes further, there is reason to think that the political viability of clientelism will continue to decline and party competition will emerge in more of the country. In addition, with economic globalization and increased openness of the Japanese economy, many formerly loyal clients of the LDP have lost their protection and, in turn, their reason for supporting the LDP. That said, as long as an LDP-led government can continue to provide enough (rural) clientelism-dependent SMDs with clientelist favors, the party will remain in a strong position.

Moves made under the Koizumi administration may weaken the LDP's capacity to maintain such bonds with clientelism-dependent regions. Especially as the economy soured, the opposition helped push the breakdown of these bonds, as it campaigned openly against the clientelist system. Many urban voters supported the opposition, in part because of its outspokenness against clientelist practices. In addition, internationally competitive business showed increasing discomfort with the clientelist system. Under Prime Minister Koizumi in the early 2000s, the LDP began taking steps to respond to this anti-clientelism backlash. Although many in the party opposed measures that could undercut the party's clientelist base, other LDP members proposed altering Japan's political economic structure, including the heavy use of public works. Many of Koizumi's efforts, including postal privatization, were slow coming. But, as the poor economy forced budget cuts, overall spending on public works declined (*Japan Statistical Yearbook*; Ogawa 2004).[15]

Koizumi's early rhetoric about reforming Japan attracted widespread support, but his actual term in office offered nearly everyone something to be unhappy about. Rural areas grew bitter over his budget cuts that directly hit their weak and dependent economies, and many rural groups even threatened to withdraw their support of the LDP (*Asahi Shinbun*, November 6, 2003, and July 13, 2004). Meanwhile, many urban groups were displeased with the LDP's inability to reform Japan's troubled economic system. After the LDP lost the 2004 Upper House election, political scientist Kabashima Ikuo commented, "People in agricultural villages expressed their opposition to the reforms led by Koizumi.... People in urban areas were disgusted by the way Koizumi has been controlled by the LDP" (quoted in *Asahi Shinbun*, English language version, July 13, 2004). Continued rural unhappiness with LDP moves could ultimately improve the opposition's fortunes substantially.[16]

Nevertheless, in general in 2003 and 2004, the LDP continued to do much better in rural areas than the DPJ (Scheiner 2003/2004, 2004). If the LDP demonstrates a capacity to reform some elements of the clientelist system without cutting off its dependent rural base, the LDP could maintain support for a long time, especially if the economy improves at all. As long as it can provide favors to its clientelism-dependent base and maintain a deep pool of strong candidates (something that is likely as long as Japanese politics remain clientelistic and financially centralized), even if it remains relatively unpopular, the LDP will hold critical advantages over the opposition. Moreover, the opposition's success in highlighting the problems of the clientelist system could hurt its ability to challenge the LDP electorally. By stimulating LDP policy reform, the opposition might make itself appear somewhat superfluous.

On the other hand, if the LDP were "too successful" in reforming its clientelist system, it could ultimately loosen the clientelist bonds that tie rural voters to the party and lead to a system in which the opposition can compete on more equal footing. In this way, should the LDP ever be able to achieve major reform, it will be the longtime ruling party itself that helps the opposition find success in Japan.

Undercutting the clientelist and/or centralized foundations of the Japanese system would generate greater willingness to support the opposition

---

[15] Ironically, although largely unreported, it appears that, even though public works spending declined overall under Koizumi, at times it actually *grew* in urban areas as building construction increased (Ogawa 2004).

[16] Despite its explicit statements about the need to eliminate clientelist practices, the DPJ took the opportunity of rural displeasure with the LDP to make overtures to the countryside, offering new support to farmers (*Asahi Shinbun*, February 20, 2004, and June 29, 2004) and small business (*Asahi Shinbun*, September 19, 2003).

throughout the country and improve opposition party chances of recruiting strong candidates. Despite these possibilities, as of 2004 the LDP still maintained numerous advantages because of the continued existence of clientelist and centralized foundations. As a result, the party had a solid base in clientelism-dependent regions and a deep pool of candidates to win it seats.

GENERAL IMPLICATIONS OF "DE-CLIENTELIZATION"
AND DECENTRALIZATION?

I have discussed a number of factors – including parliamentarism, candidate-centered elections, and institutional protections – as obstacles to party competition. In the end, however, my analysis focuses on the impact of clientelism and a centralized governmental fiscal structure.

Clientelism is the key piece in the puzzle of party competition failure. In many ways this conclusion is unhelpful for those who are trying to encourage competitive party politics; there is no clear path to developing a system founded on one politician–citizen linkage rather than another. Political engineers cannot choose to found their system on programmatic linkages and then simply enact a constitution or electoral framework to make it so. The heavily clientelist bent of Austria, even in the presence of a closed-list PR electoral system, which should privilege programmatism, demonstrates the limited impact of electoral rules.

Fiscal centralization is far more malleable: National policy makers can choose to give subnational governments greater control over resources. Although not common for a country to vary its level of centralization dramatically, it is not unusual to see countries change. Japan *increased* its level of centralization in the 1950s and early 1960s (Reed 1986), while many Latin American countries decentralized in the 1980s and 1990s (O'Neill 2002).

Nevertheless, the degree to which decentralization's effects are positive is under debate. Much economic theory predicts that decentralization improves efficiency (see, e.g., Musgrave 1959), whereas a number of political theories suggest that decentralization aids democratic consolidation and democratic practice generally (Dahl 1971; Diamond 1999) and is of benefit by encouraging policy experimentation (Tocqueville [1835] 2000). On the other hand, recent studies of decentralization indicate problems associated with the practice. Alesina et al. (1999) suggest that it hinders fiscal constraint; Treisman's (1999) work indicates ways in which it increases corruption; and Cornelius (1999) describes how it may offer legitimacy to subnational authoritarian bosses. Most disturbing, Gaitan Pavia and Moreno Ospina (1992, cited in O'Neill 2002) argue that decentralization in Colombia helped empower guerrilla movements, right-wing paramilitary units, and the narcotics trade. As O'Neill indicates, however, work on the political outcomes associated with decentralization tends to focus on extreme (whether good or bad) cases.

O'Neill's (2002) examination of decentralization in Andean South American countries offers a more systematic cross-national study and suggests a positive relationship between strong, fiscally autonomous local governments and improved democratic practice and representation. Preliminary evidence from the Andes suggests that decentralization leads to, all else being equal, increased voter participation and new party strides in subnational elections, as well as a more professionalized set of politicians entering local-level politics. O'Neill also notes decentralization's potential shortcomings: Increasingly professionalized local politics may further hinder the ability of typically excluded groups to gain subnational representation. Moreover, in presidential systems decentralization provides an opportunity for independents and "dissident" party members to use high-level subnational office positions as a springboard for a run for national presidential office, a pattern that may weaken the ability of national parties to create and promote policy coherence.

As with any proposed institution or policy shift, it is important to recognize where the shift best meshes with existing contextual realities. O'Neill finds examples of both positive and negative outcomes of decentralization within all the countries she considers, because the effects are experienced locally. It is important to understand local conditions before instituting any policy and, for those concerned about creating a more democratic society, it makes little sense to institute decentralizing reforms in a country where authoritarian bosses and guerrilla groups are known to dominate subnational arenas. It is also critical to consider carefully what the desired outcome is. In 1950s' and 1960s' Japan, which was pursuing central government-led economic growth, *centralization* made sense. Countries seeking similarly state-driven growth may be wise to follow the same path.

However, for those looking to improve democracy, decentralization offers many positive effects. It is too strong to say that decentralization simply will improve democracy; rather, we should say that decentralization should improve democracy in *particular ways*. By encouraging participation that is "closer to home," decentralization helps develop democratic values and skills (Diamond and Tsalik 1999: 121; O'Neill 2002). It increases accountability and responsiveness to local concerns (Diamond and Tsalik) and improves representativeness by offering additional channels of political access for marginalized (often ethnic) groups (Dahl 1971; Diamond 1999; Diamond and Tsalik 1999). By creating more powerful subnational governments, decentralization provides additional checks and balances on central governmental power (Diamond and Tsalik). Decentralization also offers greater opportunity for opposition entry into the political arena (Dahl 1971; Diamond 1999).

Moreover, centralized fiscal power combined with clientelism has a huge negative impact on opposition parties' ability to succeed, an impact that is devastating to the quality of democracy. E. E. Schattschneider wrote that "democracy is unthinkable save in terms of parties" (1942: 1). Nearly 20 years later (1960) he continued his discussion, noting the importance of party competition as a key to modern democracy.

In light of Schattschneider's characterization, the analysis here has potential implications for new democracies. Because many new democracies grow out of autocratic regimes with a heritage of cronyism, they are particularly likely to be clientelistic. Decentralization offers no panacea for all the ills of a democratic society. But the framers of constitutions and political structures in new democracies would do well to develop systems that decentralize financial power if they wish to avoid party competition failure of the type that I have been discussing. Political competition – competition for office and competition over ideas – is probably the greatest service parties offer a democracy. Schattschneider's words suggest that decentralization may indeed be critical, therefore, in helping to establish in developing systems – as well as established ones such as Japan's – a higher quality of democracy.

References

Akizuki Kengo. 1995. "Institutionalizing the Local System: Ministry of Home Affairs and Intergovernmental Relations in Japan." In Hyung-Ki Kim, Michio Muramatsu, T. J. Pempel, and Kozo Yamamura (eds.) *The Japanese Civil Service and Economic Development: Catalysts of Change*, pp. 337–66. Oxford: Clarendon Press.

Akuto, Hiroshi. 1996. "Media in Electoral Campaigning in Japan and the United States." In Susan J. Pharr and Ellis S. Krauss (eds.), *Media and Politics in Japan*, pp. 313–37. Honolulu: University of Hawaii Press.

Aldrich, John H. 1995. *Why Parties? The Origin and Transformation of Party Politics in America*. Chicago: Chicago University Press.

Aldrich, John H., and John D. Griffin. ND. "Blind (to) Ambition: The Emergence of a Competitive Party System in the American South 1948–1998." Unpublished manuscript, Duke University.

Alesina, Alberto, Ricardo Hausmann, Rudolf Hommes, and Ernesto Stein. 1999. "Budget Institutions and Fiscal Performance in Latin America." *Journal of Development Economics*, 59: 253–73.

Allinson, Gary D. 1993. "Citizenship, Fragmentation, and the Negotiated Polity." In Gary D. Allinson and Yasunori Sone (eds.), *Political Dynamics in Contemporary Japan*. Ithaca, NY: Cornell University Press.

Allum, Percy. 1981. "Thirty Years of Southern Policy in Italy." *Political Quarterly*, 52: 314–23.

1997. "'From Two Into One,' The Faces of Italian Christian Democratic Party." *Party Politics*, 3: 25–52.

Alvarez, R. Michael. 1997. *Information and Elections*. Ann Arbor: University of Michigan Press.

Ames, Barry. 1994. "The Reverse Coattails Effect: Local Party Organization in the 1989 Brazilian Presidential Election." *American Political Science Review*, 88: 95–109.

1995. "Electoral Rules, Constituency Pressures, and Pork Barrel: Bases of Voting in the Brazilian Congress." *The Journal of Politics*, 57: 324–43.

Ames, Barry. 2002. *The Deadlock of Democracy in Brazil*. Ann Arbor: The University of Michigan Press.

Amyx, Jennifer. 2000. "The 1998 Reforms in Japanese Financial Regulation: Collapse of the Bureaucratic-led Bargain." Manuscript, University of Pennsylvania.

Anderson, Christopher. 1995. *Blaming the Government: Citizens and the Economy in Five European Democracies*. New York: M.E. Sharpe.

Bailey, John. 1994. "Centralism and Political Change in Mexico: The Case of National Solidarity." In Wayne A. Cornelius, Ann L. Craig, and Jonathan Fox (eds.), *Transforming State-Society Relations in Mexico: The National Solidarity Strategy*. La Jolla: Center for U.S.–Mexican Studies, University of California, San Diego.

Baker, Andy, and Ethan Scheiner. 2004. "Adaptive Parties: Party Strategic Capacity under Japanese SNTV." *Electoral Studies*, 23: 251–78.

Baker, Andy, and Ethan Scheiner. ND. "Electoral System Effects and Ruling Party Dominance in Japan." Working manuscript, University of California, Davis.

Banfield, Edward, and James Q. Wilson. 1963. *City Politics*. Cambridge, MA: Harvard University Press.

Bartels, Larry M. 1988. *Presidential Primaries and the Dynamics of Public Choice*. Princeton, NJ: Princeton University Press.

Berger, Gordon Mark. 1977. *Parties Out of Power in Japan, 1931–1941*. Princeton, NJ: Princeton University Press.

Bruhn, Kathleen. 1997. *Taking on Goliath: The Emergence of a New Left Party and the Struggle for Democracy in Mexico*. University Park: Pennsylvania State University Press.

Bull, Anna. 1994. "Regionalism in Italy." *Europa*, 1 (2/3): 69–83.

Bungei Shunju. 1996. "Watashitachi wa kō kangaeru." *Bungei Shunju* August: 110–24.

Cain, Bruce, John Ferejohn, and Morris Fiorina. 1987. *The Personal Vote: Constituency Service and Electoral Independence*. New York: Cambridge University Press.

Calder, Kent E. 1988. *Crisis and Compensation: Public Policy and Political Stability in Japan*. Princeton, NJ: Princeton University Press.

Camp, Roderic Ai. 1999. *Politics in Mexico: The Decline of Authoritarianism*. New York and Oxford: Oxford University Press.

Campbell, John C. 1979. "The Old People Boom and Japanese Policy Making." *Journal of Japanese Studies*, 5: 321–58.

Carey, John, and Matthew S. Shugart. 1995. "Incentives to Cultivate a Personal Vote: A Rank Ordering of Electoral Formulas." *Electoral Studies*, 14: 417–39.

Christensen, Ray. 1998. "The Effect of Electoral Reforms on Campaign Practices in Japan: Putting New Wine into Old Bottles." *Asian Survey*, 38: 986–1004.

     2000. *Ending the LDP Hegemony: Party Cooperation in Japan*. Honolulu: University of Hawaii Press.

Christensen, Ray, and Paul Johnson. 1995. "Toward a Context-Rich Analysis of Electoral Systems: The Japanese Example." *American Journal of Political Science*, 39: 575–98.

Cornelius, Wayne A. 1999. "Subnational Politics and Democratization: Tensions between Center and Periphery in the Mexican Political System." In Wayne A. Cornelius, Todd Eisenstadt, and Jane Hindley (eds.), *Subnational Politics and Democratization in Mexico*, pp. 3–16. La Jolla, CA: Center for US-Mexican Studies, University of California, San Diego.

Cox, Gary W. 1996. "Is the Single Nontransferable Vote Superproportional? Evidence from Japan and Taiwan." *American Journal of Political Science*, 40: 740–55.

1997. *Making Votes Count: Strategic Coordination in the World's Electoral Systems*. New York: Cambridge University Press.

Cox, Gary W., and Jonathan N. Katz. 2002. *Elbridge Gerry's Salamander: The Electoral Consequences of the Reapportionment Revolution*. New York: Cambridge University Press.

Cox, Gary W., and Frances M. Rosenbluth. 1995. "Anatomy of a Split: The Liberal Democrats of Japan." *Electoral Studies*, 14: 355–76.

Cox, Gary W., Frances M. Rosenbluth, and Michael F. Thies. 1999. "Factional Competition for the Party Endorsement: The Case of Japan's Liberal Democratic Party." *British Journal of Political Science*, 29: 33–56.

Curtis, Gerald. 1971. *Election Campaigning Japanese Style*. New York and London: Columbia University Press.

Curtis, Gerald. 1988. *The Japanese Way of Politics*. New York: Columbia University Press.

1992. "Japan." In David Butler and Austin Ranney (eds.), *Electioneering: A Comparative Study of Continuity and Change*, pp. 222–43. Oxford: Clarendon Press.

1999. *The Logic of Japanese Politics: Leaders, Institutions, and the Limits of Change*. New York: Columbia University Press.

Dachs, Herbert. 1996. "The Politics of Regional Subdivision." In Volkmar Lauber (ed.), *Contemporary Austrian Politics*, pp. 235–52. Boulder and Oxford: Westview Press.

Dahl, Robert. 1971. *Polyarchy: Participation and Opposition*. New Haven, CT: Yale University Press.

Desposato, Scott W. 2002. "Parties for Rent? Ambition, Ideology, and Party Switching in Brazil's Chamber of Deputies." Unpublished Working Paper, University of Arizona.

Desposato, Scott W., and Ethan Scheiner. ND. "Resource Distribution and Party Defections in Japan and Brazil." Unpublished working paper, University of California, Davis.

Diamond, Larry Jay. 1999. *Developing Democracy: Toward Consolidation*. Baltimore: The Johns Hopkins University Press.

Diamond, Larry Jay, and Svetlana Tsalik. 1999. "Size and Democracy: The Case for Decentralization." In Larry Diamond, *Developing Democracy: Toward Consolidation*, pp. 117–60. Baltimore: The Johns Hopkins University Press.

Diaz-Cayeros, Alberto. In press. "Decentralization, Democratization, and Federalism in Mexico." In Kevin Middlebrook (ed.), *Dilemmas of Change in Mexican Politics*. La Jolla: Center for U.S.-Mexico Studies, University of California, San Diego.

Diaz-Cayeros, Alberto, Jose Antonio Gonzalez, and Fernando Rojas. 2002. "Mexico's Decentralization at a Crossroads." Working Paper #153, Center for Research on Economic Development and Policy Reform.

Diaz-Cayeros, Alberto, Beatriz Magaloni, and Barry Weingast. 2000. "Federalism and Democratization in Mexico." Paper prepared for delivery at the annual meeting of the American Political Science Association, Washington, DC, August 31–September 3.

Doi, Takeo. 1971. *Amae no Kozo*. Tokyo: Kokubun-do.

Donovan, Mark. 1994. "The 1994 Election in Italy: Normalisation or Continuing Exceptionalism?" *West European Politics*, 17: 193–201.

Downs, Anthony. 1957. *An Economic Theory of Democracy*. New York: Harper and Row.

Duverger, Maurice. 1954. *Political Parties: Their Organization and Activity in the Modern State* (translated by Barbara and Robert North). London: Methuen/New York: John Wiley & Sons.

Epstein, Leon. 1967. *Political Parties in Western Democracies*. New York: Praeger.

Esping-Andersen, Gøsta. 1990. "Single-Party Dominance in Sweden: The Saga of Social Democracy." In T. J. Pempel (ed.), *Uncommon Democracies: The One-Party Dominant Regimes*. Ithaca, NY: Cornell University Press.

Evans, Geoffrey, and Stephen Whitefield. 1993. "Identifying the Bases of Party Competition in Eastern Europe." *British Journal of Political Science*, 23: 521–48.

Fenno, Richard F., Jr. 1975. "If, As Ralph Nader Says, Congress Is 'The Broken Branch,' How Come We Love Our Congressmen So Much?" In Norman J. Ornstein (ed.), *Congress in Change: Evolution and Reform*, pp. 277–87. New York: Praeger.

Fiorina, Morris P. 1977. *Congress: Keystone of the Washington Establishment*. New Haven, CT: Yale University Press.

Flanagan, Scott. 1991. "The Changing Japanese Voter and the 1989 and 1990 Elections." In Scott C. Flanagan, Shinsaku Kohei, Ichiro Miyake, Bradley M. Richardson, and Joji Watanuki (eds.), *The Japanese Voter*. New Haven, CT: Yale University Press.

Flanagan, Scott, Shinsaku Kohei, Ichiro Miyake, Bradley M. Richardson, and Joji Watanuki (eds.). 1991. *The Japanese Voter*. New Haven, CT: Yale University Press.

Fletcher, Peter. 1967. "The Results Analyzed." In L. J. Sharpe (ed.), *Voting in Cities*, pp. 290–328. London: Macmillan.

Foster, James J. 1982. "Ghost-Hunting: Local Party Organization in Japan." *Asian Survey*, 22: 843–57.

Fukui, Haruhiro, and Shigeko N. Fukai. 1996. "Pork Barrel Politics, Networks, and Local Economic Development in Contemporary Japan." *Asian Survey*, 36: 268–86.

Fukushima, Glen S. 1989. "Corporate Power." In Takeshi Ishida and Ellis S. Krauss (eds.), *Democracy in Japan*, pp. 255–79. Pittsburgh: Pittsburgh University Press.

Furlong, Paul. 1996. "Political Catholicism and the strange death of the Christian Democrats." In Stephen Gundle and Simon Parker (eds.), *The New Italian Republic: From the Fall of the Berlin Wall to Berlusconi*, pp. 59–71. London and New York: Routledge.

Gaitan Pavia, Pilar, and Carlos Moreno Ospina. 1992. *Poder Local: Realidad y Utopia de la Descentralizacion en Colombia*. Bogota, Colombia: Tercer Mundo Editores.

Garrett, Geoffrey, and Jonathan Rodden. 2001. "Globalization and Fiscal Decentralization." Paper presented at the conference on Globalization and Governance, La Jolla, CA, March 30–31.

George Mulgan, Aurelia. 2000. *The Politics of Agriculture in Japan*. New York: Routledge.

Golden, Miriam A. 2000. "Political Patronage, Bureaucracy and Corruption in Post-war Italy." Paper presented at the annual meeting of the American Political Science Association, Washington, DC, August 31–September 3.

Gourevitch, Peter. 1978. "Reforming the Napoleonic State: The Creation of Regional Governments in France and Italy." In Sidney Tarrow, Peter J. Katzenstein, and Luigi Graziano (eds.), *Territorial Politics in Industrial Nations*, pp. 28–63. New York: Praeger.

Graziano, Luigi. 1978. "Center-Periphery Relations And the Italian Crisis: The Problem of Clientelism." In Sidney Tarrow, Peter J. Katzenstein, and Luigi Graziano (eds.), *Territorial Politics in Industrial Nations*, pp. 290–326. New York: Praeger.

Greene, Kenneth F. 2002. "Defeating Dominance: Opposition Party Building and Democratization in Mexico." Unpublished doctoral dissertation, Department of Political Science, University of California, Berkeley.

Grofman, Bernard. 1999. "SNTV: An Inventory of Theoretically Derived Propositions and a Brief Review of the Evidence from Japan, Korea, Taiwan, and Alabama." In Bernard Grofman, Sung-Chull Lee, Edwin A. Winkler, and Brian Woodall (eds.), *Elections in Japan, Korea, and Taiwan under the Single Non-Transferable Vote: The Comparative Study of an Embedded Institution*, pp. 375–416. Ann Arbor: University of Michigan Press.

Gundle, Stephen, and Simon Parker. 1996. "Introduction: The New Italian Republic." In Stephen Gundle and Simon Parker (eds.), *The New Italian Republic: From the Fall of the Berlin Wall to Berlusconi*, pp. 1–15. New York: Routledge.

Hibbs, Douglas. 1977. "Political Parties and Macroeconomic Policies." *American Political Science Review*, 71: 1467–87.

Hine, David. 1993. *Governing Italy: The Politics of Bargained Pluralism*. Oxford: Clarendon Press.

Hirano, Shigeo. 2002. "Redistributive Effects of Electoral Reform: Evidence from the Japanese Case in the 1990s." Paper presented at the annual meeting of the American Political Science Association, Boston, August 29–September 1.

Hori, Kaname. 1996. *Nihon Seiji no Jissho Bunseki: Seiji Kaikaku, Gyousei Kaikaku no Shiten* (Empirical Study on Japanese Politics: Viewpoint for Political and Administrative Reform). Tokyo: Tokai Daigaku Shuppankai.

Horiuchi, Yusaku. 2001. *Turnout Twist: Higher Voter Turnout in Lower-Level Elections*. Unpublished Doctoral Dissertation, MIT.

Horiuchi, Yusaku, and Jun Saito. 2003. "Reapportionment and Redistribution: Consequences of Electoral Reform in Japan." *American Journal of Political Science*, 47: 669–82.

Hrebenar, Ronald. 1992. "The Changing Postwar Party System." In Ronald J. Hrebenar (ed.), *The Japanese Party System: From One-Party Rule to Coalition Government*, pp. 3–31. Boulder, CO: Westview.

Huntington, Samuel. 1968. *Political Order in Changing Societies*. New Haven, CT: Yale University Press.

Igarashi Takayoshi and Akio Ogawa. 1997. *Koukyou jigyou wo dou suru ka*. Tokyo: Iwanami Shinsho.

Inoue Yoshihiko. 1992. "Kokkai Giin to Chihou Giin no Sogou izonryokugaku: Daigishi keiretsu no jisshou kenkyuu." *Leviathan*, 10: 133–55.

International Monetary Fund (IMF). Various Years. *Government Finance Statistics Yearbook*. Washington, DC: IMF.

Ishida, Takeshi. 1971. *Japanese Society*. New York: Random House.

Ishihara, Nobuo. 1986. "The Local Public Finance System." In Tokue Shibata (ed.), *Public Finance in Japan*, pp. 132–55. Tokyo: University of Tokyo Press.

Iversen, Torben. 1994. "The Logics of Electoral Politics: Spatial, Directional, and Mobilizational Effects." *Comparative Political Studies*, 27 (2): 155–89.

Jacobson, Gary C. 1990. *The Origins of Divided Government: Competition in the U.S. House Elections, 1946–88*. Boulder, CO: Westview.

Jichishō. Various Years. *Chihō zaisei hakusho*. Tokyo: Okurashō Insatsukyoku.

Jichishō. Various Years. *Chihō zaisei tōkei nenkan*. Tokyo: Okurashō Insatsukyoku.

Jichishō. Various Years. *Todōfuken ZaiseishisÛhyō*. Tokyo: Jichishō Zaiseikyoku Shidōka.

Johnson, Chalmers. 1982. *MITI and the Japanese Miracle*. Stanford, CA: Stanford University Press.

Johnson, David T. 2003. "A Tale of Two Systems: Prosecuting Corruption in Japan and Italy." In Frank Schwartz and Susan Pharr (eds.), *The State of Civil Society in Japan*. New York: Cambridge University Press.

Jones, Mark. 1997. "Federalism and the Number of Parties in Argentine Congressional Elections." *The Journal of Politics*, 59: 538–49.

Kabashima, Ikuo. 1994. "Shintou no Toujou to Jimintou Ittou Yuui Taisei no Houkai." *Leviathan*, 15: 7–31.

Kataoka, Masaaki. 1997. "Changing Local Politics: Party Realignment and Growing Competition." In Purnendra Jain and Takashi Inoguchi (eds.), *Japanese Politics Today: Beyond Karaoke Democracy*. New York: St. Martin's Press.

Kato Junko. 1998. "When the Party Breaks Up: Exit and Voice among Japanese Legislators." *American Political Science Review*, 92: 857–70.

Katzenstein, Peter J. 1978. "Center-Periphery Relations in a Consociational Democracy: Austria and Kleinwalsertal." In Sidney Tarrow, Peter J. Katzenstein, and Luigi Graziano (eds.), *Territorial Politics in Industrial Nations*, pp. 123–69. New York: Praeger.

Key, V. O. 1949. *Southern Politics in State and Nation*. New York: Knopf.

Kitschelt, Herbert. 1994a. *The Transformation of European Social Democracy*. New York: Cambridge University Press.

Kitschelt, Herbert. 1994b. "Austrian and Swedish Social Democrats in Crisis: Party Strategy and Organization in Corporatist Regimes." *Comparative Political Studies*, 27: 3–39.

1995a. *The Radical Right in Western Europe*. Ann Arbor: University of Michigan Press.

1995b. "The Formation of Party Cleavages in Post-Communist Democracies: Theoretical Propositions." *Party Politics*, 1: 447–72.

1997. "European Party Systems: Continuity and Change," In Raul Heywood, Martin Rhodes and Vincent Wright (eds.), *Developments in West European Politics*, pp. 131–50. London: Macmillan.

2000. "Linkages Between Citizens and Politicians in Democratic Polities." *Comparative Political Studies*, 33: 845–79.

Klesner, Joseph L. 1997. "Democratic Transition? The 1997 Mexican Elections." *PS: Political Science and Politics*, 30: 703–11.

Kobayashi, Yoshiaki. 1999. "Enhancing Local Fiscal Autonomy: A Study of the Japanese Case with Comparative Reference to South Korea and the

United States." In National Institute for Research Advancement (NIRA) (ed.), *The Challenge to New Governance in the Twenty-First Century*, pp. 34–71. Tokyo: NIRA.

Koff, Sondra, and Stephen Koff. 2000. *Italy from the First Republic to the Second.* London and New York: Routledge.

Kohno, Masaru. 1997. *Japan's Postwar Party Politics.* Princeton, NJ: Princeton University Press.

Kornberg, Allan, and Hal H. Winsborough. 1968. "The Recruitment of Candidates for the Canadian House of Commons." *American Political Science Review,* 62: 1242–57.

Kosai, Yutaka. 1986. *There Era of High-Speed Growth: Notes on the Postwar Japanese Economic System.* Tokyo: University of Tokyo.

Krauss, Ellis S., and Robert Pekkanen. 2004. "Explaining Party Adaptation to Electoral Reform: The Discreet Charm of the LDP?" *Journal of Japanese Studies,* 30: 1–34.

Kuroda, Yasumasa. 1974. *Reed Town, Japan: A Study in Community Power Structure and Political Change.* Honolulu: University Press of Hawaii.

Lauber, Volkmar. 1996a. "Conclusion and Outlook." In Volkmar Lauber (ed.), *Contemporary Austrian Politics,* pp. 253–61. Boulder and Oxford: Westview Press.

 1996b. "Economic Policy." In Volkmar Lauber (ed.), *Contemporary Austrian Politics,* pp. 125–50. Boulder and Oxford: Westview Press.

Lijphart, Arend, Rafael Lopez Pintor, and Yasunori Sone. 1986. "The Limited Vote and the Single Nontransferable Vote: Lessons from the Japanese and Spanish Examples." In Bernard Grofman and Arend Lijphart (eds.), *Electoral Laws and Their Political Consequences.* New York: Agathon Press.

Lowi, Theodore J. 1985. *The Personal President: Power Invested, Promise Unfulfilled.* Ithaca, NY: Cornell University Press.

Magaloni, Beatriz. 1997. The Dynamics of Dominant Party Decline: The Mexican Transition to Multipartysm. Unpublished Doctoral Dissertation, Duke University.

Manin, Bernard, Adam Przeworski, and Susan C. Stokes. 1999. "Elections and Representation." In Adam Przeworski, Susan C. Stokes, and Bernard Manin (eds.), *Democracy, Accountability, and Representation.* New York: Cambridge University Press.

Masumi, Junnosuke. 1995. *Contemporary Politics in Japan.* Berkeley: University of California Press.

Mayhew, David R. 1974. *Congress: The Electoral Connection.* New Haven, CT: Yale University Press.

McCubbins, Mathew D., and Frances Rosenbluth. 1995. "Party Provision for Personal Politics: Dividing the Vote in Japan." In Peter F. Cowhey and Mathew D. McCubbins (eds.), *Structure and Policy in Japan and the United States,* pp. 35–55. Cambridge: Cambridge University Press.

McGeveran, William A., Jr. 2003. *The World Almanac and Book of Facts.* New York: World Almanac Books.

McKean, Margaret A. 1977. "Pollution and Policymaking." In T. J. Pempel (ed.), *Policymaking in Contemporary Japan.* Ithaca, NY: Cornell University Press.

 1981. *Environmental Protest and Citizen Politics in Japan.* Berkeley and Los Angeles: University of California Press.

McKean, Margaret A., and Ethan Scheiner. 2000. "Japan's New Electoral System: La Plus ça change...." *Electoral Studies*, 19: 447–77.

Miller, William L. 1988. *Irrelevant Election? The Quality of Local Democracy in Britain.* Oxford: Clarendon Press.

Miyagawa Takayoshi. Various years. *Seiji Handobukku* (Political Handbook). Tokyo: Seiji Kōhō Sentā.

Miyake, Ichiro. 1995. *Nihon no Seiji to Senkyo.* Tokyo: Tokyo Daigaku Shuppankai.

Mizusaki Setsufumi and Mori Hiroki. 1998. "Tokuhyo deeta kara mita heiritsusei no mekanizumu." *Senkyo Kenkyu*, 13: 50–9.

Moser, Robert G., and Ethan Scheiner. 2004. "Mixed Electoral Systems and Electoral System Effects: Controlled Comparison and Cross-National Analysis." *Electoral Studies*, 23: 575–99.

In press. "Strategic Ticket Splitting and the Personal Vote in Mixed Electoral Systems." *Legislative Studies Quarterly.*

Müller, Wolfgang C. 1996a. "Political Institutions." In Volkmar Lauber (ed.), *Contemporary Austrian Politics*, pp. 23–58. Boulder and Oxford: Westview Press.

1996b. "Political Parties." In Volkmar Lauber (ed.), *Contemporary Austrian Politics*, pp. 59–102. Boulder and Oxford: Westview Press.

Muramatsu, Michio, and Ellis Krauss. 1987. "The Conservative Party Line and the Development of Patterned Pluralism." In Kozo Yamamura and Yasukichi Yasuba (eds.), *The Political Economy of Japan*, Vol. 1: *The Domestic Transformation*, pp. 516–54. Stanford, CA: Stanford University Press.

Musgrave, Richard A. 1959. *The Theory of Public Finance: A Study of Public Economy.* New York: McGraw-Hill.

Nakane, Chie. 1967. *Tate-Shakai no Ningen Kankei.* Tokyo: Kodan-sha.

Nicolau, Jairo Marconi (org.). 1998. *Dados Eleitoras do Brasil (1982–1996).* IUPERJ Universidade Candido Mendes-UCAM.

Norris, Pippa, and Joni Lovenduski. 1993. "'If Only More Candidates Came Forward': Supply-Side Explanations of Candidate Selection in Britain." *British Journal of Political Science*, 23: 373–408.

Ogawa, Akio. 2004. "Chokushi subeki 12 no shihyō. (4) Kōkyō shigyōjigyō." *Sekai*, 8: 130–1.

Okimoto, Daniel I. 1989. *Between MITI and the Market: Japanese Industrial Policy for High Technology.* Stanford, CA: Stanford University Press.

Okuda, Takako. 2001. "Mechanism and Dynamics of Japanese Clientelism: Examination of Politics of Pork Barrel Politics in the 1990s." Unpublished Master's Thesis, Duke University.

Okurashō Shukei-kyoku Chōsa-ka (ed.). 2001. *Zaisei Tōkei.* Tokyo: Okurashō Insatsu-kyoku.

O'Neill, Kathleen. 2002. "Party Deterioration or Revitalization? How Decentralization Changes Party Dynamics." Paper presented at the annual meeting of the American Political Science Association, Boston, August 29–September 1.

Organisation for Economic Co-operation and Development (OECD). 1998. "OECD Economic Surveys 1997–1998 – Japan 1998." Paris: OECD Publications.

Otake, Hideo. 1990. "Defense Controversies and One-Party Dominance: The Opposition in Japan and West Germany." In T. J. Pempel (ed.), *Uncommon Democracies: The One-Party Dominant Regimes.* Ithaca, NY: Cornell University Press.

"How a Diet Member's Koenkai Adapts to Social and Political Changes." In Otake Hideo (ed.), *How Electoral Reform Boomeranged*, pp. 1–32. Tokyo and New York: Japan Center for International Exchange.

2000. "Political Mistrust and Party Dealignment in Japan." In Susan J. Pharr and Robert D. Putnam (eds.), *Disaffected Democracies*. Princeton, NJ: Princeton University Press.

Park, Cheol Hee. 1998a. "Electoral Strategies in Urban Japan: How Institutional Change Affects Strategic Choices." Unpublished doctoral dissertation, Columbia University.

1998b. "The Enduring Campaign Networks of Tokyo's Shitamachi District." In Otake Hideo (ed.), *How Electoral Reform Boomeranged: Continuity in Japanese Campaigning Style*, pp. 59–96. Tokyo and New York: Japan Center for International Exchange.

Pempel, T. J. 1975. "The Dilemma of Parliamentary Opposition in Japan." *Polity*, 8: 63–79.

"Political Parties and Social Change: The Japanese Experience." In Louis Maisel and Joseph Cooper (eds.), *Political Parties: Development and Decay*, pp. 309–41. London: Sage Publications.

(ed.). 1990. *Uncommon Democracies: The One-Party Dominant Regimes*. Ithaca, NY: Cornell University Press.

1998. *Regime Shift: Comparative Dynamics of the Japanese Political Economy*. Ithaca, NY: Cornell University Press.

2000. "Tokyo's Little Italy." *The International Economy*, 14 (May/June): 34–7, 55.

Peterson, Paul E., and Paul Kantor. 1977. "Political Parties and Citizen Participation in English City Politics." *Comparative Politics*, 9: 197–217.

Pharr, Susan J. 2000. "Officials' Misconduct and Public Distrust: Japan and the Trilateral Democracies." In Susan J. Pharr and Robert D. Putnam (eds.), *Disaffected Democracies*, pp. 173–201. Princeton, NJ: Princeton University Press.

Piattoni, Simona (ed.). 2001. *Clientelism, Interests, and Democratic Representation: The European Experience in Historical and Comparative Perspective*. New York: Cambridge University Press.

Rabinowitz, George, and Stuart Elaine Macdonald. 1989. "A Directional Theory of Issue Voting." *American Political Science Review*, 83: 93–121.

Rabinowitz, George, Stuart Elaine Macdonald, and Ola Listaug. 1991. "New Players in an Old Game: Party Strategy in Multiparty Systems." *Comparative Political Studies*, 24: 147–85.

Ramos, Fidel V. 2001. "Good Governance Against Corruption." *The Fletcher Forum of World Affairs*, 25: 9–17.

Rallings, Colin, and Michael Thrasher. 1997. *Local Elections in Britain*. London and New York: Routledge.

Ramseyer, J. Mark, and Frances M. Rosenbluth. 1993. *Japan's Political Marketplace*. Cambridge, MA: Harvard University Press.

1995. *The Politics of Oligarchy: Institutional Choice in Imperial Japan*. New York: Cambridge University Press.

Reed, Steven R. 1986. *Japanese Prefectures and Policymaking*. Pittsburgh: University of Pittsburgh Press.

1997. "Providing Clear Cues: Voter Response to the Reform Issue in the 1993 Japanese General Election." *Party Politics*, 3: 265–77.

2001. "Impersonal Mechanisms versus Personal Networks in the Distribution of Central Grants-in-Aid to Local Governments in Japan." In Michio Muramatsu, Ikuo Kume, and Farrukh Iqbal (eds.), *Local Government Development in Post-War Japan*, pp. 112–31. Oxford: Oxford University Press.

Reed, Steven R., and John Bolland. 1999. "The Fragmentation Effect of SNTV in Japan." In Bernard Grofman, Sung-Chull Lee, Edwin A. Winkler, and Brian Woodall (eds.), *Elections in Japan, Korea, and Taiwan under the Single Non-Transferable Vote: The Comparative Study of an Embedded Institution*, pp. 211–26. Ann Arbor: University of Michigan Press.

Reed, Steven R., and Ethan Scheiner. 2003. "Electoral Incentives and Policy Preferences: Mixed Motives Behind Party Defections in Japan." *British Journal of Political Science*, 33: 469–90.

Reed, Steven R., and Michael F. Thies. 2001. "The Consequences of Electoral Reform in Japan." In Matthew Soberg Shugart and Martin P. Wattenberg (eds.), *Mixed-Member Electoral Systems: The Best of Both Worlds?* Oxford: Oxford University Press.

Richardson, Bradley. 1974. *The Political Culture of Japan*. Berkeley: University of California Press.

1977. "Stability and Change in Japanese Voting Behavior, 1958–1972." *The Journal of Asian Studies*, 36: 675–93.

1997. *Japanese Democracy: Power, Coordination, and Performance*. New Haven, CT: Yale University Press.

Richardson, Bradley, and Scott Flanagan. 1984. *Politics in Japan*. Boston: Little Brown.

Rodriguez, Victoria E. 1997. *Decentralization in Mexico: From Reforma Municipal to Solidaridad to Nuevo Federalismo*. Boulder: Westview Press.

Rodriguez, Victoria E., and Peter M. Ward. 1995. *Opposition Government in Mexico*. Albuquerque: University of New Mexico Press.

Rosenbluth, Frances McCall. 1996. "Internationalization and Electoral Politics in Japan." In Robert O. Keohane and Helen V. Milner (eds.), *Internationalization and Domestic Politics*, pp. 137–56. Cambridge: Cambridge University Press.

Sakakibara, Eisuke. 1991. "The Japanese Politico-Economic System and the Public Sector." In Samuel Kernell (ed.), *Parallel Politics: Economic Policymaking in the United States and Japan*, pp. 50–79. Washington, DC: Brookings Institution.

Salvati, Michele. 1995. "The Crisis of Government in Italy." *New Left Review*, 213: 81–2.

Samuels, David. 2000a. "The Gubernatorial Coattails Effect: Federalism and Congressional Elections in Brazil." *The Journal of Politics*, 62: 240–53.

2000b. "Concurrent Elections, Discordant Results: Presidentialism and Governance in Brazil." *Comparative Politics*, 33: 1–20.

2003. *Ambition, Federalism, and Legislative Politics in Brazil*. New York: Cambridge University Press.

Samuels, David, and Fernando Luiz Abrucio. 2000. "Federalism and Democratic Transitions: The 'New' Politics of the Governors in Brazil." *Publius: The Journal of Federalism*, 30: 43–61.

Scalapino, Robert A. 1953. *Democracy and the Party Movement in Prewar Japan.* Berkeley, University of California Press.

Scarrow, Susan. 1996. *Parties and Their Members.* Oxford: Oxford University Press.

Schattschneider, E. E. 1942. *Party Government.* New York: Rinehart.

——— 1960. *The Semisovereign People: A Realist's View of Democracy in America.* New York: Holt, Rinehart, and Winston.

Scheiner, Ethan. 1999. "Urban Outfitters: City-Based Strategies and Success in Postwar Japanese Politics." *Electoral Studies,* 18: 179–98.

——— 2003. "Political Realignment in Nagano: Hata Tsutomu and the New Opposition Challenge the LDP." In Steven R. Reed (ed.), *Creating a New Party System in Japan: Electoral Politics from 1993 through 2000,* pp. 67–83. London and New York: Routledge.

——— 2003/2004. "Kono mama de ha seiken kōtai ha jitsugen shinai." *Foresight Magazine,* 15 (12/20/03–1/16/04, Issue 1): 74–5.

——— 2004. "Minshutō ha 'Sōsenkyo' de masateru no ka." *Foresight Magazine,* 15 (8/21/04–9/17/04, Issue 9): 70–1.

——— In press. "Pipelines of Pork: A Model of Local Opposition Party Failure." *Comparative Political Studies.*

——— ND. "Clientelism in Japan: The Importance and Limits of Institutional Explanations." In Herbert Kitschelt and Steven I. Wilkinson (eds.), unpublished volume on politician-citizen linkages.

Scheiner, Ethan, Michio Muramatsu, and Ellis S. Krauss. 2004. "Incentives, Institutions, and Bureaucrat-Politician Relations in Japan." Paper prepared for delivery at the annual meeting of the Association of Asia Studies, San Diego, March 4–7.

Schlesinger, Joseph. 1966. *Ambition and Politics: Political Careers in the United States.* Chicago: Rand McNally.

——— 1991. *Political Parties and the Winning of Office.* Chicago: University of Chicago Press.

Schoppa, Leonard. 2001. "Locating the LDP and Koizumi in Policy Space: A Party System Ripe for Realignment," *Social Science Japan,* 22: 9–15.

Schumpeter, Joseph A. 1942. *Capitalism, Socialism, and Democracy.* New York and London: Harper.

Seaman, Scott R. 2003. "Crumbling Foundations: Japan's Public Works Policies and Democracy in the 1990s." Unpublished Doctoral Dissertation, Duke University.

Sellers, Jefferey M. 1998. "Place, Post-industrial Change and the New Left." *European Journal of Political Research,* 33: 187–217.

Shalev, Michael. 1990. "The Political Economy of Labor-Party Dominance and Decline in Israel." In T. J. Pempel (ed.), *Uncommon Democracies: The One-Party Dominant Regimes.* Ithaca, NY: Cornell University Press.

Sheffer, Gabriel. 1978. "Elite Cartel, Vertical Domination, and Grassroots Discontent in Israel." In Sidney Tarrow, Peter J. Katzenstein, and Luigi Graziano (eds.), *Territorial Politics in Industrial Nations,* pp. 64–96. New York: Praeger Publishers.

Shefter, Martin. 1994. *Political Parties and the State: The American Historical Experience.* Princeton, NJ: Princeton University Press.

Shugart, Matthew S. 1995. "The Electoral Cycle and Institutional Sources of Divided Presidential Government." *American Political Science Review,* 89: 327–43.

Skidmore, Thomas E. 1967. *Politics in Brazil, 1930–1964: An Experiment in Democracy.* New York: Oxford University Press.

Steiner, Kurt. 1965. *Local Government in Japan.* Stanford, CA: Stanford University Press.

Stirnemann, Alfred. 1989. "Recruitment and Recruitment Strategies." In Anton Pelinka and Fritz Plasser (eds.), *The Austrian Party System,* pp. 402–27. Boulder, CO: Westview Press.

Stockwin, J. A. A. 1992. "The Japan Socialist Party: Resurgence After Long Decline." In Ronald J. Hrebenar (ed.), *The Japanese Party System,* pp. 81–115. Boulder, CO: Westview Press.

Tanaka, Aiji, and Yoshitaka Nishizawa. 1997. "Critical Elections of Japan in the 1990s: Does the LDP's Comeback in 1996 mean Voter Realignment or Dealignment?" Paper presented at the XVIIth World Congress of International Political Science Association, Seoul, Korea, August 17–21.

Tarrow, Sidney. 1977. *Between Center and Periphery: Grassroots Politicians in Italy and France.* New Haven, CT: Yale University Press.

——— 1978. "Introduction." In Sidney Tarrow, Peter J. Katzenstein, and Luigi Graziano (eds.), *Territorial Politics in Industrial Nations,* pp. 1–27. New York: Praeger Publishers.

——— 1990. "Maintaining Hegemony in Italy: 'The Softer They Rise, the Slower They Fall!'" In T. J. Pempel (ed.), *Uncommon Democracies: The One-Party Dominant Regimes,* pp. 306–32. Ithaca, NY: Cornell University Press.

Tatebayashi, Masahiko, and Margaret McKean. 2002. "Vote Division and Policy Differentiation Strategies of LDP members under SNTV/MMD in Japan." Paper presented at the annual meeting of the Association of Asian Studies, Washington, DC, April 4–7.

Tocqueville, Alexis de. [1835] 2000. *Democracy in America.* New York: Bantam Books.

Treisman, Daniel. 1999. "Decentralization and Corruption: Why Are Federal States Perceived to Be More Corrupt?" Paper presented at the annual meeting of the American Political Science Association, Atlanta, September 2–5.

Verdier, Daniel. 1995. "The Politics of Public Aid to Private Industry: The Role of Policy Networks." *Comparative Political Studies,* 28: 3–42.

Ward, Peter M., and Victoria E. Rodriguez (with Enrique Cabrero Mendoza). 1999. *New Federalism and State Government in Mexico,* U.S.-Mexican Policy Report No. 9. Austin: Lyndon B. Johnson School of Public Affairs, The University of Texas at Austin.

Watanuki, Joji. 1991. "Social Structure and Voting Behavior." In Scott C. Flanagan, Shinsaku Kohei, Ichiro Miyake, Bradley M. Richardson, and Joji Watanaki (eds.), *The Japanese Voter.* New Haven, CT: Yale University Press.

Waters, Sarah. 1994. "'Tangentopoli' and the Emergence of a New Political Order in Italy." *West European Politics,* 17 (1): 169–82.

Weiner, Robert. 2003. "Anti-competition in 'Competitive' Party Systems." Unpublished Doctoral Dissertation, University of California, Berkeley.

Wertman, Douglas A. 1993. "The Christian Democrats: A Party in Crisis." In Gianfranco Pasquino and Patrick McCarthy (eds.), *The End of Post-War Politics in Italy: The Landmark 1992 Elections,* pp. 12–30. Boulder, CO: Westview Press.

Woldendorp, Jaap, Hans Keman, and Ian Budge. 1998. "Party Government in 20 Democracies: An Update (1990–1995)." *European Journal of Political Research*, 33: 125–64.

Woodall, Brian. 1996. *Japan Under Construction: Corruption, Politics, and Public Works*. Berkeley: University of California Press.

Woods, Dwayne. 1992. "The Centre No Longer Holds: The Rise of Regional Leagues in Italian Politics." *West European Politics*, 15 (2): 56–76.

Yamada Masahiro. 1998. "Nukaga Fukushiro: Climbing the Ladder to Influence." In Otake Hideo (ed.), *How Electoral Reform Boomeranged*. Tokyo and New York: Japan Center for International Exchange.

Yomiuri Shinbun. Various years. *Bun'yabetsu Jinmeiroku* (Key names in various fields).

Yonehara, Junshichirō. 1986. "Financial Relations Between National and Local Governments." In Tokue Shibata (ed.), *Public Finance in Japan*, pp. 156–79. Tokyo: University of Tokyo Press.

Zenkoku Kakushin Shichōkai. 1990. *Shiryo Kakushin Jichitai*. Tokyo: Nihon Hyoronsha.

Zariski, Raphael. 1984. "Coalition Formation in the Italian Regions: Some Preliminary Findings and Their Significance for Coalition Theory." *Comparative Politics*, 16: 403–20.

Index

clientelism (*cont.*)
  Japanese, 69–70
  linkage and, 65–6, 74, 78–82
  local politics and, 22–3, 74
  maintenance of, 219–20
  material benefits of, 15
  measure of, 16
  mechanisms of, 64, 70–1
  methods of, 3
  in Mexico, 4
  monitoring in, 15–16, 65–6
  opposition parties and, 18, 23
  opposition to, 47, 180
  origins of, 75, 76–8
  outrage against, 86
  partisanship and, 95
  peasants and, 66
  personalistic politics v., 108
  phasing out of, 200
  predominance of, 219
  procedural definition of, 14–16, 70,
    72, 79, 85, 162, 213
  programmatic politics v., 15, 16
  protection of, 8, 18, 23–6, 28–9, 88,
    223
  reform of, 219
  resource control and, 76–8
  rifts within, 24–5, 29
  role of, 63
  Single Non-Transferable Vote in
    multi member district and, 64,
    75
  socioeconomics and, 76–8
  support for, 5, 86–7, 179, 220, 223
  symbolic, 69
  "tracers" of, 162
  undercutting of, 200
  unpopularity of, 217
  viability of, 24, 228
  voters and, 164
  votes and, 172
  weaknesses of, 11
clientelist/anti-market-liberalization
    policy kit, 165
coalitions, 31, 103
  anti-LDP, 222
  socioeconomic, 17

collective goods, 95
  distribution of, 21
  "collective-goods policies," 18
Columbia, 74, 230
  local politics in, 141
competition
  clientelism and, 13
  dominance and, 11–12
  failure of, 11
  importance of, 7–30
  incentives of, 7–8
  lack of, 218
  levels of, 8–13
  natural selection in, 8
  opportunity for, 30
  political party, 25, 29–30
  substantial, 10–11
  two-party, 24
  urban areas and, 48
  weak, 12–13
  zones of, 19, 23–6, 29
conservative
  progressive v., 203
Conservative Party, Japan, 43
  alternative of, 45
Conservative Party, U.K., 10,
    100
consolidation
  incentives toward, 186–7
  public financing and, 187
Constitution, Japan
  American imposition of,
    46
  "peace" clause, 195–6
  revision of, 198, 200, 202
  Socialist Party and, 46
construction
  clientelism and, 72
  firms, 112
  projects, 161
contractors, 159
Cornelius, Wayne A., 230
corporatist system, 154
corruption, 1, 33, 48, 59
  anger over, 82
  backlash against, 216
  cost of, 86